A STONE
SPEAKS

THE VOICE OF THE KOTEL

A STONE SPEAKS

THE VOICE OF THE KOTEL

ISRAEL RUBIN

MOSAICA PRESS

Mosaica Press, Inc.

© 2014 by Israel Rubin

Edited by Doron Kornbluth

Typeset and designed by Rayzel Broyde

ISBN 13: 978-1-937887-33-9   ISBN-10: 1937887332

Published and distributed by:

Mosaica Press, Inc.

www.mosaicapress.com

info@mosaicapress.com

Other works by this author:

The How and Why of Jewish Prayer (2012)

תהילים קב:טו כי רָצוּ עֲבָדֶיךָ אֶת אֲבָנֶיהָ וְאֶת עֲפָרָהּ יְחוֹנֵנוּ

"For Your servants desired its stones
and favored its dust."

(Psalms 102:15)

This volume chronicles the history[1] of the
Western Wall — Kotel, or *Ha-Kotel Ha'Ma'aravi*
in Hebrew — as told by one of the huge stones
that make up the Wall. It faces the plaza where
Jews (and often non-Jews) from around the
world come to pray or petition G-d.[2]

"There are men with hearts of stone and there
are stones with human hearts."[3]

---

[1] A note about dates in this book: A number of the dates, mainly those of ancient times and years prior to the Common Era, are inexact. Some are in dispute between Jewish scholars and between Jewish and non-Jewish historians. There is also the ambiguity of the calendar and the imprecise documentation throughout Jewish history. The author has tried his best to verify the correctness of the dates in this book. The chronicles of this extensive time frame is conditional on the uncertainty expressed above.

[2] The word "G-d" is used interchangeably with HaShem (The Name), which some prefer.

[3] By Yossi Gamzu, as it appeared in "Reflections - Stones With a Human Heart." Reprinted with permission from the Western Wall Heritage Foundation; permission requested from Jerusalem Diaries.

ZOOMING IN ON WOMEN'S PRAYER SECTION

Women and girls are wholeheartedly welcome to pray at the Kotel, just like men. Since 1967, when Israel regained control of the Kotel, there has been a mechitzah at the Wall. Prior to 1967, restrictions imposed by foreign rulers prohibited setting up a mechitzah. True, photos dating back more than 160 years do show men and women praying together. Nevertheless, we have a tradition, authenticated in halachah (Jewish religious law), for the preservation of modesty and humility that deems public and loud women's prayer inappropriate in the presence of men.

Table of Contents

ACKNOWLEDGMENTS

I offer thanks to HaShem Yitborach, Almighty G-d, and the Ultimate Source of everything, for having kept me alive, sustained me and enabled me to see the completion of this work. *Sh'Hecheyanu…*

To my beloved wife, Blossom, I am grateful for many things — especially her encouragement, patience, love, and support. I have been blessed with a wonderful *eishet chayil* for more than fifty-four years [*ad me'ah v'esrim*], whose considerate indulgence and tolerant understanding of days spent researching, writing, and rewriting this volume make her a true partner in this venture. May HaShem bless her, our children, grandchildren and great-grandchildren, together with Jews everywhere. May we be privileged to experience the coming of *Mashiach* speedily, in our days.

An off-the-cuff comment made by one of my grandchildren about the Kotel led me to envision the narrative that is related in this book. The anthropomorphic literary device, i.e., attributing human characteristics and human behavior to an inanimate stone, was of my own making. Since its publication in 1987 by the Israel Ministry of Defense Publishing House, I have treasured a book, *The Western Wall (Hakotel),* which I have read and re-read. The three authors Meir Ben-Dov, Mordechai Naor, and Zeev Aner, have done an outstanding job of bringing together excellent photographs and text about the Kotel. Those who do not possess this gem should make every effort to obtain a copy before it goes out of print. It belongs in your library.

I would like to acknowledge the help and encouragement of many individuals. Many people helped bring this book to completion. I want to thank the entire staff of Mosaica Press, and Rabbi Yaacov Haber and Rabbi Doron Kornbluth. Rabbi Kornbluth edited the entire book and gave me his invaluable advice. I hope to give Mosaica Press the opportunity to publish my forthcoming books.

I want to thank those who granted me permission to reprint their stories and essays. These include:

Sarah and Dov of the Western Wall Heritage Foundation; Israeli Ministry of Defense; Rabbi Moshe Kolodny of Agudath Israel of America; Rabbi Abraham J. Twerski (*A Sincere Dialogue With G-d*); Chana Benjaminson of Chabad.org; Aish HaTorah; Rabbi Moshe Newman of Ohr Somayach; Dr. Moshe Amirav ("A Paratrooper Describes his First Minutes at the Wall"); Abraham Duvdevani ("First Encounter with the Wall"); Avraham Schecter ("Was I Dreaming? Was it Real?"); Jewish Lights Publishing; Yehuda Ha-Ezrachi ("The Soldiers Are Weeping"); Yossi Gamzu (*Reflections — Stones With a Human Heart*); Rabbi Zvi Yehuda (*Shofar*); Hillel Fendel (Israelnationalnews.com); Joseph Hermoni of Kibbutz Ayelet haShachar ("The Heart of the Matter"); Deborah (Shapiro) Hemstreet ("Kotel, Kotel, Kotel — A Poem"); Ilan Braun (Singing Stones of the Kotel); Barbara Sofer; Heddi Keil ("My Awesome Visit to the Western Wall Tunnels"); Miriam Herschlag of *The Times of Israel*; HebrewSongs.com (http://www.hebrewsongs.com/song-haKotel.htm) for the Gamzu poem; Jenna Hopp (Yom Kippur at the Kotel); Judy Lash Balint (Winds of Remembrance — *Shoah* Commemoration); Jared Zaifman (*Ani Zocher*) and Prof. Todd Bolen (Pictorial Library of Bible Lands).

And to those who have passed on to *Olam Haba, z"l*: Chaim Hefer ("The Paratroopers are Crying"); Defense Minister Moshe Dayan; Prime Minister Levi Eshkol; Yitzchak Rabin ("No Time for Weeping"); Rabbi Mendel Weinbach (*A Return to Jerusalem*); Rabbi Moshe Tsvi Segal (The *Shofar* and the Wall).

To Ania Likhtikman for the illustrations depicting the quarrying, transporting, and erecting of the huge stones.

PREFACE

This book is an outpouring of the flood of images that have filled my mind over the past twenty centuries.[4] No camera has ever been invented that can capture all that I have seen and experienced. I have encountered the full spectrum of happenings — from the sad, heartbreaking, and distressing to the happy, joyful, and lively — that have marked the years. I have chronicled every episode and can verify its authenticity. No, I did not take down notes nor was I able to make a recording or video; there was never a need to. I have been blessed with an extraordinary memory, as you shall soon see. My powers of recall are staggering. It is now time to communicate my feelings and share some of my memories.

The Divine Presence has never left us stones of the Western Wall. Here at the Wall, you will come into contact with something both palpable and ethereal. You will be able to experience a feeling both profound and inexplicable. Perhaps for the first time, you will sense the real essence of life.

What is Our Story?

"It's the story of this place, the stories we will know but seldom speak of anymore: A people exiled from its homeland for 2,000 years; a people that kept a dream alive; that clawed its way back into the homeland through all sorts of extraordinary means; that breathe new life into an ancient, mostly moribund language; that restored immediacy to Jewish memory; that created Jewish communities of urgent purpose, fashioning a Judaism of activism and Jewish lives, with responsibility for our own

---

4   The stone was born in 19 BCE, or 2033 years ago

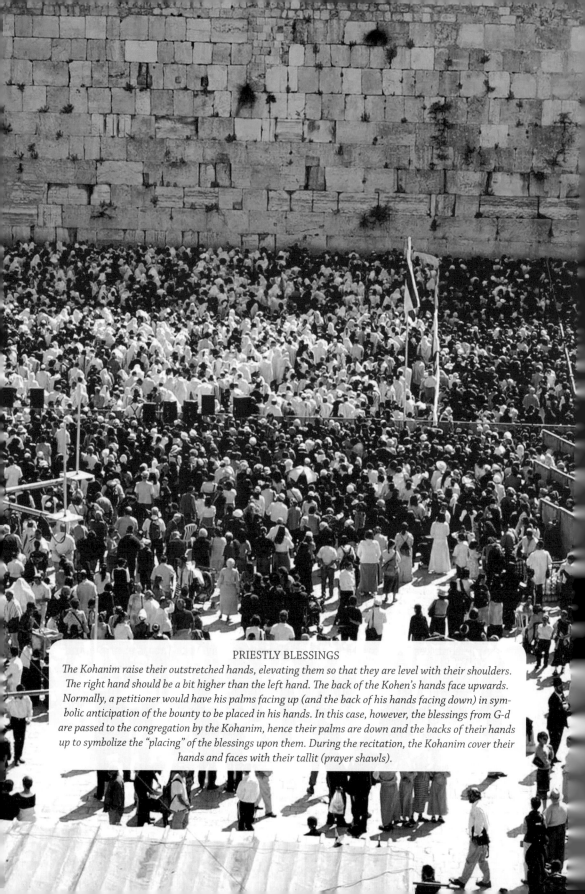

PRIESTLY BLESSINGS

The Kohanim raise their outstretched hands, elevating them so that they are level with their shoulders. The right hand should be a bit higher than the left hand. The back of the Kohen's hands face upwards. Normally, a petitioner would have his palms facing up (and the back of his hands facing down) in symbolic anticipation of the bounty to be placed in his hands. In this case, however, the blessings from G-d are passed to the congregation by the Kohanim, hence their palms are down and the backs of their hands up to symbolize the "placing" of the blessings upon them. During the recitation, the Kohanim cover their hands and faces with their tallit (prayer shawls).

Note to Reader
Humanized Stone

The author has attributed human characteristics to an inanimate stone. While careful not to depict the stone with human form (which could violate the commandment that reads, in part, "You shall not make yourself a carved image nor any likeness of that which is in the heavens above or on the earth below,")[6] he has ascribed human emotions and motives to the stone.

This literary device to tell a story may be unusual, but the author felt that such a personification, enabling the stone to talk and feel like a human, would enhance the narrative. The use of anthropomorphic language that suggests that inanimate objects have intentions and emotions may very well be deprecated as flippancy, indicating a lack of seriousness. Far from it. The subject matter is too serious a matter to be treated frivolously.

Needless to say, the reader is cautioned to avoid assumptions that a stone can honestly share any of the same mental, social, and emotional capacities of humans. Indeed, employing anthropomorphic elements may be seen as representing facets of human personality and character. He has used anthropomorphic language in metaphor to make the narrative more humanly comprehensible or memorable, especially for the younger reader.

---

6   The full text from Exodus (20:4-6) reads, "You shall not make yourself a carved image nor any likeness of that which is in the heavens above or on the earth below or in the water beneath the earth. You shall not prostrate yourself to them nor worship them, for I am HaShem, your G-d, a jealous G-d, Who visits the sin of fathers upon children to the third and fourth generations, for My enemies; but, Who shows kindness for thousands [of generations] to those who love Me and observe My commandments."

MEN'S AREA FILLED TO CAPACITY

On the Three Pilgrimage festivals, as well as during Rosh Hashanah and Yom Kippur, thousands come from all over Israel, as well as from around the world, to the Western Wall in order to be close to the where the Holy Temple stood. Tradition has it that the Shechinah (Divine Presence) hovers above the Kotel area.

CHAPTER I

ברוכים הבאים

ברוך הבא

***Baruch Haba!* Blessed is he who comes!**

Welcome and Shalom!

The Wall and I!

I am one of the huge stones that make up the Kotel. Yes, you can find me and my fellow stones at the Western Wall Plaza. We are here 24/7, 365 days a year. I invite you to come and visit. You cannot miss us. Just look for the huge stones bathed with the soft golden glow of Jerusalem. Yes, at times it is a very busy place, with people coming and going all day long. Do not let that deter you. As you approach, you will be surrounded by the sound of men, women, and children praying. If you have ever dreamed of being connected to G-d, this might very well be the place to start.

HAGBAH – ELEVATION OF TORAH SCROLL
In Sephardic tradition (shown in photo) there is no separate gelilah since the scroll is encased in a wooden frame. Hagbah is done prior to the Torah reading.

If you are one of the countless visitors who come to us at the most visited site in the Holy Land, you may have touched and kissed me as you stood to pray or recite Psalms. If you have not yet been here, possibly your parents, grandparents, or those that came before them were here to touch and caress me. Moreover, even though millions of Jews throughout history were unable to come to Jerusalem from their countries of dispersion, when praying they would always face Jerusalem. And, indeed, they did manage to visit — in their dreams and prayers.

To this day, the strong spiritual magnet that is the Kotel draws thousands of tourists visiting Israel from all over the world. The enticement is more than a visit to another archaeological site. Can you feel it? That special power that draws you to the Kotel stems from the special holiness that defines the Kotel. I have witnessed throughout the centuries how people pour out their hearts to G-d, in a variety of languages, at all hours of the day and night. Only at the Kotel can they experience this inexplicable sensation and response. The encounter is as mysterious as it is baffling. Young and old, pleading and questioning as they come face to face with the closest physical symbol of G-d's Presence on earth. After just under two thousand years, the Western Wall is still standing. What a powerful symbol of endurance!

What is my role, an ancient stone that has lived through 2,000 years of Jewish history? What is it that has gripped me for so many centuries? It is nothing less than a history gorged with the blood and tears of human misfortune that has haunted me for two millennia. I am more than just a bystander. At times, I was an eyewitness; at other times Jews leaned on me, crying uncontrollably as they related their recurring nightmares of the many catastrophes and tragedies that have weaved a tear-soaked and blood-stained pattern through the fabric of "the Chosen People." Try as I might, I could not hide the battles going on inside of me. I could not erase the expressions of horror and terror on the faces of those whose tears have drenched me. While my faith in G-d has never wavered, I have never been able to shake off the feeling of dread and anticipation that might, G-d forbid, signal another gruesome event.

We, Stones of the Kotel, Celebrate Life.

But we cannot forget the many tragedies that befell the Jewish people: first and foremost the destruction of the First and Second Temples in

CHILD PRAYING AT THE KOTEL
From an early age, Jewish children are taught to recite simple prayers. Here a young boy with peyot (sidelocks) prays from a siddur (prayer book).

Jerusalem, the subsequent exile of the Jews from the land of Israel, the Roman massacre of over 100,000 Jews at Beitar in 135 CE, and the expulsion of Jews from Spain in 1492. Many have come, especially on the sad day of Tisha b'Av, to mourn those calamities that befell our people. There are many — too many — other national calamities whose memories drenched the Kotel with heart-rending tears. Are you aware that over one-quarter of the Jewish inhabitants of Germany and northern France were slaughtered in the First Crusade? That the resulting expulsion of Jews from England, France, and Spain snuffed out the lives of at least another 25,000 Jews? Surely you remember the Nazi brutality of the *Shoah,* in which more than 6 million Jewish men, women, and children were dehumanized and savagely murdered.

While never forgetting the above calamities, G-d has provided us with a sense of balance.

Baruch HaShem (Praise be to G-d), there is much to celebrate. We not only celebrate the Three Festivals, but also Rosh Hashanah, Yom

Kippur, Chanukah, Purim, and other important events of Jewish history throughout the year. The Kotel is transformed on Shabbat. This day, with its overtone and meaning, is one of the most important elements of Jewish survival. It is on Shabbat that I see a remarkable change in the crowd that approaches the Kotel. I notice a rejuvenation, almost like magic. See that man? I know how poverty-stricken he is, begging for a handout on weekdays. But on Shabbat, as if by a miracle, he is transformed into a man of self-esteem and pride. On Shabbat, he is a true king.

Today, there are more than 10 million visits to my Wall every year.[7] As you read this book, you will better appreciate why the Western Wall in Jerusalem is so special and sacred. Hopefully, you will identify with the millions of people who believe the Divine Presence still rests at the Western Wall in an incomparable way.

The Western Wall is the holiest of Jewish sites, revered because it is a remnant of the Herodian retaining wall that supported the Second Temple.[8] Many have dubbed it the "Wailing Wall" because for centuries Jews have gathered here to weep over the destruction of their Holy Temples. Since the 1967 liberation of Jerusalem, the large open area that faces the Western Wall serves as a roofless synagogue capable of accommodating tens of thousands of worshippers. Prayers continually take place here well into the night. It is the scene of special services, some of which I will describe below.

We, the stones of the Kotel, are the last recognized and accessible vestige of the Holy Temple, linking past generations with those who come today and with those who will be inspired to come in the future. People are motivated to pray at the Wall because it is the closest point to the Holy of Holies, the holiest part of the ancient Holy

---

7   According to *Arutz Sheva* (http://www.israelnationalnews.com/news/news.aspx/165677), there were "10.5 million Kotel visits in 2012 (based on police data). These include regular worshippers as well as tourists and other visitors." Another newspaper (*Israel Hayom*, July 13, 2011) reported 10 million, compared with only 2.3 million in 2003.

8   Note that the Western Wall is not a remnant of either of the ancient Jewish Temples. It is one of the retaining walls of the Temple Mount. The southern and eastern walls are well preserved and can be seen in large part, even today. One of the major recent attractions there is the Davidson Center, which comprises the Southern Wall of the Temple Mount, together with a portion of the Western Wall.

Temple, which today is covered by a Muslim shrine. The custom to pray at the Wall started around 300 CE after our sages declared that HaShem's (G-d's) presence still hovered above the spot of the Holy of Holies.[9]

---

9   The first source mentioning Jewish connection to the Western Wall goes back to the 4th century. Following the destruction of the Second Temple, Jews used to pray at the Mount of Olives, and when permitted by foreign rulers, prayed on the Temple Mount itself. [Neusner, Jacob (2001). "Judaism and the Land of Israel." *Understanding Jewish Theology*. Global Academic Publishing, pp. 79. See also Harman, Graham (2008). "The Holiness of the "Holy Land." *A History of Palestine*, Princeton University Press. pp. 24.] In the 12th century, Benjamin of Tudela mentions Jews coming to the Western Wall for prayers and to the "Mercy Gate," but it is possible that the other walls to the south and east also served a similar purpose. What is apparent is that only from the 16th century did Jews prefer to pray at the Western Wall.

CHAPTER II

ASSEMBLING FOR EVENING PRAYERS — 2002
[Photo courtesy Amos Ben Gershom; Government Press Office] [Code: D 742-051]

The advent of night, representing (according to some) "darkness, judgment and suffering," brought with it a yearning for G-d's mercy. These two verses (v'Hu Rachum… and Adon-oi…) whose themes are pleading for mercy, are most appropriate because they consist of thirteen words, corresponding to G-d's Thirteen Attributes of Mercy. In this photo, men are assembling for the nighttime prayer.

You!

Yes you!

Please come closer. If you are genuinely seeking to communicate with G-d, let me help you. Rub your hands on one of the stones. Notice how

the stone has been rubbed smooth by fingers that have caressed them in prayer and supplication. Close your eyes and try to concentrate. As you pray, try to recognize your dependence on G-d. I admit that it is not easy. It is an exercise in humility that will help you communicate better with G-d. You will be surprised at the results. Prayer, whether fixed or spontaneous, will ultimately transform you. Many others, just like you, each with his own struggles, came here and rubbed these very stones over the past twenty centuries. With time and focus, I promise you that you will experience a religious high. The Wall is here for you. G-d is here for you.

You have now joined the never-ending stream of people coming to our ancient Wall. Is there any better proof of how important the Kotel still is to millions of people? The Wall is in fact the most important religious site in Israel. Did you know that more than half of the Wall, as well as its seventeen courses[10] located below street level, date back more than 2,000 years? That was about the time when I was "born" and placed in the Wall, being erected by one of the builders of Herod the Great around 19 BCE. My fellow stones and I cannot say that we witnessed the Jewish people's birth, but we have witnessed its repeated exile, subjugation, and redemption. From our place in this tiny part of the world, we have observed the coming together of the Jewish nation's past with its aspirations for the future.

Although Jews have journeyed to this holy place as far back as the 4th century, it appears that the main shift in pilgrimage from the Mount of Olives to the Kotel occurred in the sixteenth century.[11] Therefore, whether you come as a worshipper, a pilgrim, or a tourist, sit back and enjoy a most sensational experience. Using your power of imagination, I will accompany you as we go back through history from the time I was "born" in 19 BCE to the present. This will be more than just a learning session. It may revolutionize your understanding of Jerusalem — a city

---

10   Rows of bricks (continuous horizontal layers) are called *courses*. They are laid on top of one another to build up a wall.

11   "It is known that in the past sanctity was not attributed to the Wall, and the [early] written sources and writings left by Jewish visitors in the Middle Ages testify that the Western Wall was no more important than the other walls of the Temple Mount," according to Dr. Gabriel Barkay, a professor of archaeology at Bar-Ilan University, in an article in the journal *Ariel* in July 2007.

that has experienced more struggles in the last 3,000 years than any other city in the world.

Together, we will share the feelings of those whose lives were trampled as twenty-six empires dominated Jerusalem, suppressing her native population and demolishing the Jewish capital to the ground at least five separate times. You will get a sense of why Jerusalem, which is mentioned in the Bible 669 times, has been the center of Israel's worship and the focal point of Jewish religious life. Together we will relive the liberation of Jerusalem in 1967 CE. You will be there vicariously as Jews all over the world celebrate this joyous and momentous occasion. I joined my fellow stones to thank G-d for this great gift.

FATHERS PLACING HANDS ON SONS

The only lingering trace of 3,300 year-old worship service in the Holy Temple (Beit Hamikdash) is the mitzvah of Nesiat Kapayim — the duty of the Kohanim to lift up their hands and bless the Jewish people with the three verses recorded in the Torah. G-d, in turn, blesses the Kohanim for their performance of this mitzvah. When the congregation listens and responds to the blessings recited by the Kohanim, they are then participants in the mitzvah of the Kohanim to bless the Jewish people. The custom is for the father to place his hands on the heads of his sons during this ritual.

Remember that first time you came to the Kotel? Recall that feeling of wonder, thank Remember that first time you came to the Kotel? Recall that feeling of wonder, admiration, and respect? I have seen it on the faces of first-time visitors as their eyes scan from side to side and from top to bottom. While you may not see it or recognize it, I can probe beyond the surface appearance into the inner recesses of the visitor's heart. Where else can one experience the emotional charge of that first visit to the Kotel, the foremost remnant of the Temple Mount area?

This was the spot where King Solomon built his Temple. This was the heart of the Jewish nation. This was fated to be a place where people felt stirred to talk to HaShem. It was destined to be a place where no one would feel alone. At the Temple's inauguration, King Solomon pleaded with G-d to be especially attentive to prayers originating from this place. As you stand at the Kotel, try to sense that strong feeling, that closeness to HaShem. Our sages assured us that despite the destruction of the Temple, the *Shechinah* (the Divine Presence) has not left the site, consistent with G-d's promise to King Solomon: "*My eyes and heart will be there at all times*" (1 Kings 9:3; 2 Chronicles 7:16). You are standing not far from where the prophets Ezra and Nehemiah rebuilt the Temple in the days of King Cyrus of Persia.

In truth, I don't have any firsthand information prior to when I was "born," but I can pass along to you what I have heard from very reliable sources. So let's take a cruise together down history's river and sketch out the highlights of those most important events in the history of Jerusalem, the Temple, and the Wall.

Building and Destruction

Let us start with the reign of King David, who conquered Jerusalem in the year 1000 BCE. His son Solomon built the First Temple forty years later. In 721 BCE, the Assyrians conquered the north of Israel, forcing thousands of refugees to flee to Jerusalem. Twenty years later, Sennacherib, the Syrian ruler, besieged Jerusalem but miraculously did not manage to enter its Walls. Still, roughly one hundred years later, in 586 BCE, the Babylonians destroyed Jerusalem and exiled its Jewish population.

The Persian Period (starting in 539 BCE) witnessed Cyrus the Great beating the Babylonians and allowing the Jews to rebuild the sacred Temple. Led by the prophets Ezra, Nehemiah, and Zerubavel, returnees from the Persian Exile enthusiastically began construction. Despite the attempts of the Samaritans to stop them, they completed the task in 349 BCE.

Times were good. The return to the Holy Land, the relative calm under the protection of a benign Persian ruler, and the glory of a rebuilt Temple all contributed to the feeling that G-d was with the Jews. Under the guidance of Ezra and Nehemiah, the exultant community felt safe. The pulsating spirit seemed to confirm Jeremiah's prophecy (pronounced before the destruction of the First Temple):

"For so said G-d: For at the completion of seventy years of Babylon I will remember you, and I will fulfill My good word toward you, to restore you to this place" (Jeremiah 29:10).

In 332 BCE, Alexander the Great conquered Jerusalem. He was good to the Jews but his reign was followed by that of Seleucid ruler Antiochus IV, which was a sad time for Jews. The Temple was desecrated and every effort was made to suppress Jewish religious identity. This led to the revolt by Judah Maccabee, who rededicated the Temple and re-established Jewish independence. The Chasmonean Period, which we commemorate every Chanukah, lasted only from 167 BCE to 37 BCE. It was a great victory for the Jews, but sadly ended with the capture of Jerusalem by the Roman general Pompey in 63 BCE and its destruction in 70 CE.

Romans, Christians, and Muslims

As we make our way through the centuries, you will identify with the ancient Jews who witnessed the building and later the destruction of the First Temple and their expulsion from Jerusalem. We will experience the various attempts to rebuild the destroyed Temple as they sought permission for Jews to pray at the Temple Mount. Hadrian, in 118 CE, gave the Jews authorization to return and rebuild their Holy Temple, only to see that permission effectively revoked.

I will escort you through the years of the Bar Kochba revolt in 132 CE and consequent Roman brutality. The Jerusalem timeline following the Roman devastation of the city in 134 CE until the year 614 CE can best be described as a period of wretchedness and gloom. The year 614 CE raised some of our hopes as the Persian Empire captured Jerusalem. The outraged Byzantines recaptured the city a year later and held it until the Arab takeover of Jerusalem in 637 CE. By and large, the Muslims did not harass the Jews during this period. Their enmity was directed against the Christians. They built the Dome of the Rock (688 to 691 CE) on top of our holy Temple Mount and proclaimed Jerusalem as Muslim's third holiest site after Mecca and Medina.[12] Almost 500 years later, the Fatimid leaders of Jerusalem began harassing Christian pilgrims and destroyed the Church of the Holy Sepulcher, which triggered the Crusades. Once again, Jerusalem was conquered, this time by the Crusaders in 1099 CE. For the next eighty-eight years, our beleaguered city was the capital of the Latin Kingdom of Jerusalem until the Muslim Saladin recaptured the city in 1187 CE. In essence, various Muslim groups ruled Jerusalem for almost 1,100 years,[13] interrupted by a short period of Crusader rule.

---

12 Medina was one of the allegedly "purely Muslim" cities that actually was first settled by Jewish tribes. (Salo W. Baron, *A Social and Religious History of the Jews.* New York: Columbia University Press, 1937. Vol. 1, pp. 308T)

13 The Byzantines lost the Levant to the Arab-Islamic Empire in 638 CE. With the exception of the Crusader period (1099-1291 = 212 years), various Muslim dynasties controlled Palestine until the Ottoman Turks, who were Muslims, gained control from 1517 to 1917. From 638 to 1917, excluding 212 years, comes to 1067.

CHAPTER III

Jerusalem and The Wall

Jerusalem, Israel's capital, is home to almost 800,000 people, 65 percent of whom are Jews and 32 percent Muslims. It was the capital of our nation between 1000 BCE and 586 BCE, and again between 515 BCE and 70 CE. Throughout the centuries, Jerusalem has known many foreign rulers, but only the Jews have ever claimed it as their capital. Jews living in Jerusalem today represent a historical and spiritual link with the Jews of 3,000 years ago when King David made it his capital.[14] No other nation, people, religious or ethnic group can make this claim. For three millennia, Jerusalem has always been the focal point of Jewish national and religious aspirations for Jews dispersed throughout the world. The holiest shrine for Jews was the *Beit Hamikdash* (the Holy Temple). Jew and non-Jew alike admired its splendor and magnificence. However, for Jews throughout the world, the paramount importance of the site was its degree of sanctity. The Temple encapsulated everything that was most sacred in Judaism.

Place of Jewish Worship

I do not want to mislead you into thinking that the Kotel was always the preferred gathering place of Jewish worship. Following the destruction of the Temples and the banishment of the Jews from Jerusalem, the

---

14   *Jerusalem: the Eternal Bond; An Unbroken Link with the Jewish People*. Ruth Charif and Simcha Raz (Editors), Ruth P. Goldschmidt-Lehmann (Translator) and one more

preferred central place of assembly for Jews to recall the Temple's glory was the Mount of Olives. In fact, the Western Wall came to be regarded as the people of Israel's most sacred site only in the 16th century. Prior to that, though Jews *did* come to this spot on occasion, for the most part, a Jew who wanted to mourn the destruction of the Temple or to beseech G-d went up to the Mount of Olives and faced the Temple Mount.

From the 4th to the 7th century, the Christian-Byzantine rulers banned Jews from residing or visiting Jerusalem. The restriction was lifted for one day — the ninth day of the Hebrew month of Av — to permit Jews to mark the anniversary of the Temple's destruction. During the entire period of Roman and Byzantine rule, when the Jews were limited from entering the walled city of Jerusalem, they could only look out upon the Temple Mount from the Mount of Olives. Only with the Muslim conquest of Jerusalem in 638 CE were Jews once again permitted to reside in the city, settling in what is now called the Jewish Quarter. With the onslaught of the Crusades, Jews were again banned from Jerusalem. When the Muslims recaptured Jerusalem, Jews were once again permitted to return to their Holy City.

AERIAL VIEW OF BOTH MEN'S AND WOMEN'S SECTIONS
The Western Wall accommodated over one and a half million visitors during the holiday of Succot (Tabernacles). The Western Wall Heritage Foundation reports "that the High Holidays season and Succot hold the record for most people arriving at the Western Wall, coming to pray and connect with G-d at the holiest place for the Jewish People, especially taking into consideration over 300,000 tourists from abroad who come to visit."

With the passage of time, the perimeter of the Old City constricted in size, leaving the southern wall of the Temple outside the city's protective walls. It was dangerous for Jews to venture outside the Old City's walls. That is when the Western Wall of the Temple Mount was designated as the traditional place of worship. Some historians suggest that this alternative was decided upon when Ramban (Nahmanides) renewed Jerusalem's Jewish settlement in 1267 CE.[15]

CLOSE-UP OF KOTEL SHOWING KVITTELS IN CREVICES
For centuries, Jews have inserted written notes with a petition prayer (kvittel) into crevices of the Western Wall. Because of their intrinsic inviolability, these notes are not thrown away when they fall to the ground. This custom has also been taken on by Christian and foreign dignitaries as well. Each year more than a million kvittels are placed in the crevices of the Kotel. Twice a year, the Rabbi of the Kotel and his assistants collect the notes left in the Wall and bury them in the Jewish cemetery on the Mount of Olives.

The Wall is like a Magnet!

Has anyone ever visited Jerusalem without coming to the Western Wall? Men and women, boys and girls, old and young, religious and secular, come

---

15   According to the website, http://www.jewish-quarter.org.il/sargel.asp, 70 Jewish families were permitted to reside in the Jewish Quarter by paying as poll tax.

before us and stand in awe and trepidation. Over the centuries, hundreds of thousands of written prayer petitions — called *kvittels* in Yiddish — were folded and stuffed into the crevices between the stones. I can bear witness to the countless tears that have been shed as the *kvittels* were inserted into the Wall. Whether a petitioner was asking G-d for a speedy recovery for a sick person, or praying that he / she might finally find a soul mate, or simply asking for G-d's help with a personal problem, the *kvittel* somehow serves to "wrap up" one's prayers. The physical act of writing and inserting it into the Wall, in some way, gave the troubled petitioner a feeling that relief might be on the way now that he has shared his burden with G-d. Psychologically, that is a powerful mechanism. I recommend that you prepare the *kvittel* note prior to arriving at the Kotel. Of course one does not need to write anything — simply speaking to G-d is fine. Still, it is a beautiful custom. You may always write one on the spot if you have a pen and paper. The *kvittel* may be written in any language. Periodically, the Rabbis in charge of the Kotel collect the prayer notes to make room for more, and bury them on the Mount of Olives. The *kvittels* are never burned or discarded.

SHACHARIT (MORNING PRAYERS)
Literally, the "prayer of dawn," this daily morning service is not only the most multifaceted, but also the longest and most detailed of the three fixed daily prayers. Tradition has it that Shacharit was ascribed to our forefather Abraham, based on Genesis (19:27). The men of the Great Assembly instituted the mandatory recitation of Shacharit to take the place of the daily morning sacrifice.

For hundreds of years, those who could not physically come to the Kotel sent carefully written *kvittels* with emissaries who would travel to various Jewish communities in Europe and America, soliciting money for their impoverished brethren in Palestine. These *shluchim* (charity solicitors) would relate their experiences while visiting the Kotel. More often than not, these emissaries came back with meager contributions but with stacks of *kvittels* to be placed in the crevices of the Wall. Now, fast-forward to the 21st century where those unable to visit us at the Kotel use modern technology to "send a *kvittel.*" The staff of the Western Wall dutifully stuffs the petitions into the gaps in the Wall. Just last week, someone approached and held a cell phone against one of the stones. The petitioner, speaking in a foreign tongue, was begging HaShem to heal his sick parent. And why not? We welcome any innovation that will help a petitioner communicate with his Maker!

MAN WITH FOUR SPECIES ON SUCCOT-1995
[Photo courtesy Moshe Milner, Government Press Office] [Code: D81-105]
During the holiday of Succot, it is a mitzvah for every Jew to take hold of the arba minim (the "Four Species"), which are held together and waved in six directions. By waving the four species of the Lulav (the branch of the date palm), the etrog (the citron fruit), hadassim (three myrtle twigs), and aravot (two willow branches), the Jew affirms the dominion of G-d who created these (and all) species above Nature.

Stones with Feelings

You may snicker when I tell you that we Kotel stones have feelings. These emotions have been locked up inside us as though trapped inside our own heads. Until now, I have not been able to talk about them. Now that my emotions have reached the bursting point, I cannot contain them any longer. I desperately need to share what is really happening to my city and country.

"Stop right there," you insist. "Stones are inanimate objects and have no feelings!"

By the classic distinction between animate and inanimate, you are right. A stone is dead. Still, the differentiation is relative, and very much a matter of perception. I will concede that we stones are inert and lifeless.

Nevertheless, I hope to convince you that I, and many of my fellow stones, are in a sense very much alive. We are conscious and attentive to what is going on around us. We talk with each other, though, try as you may, you will not be able to hear our conversation. We speak by means of "stone-talk," in a slower time frame than your own language. So, for now, humor me and permit me to go on.

My heart (yes, we stones have hearts too!) is bursting with excitement to tell you my story. The cumulative happenings of 2,000 years have been confined within me. I'll split open if I cannot finally come out and divulge what has happened to my beloved Jerusalem. I may be made of stone rather than from flesh and blood, but I belong here. I, too, am an heir to the history of our Judaic ancestors, to the continuing power of the Judaic vision. There is a destiny that joins my fate to the fate of the Jewish people, and especially to its Torah, its land, and its culture.

How many times, over the centuries, have I heard the beautiful chanting of the verses from Shir HaShirim (Song of Songs) [2:8-9]:

The voice of my Beloved! Behold, it came suddenly
to redeem me,
as if leaping over mountains, skipping over hills.
In His swiftness to redeem me, my Beloved is like a
gazelle or a young hart.
I thought I would be forever alone, but behold! He
was standing behind our Wall, observing through
the windows, peering through the lattices.

In commenting on the above, the *Midrash Rabbah*[16] says:
"*Behold! He was standing behind our Wall*" — this refers to the Western

---

16   *Bamidbar* (Numbers) *Rabbah* 11:2. It refers back to Shir HaShirim (2:9).

Wall of the Temple. Why so? Because G-d has sworn that it will never be destroyed. "Because the *Shechinah* is in the West."

HaShem's Presence hovers around the Western Wall. To quote the *Midrash Rabbah* (Exodus 2:2):

Rabbi Eleazer said: "The Divine Presence never departed from the Temple, as it is written, 'For now I have chosen and sanctified this house so that My name shall be there forever and My eyes and My heart will be there all the days' (2 Chronicles 7:16)... Even when [the Temple] is destroyed, it remains in its sanctity... Even when it is destroyed, G-d does not leave it."

I'm nostalgic for those old days when Sephardic Jews would come to the Kotel on Friday evenings and sing in unison Shir HaShirim, which was hailed by Rabbi Akiva as the Torah's "Holy of Holies." The Wall mentioned by King Solomon was the Western Wall of the Temple Mount,[17] which is the last vestige of the Temple Mount still intact after 2,000 years following the Temple's destruction. That is why the mystical book of the *Zohar* asserts that "The Divine Presence has never departed from the Western Wall."

---

17   While portions of the eastern and southern walls of the Temple Mount do exist, the depiction "the Divine Presence has never departed..." has never been ascribed to them.

KVITTEL HANGING BY RED THREAD
Written prayer petitions, called kvittels in Yiddish, are folded and stuffed into the crevices between the stones. Countless tears have been shed as the kvittels are inserted into crevices in the Wall. Whether a petitioner is asking G-d for a speedy recovery for a sick person, or praying that he / she might finally find a soul mate, or simply asking for G-d's help with a personal problem, the kvittel somehow serves to "wrap up" one's prayers. The photo shows a novel approach to bypass the problem of the crevice being often jam-packed with notes.

CHAPTER IV

The Noise that Time Makes

Did you ever hear the noise that time makes?[18]

Yes, the passage of time does create a certain noise. Most of you, when you come to the Kotel, hear a cacophony of noise. Only very late at night or in the early hours of the morning is there anything resembling stillness. On the other hand, we stones are quite different. Our ears are attuned to different types of sounds. We can differentiate between noise and resonance; between hum and song; between echo and reverberation. Our built-in antenna detects the sound of prayer, even quiet or silent prayer. We stones can hear time's footsteps as they pass in front of the Western Wall.

G-d, in His infinite wisdom, gave to each individual a unique vocal tone, timbre, and quality. In addition, Sephardim, Ashkenazim and Yemenites, to mention just a few, pronounce Hebrew differently. We have had to contend with hundreds of different languages over the centuries. Jews have been coming here and articulating their prayers in their native tongues. Within each foreign language, we have had to cope with different dialects, colloquial speech, unusual idioms, and, most unfortunately, slang. It has not been easy deciphering this great variety of vernacular spoken in our presence. We have had to struggle and sort out the many styles of expression,

---

18   Credit to Dr. Merrill Moore, whose sonnet, *The Noise that Time Makes*, was the inspiration for this thought.

articulation, intonation, and inflection. Especially challenging are those who come with a drawl, a twang, or a brogue. Not that we are complaining, but at times it has been difficult to grasp a given petitioner's message. It's more than a question of diction, or the cadence, or the modulation of a petitioner's voice. We have had to put up with barely audible speech and at times with deafening cries from the heart. Some people have built-in megaphones and are not hesitant about using them. Yet we have never complained. Our task has always been to be good listeners, not eavesdroppers. We listened to the prayers, petitions, and pleas, fully aware that these conversations were meant for the Divine Presence. Where a prayer was specifically addressed to us, we automatically beamed it up towards Heaven. Over the many centuries, we have been bombarded with assorted and diverse petitions. The volume of the petitions has increased exponentially since 1967. Yet despite that deluge, we have not been overwhelmed. Patiently, we have "processed" each plea with sensitivity and urgency. Every supplicant who comes to the Kotel to beseech or implore deserves to have his entreaty heard by HaShem, Whose Presence continues to hover over the Western Wall, as it has for millennia.

Yes, we have come in contact through the centuries with so many different Jews, may HaShem bless them all. It is this diversity that has forged what we might call the "Living Pulse" of the Kotel.

With each worshipper coming to the Kotel, with each *kvittel* inserted into one of the crevices of my Wall, I feel reinvigorated knowing that the Western Wall is marvelously near to the spot where the *Kodesh Hakodashim* (Holy of Holies) stood. The destruction of this innermost chamber of the *Beit haMikdash* (the Holy Temple) has not diluted any of the original sanctity. Rest assured that I will be around to witness the future Third Temple. My fellow stones and I continue to feel the strong spirituality emanating from the place of the Temple.

Imagine, if you will, windows to HaShem that are wide open to every sincere worshipper. That is the secret channel of communication between man and his Creator. Whether by means of verbal prayers or written notes stuffed into the Wall, you and millions like you have been petitioning HaShem for countless generations throughout the many centuries. My fellow stones and I are proud witnesses, ever ready to testify that the soul, the life-force of the Jewish nation, will never be destroyed.

VATIKIN – SUNRISE PRAYERS - 1989

[Photo courtesy Yaacov Saar; Government Press Office] [Code: D 212-065]

The Talmud describes the ideal time for reciting the morning Shema as just before sunrise so that the silent Shemoneh Esrai (Amida) prayer begins with the rising sun. The word "vatikin" commonly refers to the early-morning prayer service itself, and not to its stricter meaning of referring to the men who gather before sunrise to pray then. The very early morning minyan is also called "netz," an abbreviation of "Hanetz Hachama," which means sunrise. Photo shows vatikin men assembling for prayer.

CHAPTER V

Bad News / Good News

Does bad news travel faster than good news? Does information about misfortune spread more quickly than good news? Is it because it seems to be more interesting and it makes people angry? Or because bad news tends to make people seek revenge and thus they want to broadcast their opinions and feelings about the matter?

Good news is usually simple and easy to explain. Bad news leaves many questions.

I don't know the answer to the above questions. Perhaps the answer lies in the Judaic concept of *"Kol Yisrael arevim zeh la'zeh,"* which means that "all Jews (or all the people of Israel) are responsible for one another."

We Jews (yes, I'm included) recognize the need to rely on ourselves and HaShem rather than waiting for the nations of the world to save us. The *Shoah* (Holocaust) confirmed the truth of how much we were cut off and separated from other nations. As you read this book, try to experience (vicariously, fortunately) the calamities, adversities, and tribulations that have plagued our people from time immemorial.

Here, lodged between my brother and sister stones at the Kotel, I have heard news, both good and bad, from the many who have come to visit and pray. Assuredly, much of it is hearsay — information heard by one Jew from another Jew about some event where the first person had no direct experience. However, the same news coming from numerous people over an extended period of time lends a degree of validity to authenticate the initial reports.

Jews from the four corners of the world have been drawn to the Kotel for such a long time; were we to record their conversations before and after prayer, we would fill countless volumes. What follows is a cross-section of what I have heard in many languages from these visiting Jews. It is not intended to be a complete narration. Hopefully, through my narration, you will experience, in some way, the sufferings and joys as time went by. Use your power of imagination to actualize your involvement in these events over the continuum of space-time, allowing you to travel from one time to another and from one place to another.

READING THE SEFER TORAH
Portions (known as a sedra or parashah) from the Torah are read from a scroll every Monday and Thursday, on S mornings and afternoons, on Rosh Chodesh, holidays, Rosh Hashanah, Yom Kippur and fast days. These public r have been prearranged more than 2,000 years ago so that the entire Torah is read consecutively each year.

A Bit of History

Before I continue, let's explore a bit of history as it relates to the Western Wall and the Holy Temple. It appears that much has happened during the many years that I was still buried in a mountain of stone. The Exodus from Egypt occurred in the year 1312 BCE. Throughout many of the years since, alien rulers conquered the Land of Israel and the Jews were a subjugated people.[19]

Early Period: Prior to 1025 BCE

There are archaeologists who claim that Jerusalem was occupied as far back as the fourth millennium BCE.[20] According to the *Tanach*, Jerusalem was peopled by a Canaanite tribe (Jebusites) prior to its takeover by King David,[21] who built a wall around the city.

1150–1025 BCE

During this period, the people of Israel were led by the biblical Judges.

1025 BCE

The first Jewish monarchy was established by King Saul in 1025 BCE, after a period of tribal self-rule and ad-hoc administration by the Judges. Faced with intense danger from foreign armies, the tribes united. The prophet Samuel anointed Saul (from the tribe of Benjamin) as the first king of a united kingdom of Israel. The concept of kingship encountered the opposition of many. They were reluctant to ascribe to any individual the status of reverence and power that was meant to be reserved for HaShem. Despite their hesitation, increasing pressure from

---

19   Because of disagreements between *Seder Olam Rabbah*, biblical scholars, historians and archaeologists, dates throughout this book cannot be authenticated.

20   "The City of David Archaeological Park holds some of the earliest artifacts in Jerusalem's history. There are exhibits dating back to the fourth millennium BCE, all the way to the Byzantine era during the Middle Ages. Visitors to the City of David will first notice large city walls, a 13-meter stone building constructed in the 11th and 12th centuries BCE during the Jebusite period, as well as the remains of homes destroyed during the destruction of the First Temple by the Babylonians in 586 BCE." (From City of David website)

21   I Kings 9:20 states that Jerusalem was known as Jebus prior to David's conquest.

the Philistines and other neighboring tribes drove them to accede to a united monarchy. King Saul's reign was short-lived, though, due to his disobedience to HaShem.

1010–970 BCE

It was David, successor to King Saul, who in 1006 BCE forged a strong unified confederation of the twelve tribes, and in 1003 BCE established Jerusalem as the capital of the united kingdom of Israel — more than 3,000 years ago! Prior to that, Hebron had been our capital, and preceding Hebron, Gibeah had been the capital of the united kingdom under Saul.[22] Thanks to King David's exceptional success in uniting the Israelite tribes, he was able to defeat such bitter enemies as the Philistines. The united kingdom of Israel grew into a regional power with secure borders, prosperity, and ascendancy over the surrounding nations.

970–931 BCE

King David's son Solomon succeeded his father as monarch. Peace, prosperity, and cultural expansion marked his reign.

950 BCE

King Solomon began construction of the Holy Temple. It took eleven years to build, during which time it only rained in Jerusalem at night so as not to hold up construction. With its completion, Jerusalem became the spiritual and political capital of the Jews. It remained so until the city fell to the Babylonians in 586 BCE when they utterly destroyed the Temple.

930 BCE

In 930 BCE, following King Solomon's death, the Jewish kingdom came apart. Under Solomon's son Rehoboam, the country split into two kingdoms: Israel (including the cities of Shechem and Samaria) in the

---

22 Hebron had been the capital of Judah under David and Machanaim had been the capital of the northern kingdom of Israel under Ish-bosheth. *Tanach* indicates that Shiloh had also been the national (religious) capital.

north, and Judah (containing Jerusalem) in the south. Additionally, most of the non-Israelite provinces faded away from our control.

929–721 BCE

While the weakness and bad judgment of Rehoboam set off the break-up between north and south, the underlying cause was entrenched in the idolatry of Solomon's wives. Further infuriating many Jews was the decision of Jeroboam, king of the northern country Israel, to set up an alternative place of worship in the north. Hoping to discourage Jews in the northern kingdom from departing to Jerusalem on the Three Festivals — Passover, Shavuot and Succot — he erected two temples in Beit El and Dan. His maddening resolve to set up golden calves in these temples was a deliberate violation of the commandment against graven images. His schemes opened the flood-gates to idolatry. In the ensuing quarter of a century, nineteen different kings ruled the northern kingdom of Israel — all of whom were evil and corrupt idolaters. Some were ruthless and merciless, leading the Jewish people into idolatry.

The northern kingdom of Israel, weakened by the resulting divisiveness, idolatry, and rejection of HaShem, continued as a sovereign state until 721 BCE when it was conquered by the Assyrian Empire. The kingdom of Judah (Southern Kingdom) survived as an independent state until 586 BCE, when it was conquered by the Babylonian Empire.

721–715 BCE

In 721 BCE, the Assyrian army conquered the northern kingdom (Samaria) and forcibly marched the Israelites into captivity and, ultimately, dispersal. Many Jewish refugees fled to Jerusalem. The remaining Jewish kingdom of Judah in the south was nothing more than a vassal state to Assyria, which forced its inhabitants to pay a large annual tribute to this dominant power. Two kings, Ahaz and his son Hezekiah (Chizkiyahu), ruled it as co-regents.

715 BCE

In 715 BCE, Ahaz died. His son Hezekiah was left as the only regent of the southern kingdom of Judah. Hezekiah was a righteous king who empowered an all-encompassing atmosphere of religious change. He began a system of far-reaching religious reforms. He reestablished the daily services in the Holy Temple, restored the worship of HaShem, G-d of Israel, in accordance with the Torah, cleansing the Temple of all alien elements, and restoring Torah observance. He enthusiastically ordered the obliteration of the many idols, and chopped down the many trees of idolatry. He conquered the Philistine-controlled lands in the Negev desert and formed pacts with Ashkelon and Egypt. Still, his boldest move was to refuse payment of tribute to Assyria.

701 BCE

In 701 BCE, Hezekiah, king of Judah, having witnessed the destruction of the Northern Kingdom of Israel by the Assyrians in 720 BCE and the assault and siege of Jerusalem by Sennacherib in 701 BCE, initiated a war against the Assyrian Empire.

Despite the support of Egypt and Babylonia, the rebellion was not successful. Sennacherib retaliated by ransacking several cities in Judah and attacking Jerusalem. His siege of Jerusalem failed when HaShem dispatched an angel who struck down 185,000 men in the Assyrian camp.[23] The Assyrians claimed that Sennacherib lifted the siege of Jerusalem after Hezekiah surrendered and agreed to pay tribute. *Tanach* [24] supports this claim, describing Hezekiah's payment to Sennacherib's "with three hundred talents of silver and thirty of gold in tribute." Still, the royal treasury of silver was not sufficient. Hezekiah had to raid the Temple treasury and strip the gold from the doorposts of the Temple. Even after receiving the extorted payment, Sennacherib, the king of Assyria, continued attacking Jerusalem. The Southern Kingdom of Judah, survived for more than another century.[25]

598–587 BCE

In an attempt to increase his influence, Nebuchadnezzar, king of Babylonia, launched several military campaigns against the kingdom of Judah. The Babylonian attack resulted in the capture of Jerusalem in 597

---

23   2 Kings 19:35

24   2 Kings 18:14–16

25   There were assertions that Assyria launched a second campaign against Judah.

BCE and ousted then king Jehoiakim. Zedekiah was set up as a tributary king that same year. Zedekiah revolted, bolstered by an alliance with Egypt. Infuriated by Zedekiah's rebellion, the king of Babylonia initiated a siege of Jerusalem in 589 BCE. Nebuchadnezzar sent his forces capturing Jerusalem a second time in 587 BCE, ending Zedekiah's reign.

586 BCE

When they first attacked Israel, the Babylonians did not destroy the Temple or banish the Jews into exile.[26] However, when they defeated Zedekiah in 586 BCE, they destroyed both the city of Jerusalem and the Temple. The cream of Jerusalem's inhabitants, including 10,000 of the best and brightest Jews, was exiled to Babylon. Without delay, these exceptional Torah scholars created an organizational structure for the continuation of a Torah way of life in their new land of exile. (These were the Jews who chose to remain in Babylonia even after Cyrus granted them the choice to leave for Israel.) Babylonia developed into the center of Jewish rabbinic authority, whose descendants were the core of the great Jewish revival and where, many years later, the Babylonian Talmud was written in 500 CE.

The later ravaging of Jerusalem, the destruction of the First Temple, and the banishment of much of its traumatized population marks one of the saddest periods in Jewish history. Jeremiah prophesied that the captive Jews would return to Jerusalem after seventy years of exile. HaShem, through his prophets Ezekiel and Daniel, heartened us not to give up hope but to continue to trust in Him. This seventy-year period of captivity saw the fall of Babylonia to the conquering Persians. Thankfully, no longer would the Babylonians exercise power to subjugate others.

562 BCE

Nebuchadnezzar died. Undeniably, Nebuchadnezzar was the ruler of the most powerful empire in the world at that time. Babylon was considered the center of the universe. After the exile of the Jews to Babylon, the Land of Israel faded in significance.

---

26   http://www.aish.com/jl/h/cc/48949881.html

539 BCE

However, the story changed following Nebuchadnezzar's death in 562 BCE. His irresponsible successors weakened the previously forceful kingdom. The cunning Persians seized their chance and conquered the unstable Babylonian Empire, in the process gaining Jerusalem. The fall of Babylon was complete.

538-516 BCE

The Persian period lasted from 538 BCE to 332 BCE.

After overthrowing the Babylonians, the king of Persia, Cyrus the Great, liberated the exiled Jews. We were not only free to return to Israel, but Cyrus issued a proclamation that the Temple was to be rebuilt. In 537 BCE, 40,000 Jews opted to leave Babylon and return to Jerusalem. Regrettably, there were Jews who chose to remain in Babylon, which evolved into a hub of Jewish culture and wealth. Babylonian Jews were permitted to give silver, gold, and other possessions to the *Beit haMikdash* (The Holy Temple) in Jerusalem. Jerusalem was restored to Jewish quasi-sovereignty by Cyrus the Great.

It appears that Cyrus (Koresh in Hebrew) was close to a number of Jews and appreciated the wisdom of the Jews. He valued their expertise in international trade and commerce and saw that the Jews, dispersed throughout many lands, could be instrumental in helping him create a new empire. I have heard that the Babylonian Jews helped him plan and bring about the conquest of Babylon. Unlike past conquerors, Cyrus came as a progressive and open-minded liberator. He was spellbound by the beauty and wealth of Babylon.

Thanks to its policy of tolerance and respect, the Persian Empire lasted more than 1,000 years.[27] It was a good time for Jews. Jewish communities and institutions sprang up throughout the Persian Empire. The *Gomel*, the Hebrew blessing for deliverance, was on the lips of many as they came to the Kotel to thank HaShem.

The Jews of Babylon welcomed Cyrus and helped him because he emerged as their liberator. While the Jews were generally left alone and

---

27   "After the fall of Jerusalem, Babylon would become the focus of Judaism for more than a thousand years, and the place where Jews would acclimate themselves as a people without a land." http://www.pbs.org/wgbh/nova/ancient/rise-judaism.html

tolerated by the Babylonians, the fact remains that it was the Babylonians who had destroyed the Holy Temple, plundered Jerusalem, exiling much of its population, and leaving the city as a wasteland of rubble. Now you can understand why Cyrus was so willing to reward the Jews, allowing them to return to Jerusalem. If not for the Jews, he may not have been able to enter Babylon peacefully. It was the Jews whose counsel he sought. The Jews aided and guided him. Their planning and management not only neutralized any anti-Persian opinion, but also succeeded in gaining support from the inhabitants of this city. The Jews generated pro-Persian sentiment in the city and opened the gates for him.

Jerusalem Was In Ruins

The sight that greeted the returning Jews was bittersweet. Jerusalem was in ruins, a city plundered and pillaged beyond description. Its Holy Temple was destroyed, its heart and soul torn apart. Most of its inhabitants were non-Jews who holed up in underground caverns built to catch and store rainwater, their lives marked by fear.

What were they afraid of? For seventy years, gangs of robbers, bandits, and assorted reckless and violent criminals continued to loot Jerusalem and terrorize its few inhabitants. The Holy Temple stood in ruins, stripped of every bit of metal and finished stone. The magnificent homes of the Jewish upper-class had been denuded. Nothing of any value remained. Jerusalem was an apparition, home to memories and recollections of a glorious past. The few thousand inhabitants that remained steered clear of the lifeless city. They lived in the hills around Jerusalem, eking out a living from the parched and broken agricultural terraces.

The Jews returning from Babylon, on the other hand, were determined to settle in Jerusalem — home of their ancestors, site of the Holy Temple and the most appropriate setting for a renewal of their religious practices. Just picture the scene: tens of thousands of exiles returned. Hunger and despair gripped them as they repaired their broken homes during the day and crowded together at night behind barricaded doors. This sense of misery and despondency was highlighted as howling jackals roamed outside, terrifying the sleep-disturbed children. Adults, too, were unable to sleep fearing the bands of robbers who roved freely just outside the homes of these defenseless returnees. A sense of depression filled the air, puncturing any hope of recreating a Jewish homeland and rebuilding the Temple. The grim news filtered back to Babylon.

Ezra: A Priest and A Scribe

The gloomy news troubled Ezra, an outstanding man of influence in the Persian court. Ezra, a priest and a scribe, was both a Jewish religious leader and a reformer. Ezra was a *Kohen*, that is, a member of the priestly family of Aaron. He felt drawn to his brethren in Jerusalem and pleaded with the Persian king for permission to leave Babylon and settle in Jerusalem. The king eventually agreed and appointed Ezra as a high-ranking officer in the Land of Israel, with powers to appoint judges and officers of the law and to levy monetary fines, impose banishment, and even to impose the death penalty, if necessary. Ezra, accompanied by thousands of passionate Jews, abandoned the comforts of Babylon to begin a new life in the Holy Land.

Upon arrival, Ezra was appalled to discover the extent to which the Jews had assimilated.[28] Many had intermarried with the Samaritans and had neglected the great spiritual heritage of their ancestors. Most of the younger generation grew up ignorant of their rich spiritual tradition. The children did not even speak Hebrew.

Ezra issued an ultimatum, compelling all Jewish men to divorce their non-Jewish wives. Failure to comply with this decree would result in the men's exclusion from the community. For the matter of spiritual survival, no compromises could be made. While Ezra succeeded in imbuing the Jewish inhabitants with genuine repentance, it also brought upon them the wrath of the Samaritans. Enraged, they attacked the peaceful inhabitants of Jerusalem, destroyed the protective walls of the city, and ravaged many homes. Once again, the Holy City of Jerusalem saw their Jewish populations shrink as frightened Jews fled. Once again, many Jews began to seek the friendship of the powerful Samaritans, and Ezra's

---

28 "When Ezra did arrive in the Land of Israel, he saw a Jewish community that had broken down spiritually. Some traditional sources suggest that the intermarriage rate was as high as 85-90%. The situation was so bad that the High Priest — whom all the Jewish people looked to for spiritual leadership — had sons who married non-Jewish women."(http://www.jewishhistory.org/ezra-and-nehemiah/)

strenuous efforts to stem the tide of assimilation seemed all but fruitless.[29] For twelve years, the state of affairs worsened. It was Nehemiah, Ezra's colleague, who succeeded in turning the situation around.

Nehemiah Arrives

When Nehemiah, the royal cupbearer to the Persian king, learned of the terrible situation in Jerusalem, he received the king's permission to join Ezra in Jerusalem. The king (who was favorably disposed to Nehemiah) not only granted him leave of absence, but also appointed him governor of Judea with authority to restore Jerusalem. Furthermore, he provided Nehemiah with a military escort and royal documents ordering the various provinces to assist him.

Nehemiah's sweeping power, buttressed by the small Jewish military force with him, instilled the city's residents with a renewed sense of hope. He persuaded the inhabitants to rebuild the walls and gates of the city. *Tanach* tells us that the walls surrounding the vicinity were completed in a time span of fifty-two days. In order to discourage the roving bands of bandits, Nehemiah organized a militia to patrol the walls.

Having secured the city, Nehemiah successfully induced additional Jews to move to Jerusalem — both from Babylon and from other cities of the Diaspora. It was Nehemiah's successful restoration of Jerusalem that laid the foundation for the survival of the Jewish people in Jerusalem.

Kol HaKavod (Bravo)!

Ezra and Nehemiah, you have earned my respect for all your efforts in reestablishing an embryonic Jewish state, small but viable. It had a population of approximately 100,000 Jews, most of whom lived within the city of Jerusalem. Thanks to both of you for reinvigorating the Jewish community in Jerusalem;[30] the heretofore ghostly city was now alive. The reconstructed Temple once again reverberated with the sacrificial worship led by the High Priest. The rebuilt walls of the city were

---

29 http://www.chabad.org/library/article_cdo/aid/111905/jewish/Ezra-the-Scribe.htm

30 Initially it was solely Ezra. But later on, it appears from the book of Nehemiah that both contributed to the teaching of Torah and its commandments to the people and in the dedication of the Wall. Their joint efforts succeeded in restoring Jewish life to Jerusalem.

no longer vulnerable; the giant gates opened and closed as before as peace reigned for the Jews, safeguarded by the mighty Persian Empire. Even the cruel Samaritans relented and took a softer line toward the Jews. Jerusalem was now a hub of commerce and interaction with Jewish communities in Asia, Europe, and North Africa. It was a good time for the Jews of Jerusalem.

At the head of the first wave of returning Jews was the high priest Zerubavel. The king of Persia supported the rebuilding project and sent back with the returnees the sacred vessels that had been taken from the Temple, as well as a substantial sum of money for the building materials. What Daniel had prayed for and prophesied was about to be realized. This was a turning point for the Jewish world. HaShem works in mysterious ways. HaShem motivated Cyrus, the king of Persia, to issue his famous edict, as described in Ezra (1:2): "Thus saith Cyrus, king of Persia: All the kingdoms of the earth hath the Lord, the G-d of heaven, given me; and he hath charged me to build Him a house in Jerusalem, which is in Judah."

While the rebuilding of the Second Temple began in 537 BCE, it really did not get under way until 520 BCE and was only completed in 516 BCE. The rebuilding of the Temple was approved by Cyrus the Great[31] and endorsed by Darius the Great.[32]

Alas, the peace and quiet that the Jews of Jerusalem would enjoy for more than a century would soon end. The century that witnessed the reconnection of a people with its ancient homeland after the brutal exile faded from memory. The vast Persian Empire, which Cyrus created, was conquered by the armies of Alexander the Great.

521–520 BCE

What excitement was in the air as work began to rebuild the Temple! Waves and waves of worshippers came to witness the beginning of the reconstruction. What joy, what euphoria! HaShem works in mysterious ways. The depressing, inconsolable mood following Nebuchadnezzar's destruction of the Temple had been replaced by a feeling of elation.

---

31   The founder of the Persian Empire under the Achaemenid dynasty.

32   Darius I, king of Persia, whose reign lasted from 522 to 486 BCE.

But not everyone was happy. Non-Jews from Samaria (and elsewhere) did everything in their power to thwart the rebuilding. Powerful petitions to Persian rulers such as Xerxes (Ahasuerus), Artaxerxes, and even Darius sought to foil and obstruct the project. In fact, construction of the new Temple began around 537 BCE, but work stopped and did not resume until 520 BCE. With every bit of news, the mood fluctuated. Especially during the reign of Ahasuerus, jubilation turned to gloom. Fortunately, Darius not only upheld the original decree but also provided additional financial aid.

I can attest to the fact that the rebuilt Temple in Jerusalem remained standing from 515 BCE until 70 CE, during which time it continued to serve as the center of Jewish worship with its focus on *korbanot* (sacrificial offerings). The prophet Ezra describes the building of the Temple. Two leaders of the Persian Empire, both sympathetic to the Jews — Cyrus the Great and Darius the Great — were the instruments by which HaShem re-established the Holy Temple.

515 BCE

Baruch HaShem, the reconstruction of the Temple was triumphantly completed in 515 BCE.[33] The joyous dedication of the second *Beit haMikdash* under Zerubavel, on the site of the First Temple in Jerusalem, was celebrated after four years of work. Zerubavel, the governor of Judah who led the first group of Jewish returnees from Babylon in the first year of Cyrus' reign, was also the one who laid the foundation for the Second Temple.

---

33 Conflicting dates among Jewish historians place the date of dedication at 520 BCE and destruction at 70 CE. Chabad maintains that the dedication was in the year 3412 from Creation, placing the dedication in the year 349 BCE. This stems from their belief that the First Temple was built in 833 BCE. Most authorities maintain that King Solomon completed the First Temple in 960 BCE and that it was destroyed in 586 BCE. See also Ezra 5.6-6:15; https://www.jewishvirtuallibrary.org/jsource/History/Persians.html; Also http://judaism.about.com/library/1_jerusalem/bl_jerusalemhistory2.htm Also Goldwurm, Hersh. *History of the Jewish people: the Second Temple era*, Mesorah Publications, 1982. pg. 213

397 BCE[34]

Ezra reconstituted the scattered Jewish community based on the Torah, stressing adherence to the halachah (Jewish law). He earned the respected title of "scribe" in the Jewish tradition. Ezra set up the Great Assembly of scholars and prophets, the precursor of the *Sanhedrin*, as the last word on questions of religious law. It was the Great Assembly that initiated many elements of existing traditional Judaism, such as public readings of the Torah, the *Shemoneh Esrai* (*Amida*), as well as establishing the feast of Purim.

332–63 BCE

The era known as the Hellenistic Period spans almost 270 years from the time Alexander the Great defeated the Persian King Darius and captured Jerusalem. The Jews had no standing army to speak of. They had a small militia that defended the gates of Jerusalem and a small band of soldiers on horseback trained to trounce the roving bands of bandits operating in the Judean hills. These comparatively tiny forces were no match for the tens of thousands of Greek soldiers trained with an unparalleled and innovative weapon — the phalanx. The phalanx was a human machine: a close-ranked rectangular formation consisting of 256 men who fought eight- or sixteen-men deep and in a frontage of thirty-two or sixteen men accordingly. Each soldier carried as his primary weapon a six- to ten-foot-long spear.[35] The Jews, having experienced devastation of previous wars in the past and cushioned by generations of peace, had little inclination for war. Thus it was understandable that the Jews offered no resistance and became part of the Greek Empire.

The Jews enjoyed 300 years of peace, from the time of their return from the Babylonian exile to the end of the Ptolemaic Empire.[36] During

---

34   Scholars are divided over the chronological sequence of the activities of Ezra and Nehemiah. According to *Tanach*, Ezra came to Jerusalem "in the seventh year of Artaxerxes the King." Does the passage refer to Artaxerxes I (465-424 BCE) or to Artaxerxes II (404-359 BCE)? Because of this uncertainty, we therefore do not know whether the date of Ezra's mission was 458 BCE or 397 BCE.

35   Actually there were two types of spears: A short stabbing spear fitted with an iron head for thrusting in melee combat, and a longer spear eight- to ten-feet-long intended for throwing — much like the javelins.

36   320 BCE

this period, Jewish ritual practices were reinstated, sacrificial offerings resumed in the Temple, the Jewish population increased dramatically, and the land was fruitful. Jews teamed up with the Phoenicians to expand international trade and Jewish colonies were to be found in ever-distant lands. The mechanism of international trade required a wide-reaching structure of reciprocal confidence and reliance and a commonality of language. Only because the Jewish people were dispersed as they were could they make such a network. Bound by the moral and ethical code of the Torah, the Jews provided a strong social unit. This facilitated universal banking and international commerce.

Still, there was a price to pay for these material comforts. Alexander the Great initiated a process of Hellenization. Even after the division of the kingdom between Egypt and Syria, the process of Hellenization continued. Antiochus IV,[37] king of the Syrian-Greek (Seleucids)[38] Empire, banned the observance of three elemental *mitzvot: Brit Milah* (circumcision), Shabbat and Rosh Chodesh (the New Moon). Outlawing these Torah commandments triggered the successful rebellion that we celebrate on Chanukah. Throughout the land, and especially in Jerusalem, the impact of the "Greek way of life" permeated the Jewish psyche. This included placing importance on the gymnasium — a social center and training ground for athletic fitness that promoted the public display of the naked human body. Many Jews, seeking to hide their circumcision, opted for painful reverse surgery to appear uncircumcised. Other signs of voluntary Hellenization were evident in the use of Greek language, adoption of Greek clothing styles, and the appearance of priests at arena games, often neglecting their Temple obligations.

323 BCE

Alexander the Great, the Macedonian king who defeated his Persian Empire, died at the age of 33. His death is shrouded in mystery. Many believe that he did not die of natural causes.

---

37 His full name was Antiochus IV Epiphanus

38 A Hellenistic state (Syrian-Greek) ruled by the Seleucid dynasty following the division of the empire created by Alexander the Great.

320–198 BCE

The age of Alexander, brief as it was, and his defeat of the 200 year-old Persian Empire, marks a defining moment in the history of the world.

Alexander, one of history's greatest generals, was dead. Numerous wars of succession broke out and lasted for twenty years following his death. The Ptolemiesin Egypt succeeded in seizing Jerusalem on a Sabbath day following a pretense that Ptolemy I[39] wished to bring a sacrificial offering to the Temple. He deceived the Jews, who did not want to fight on the Sabbath day.

Josephus (not always the most reliable of historians) claims that Ptolemy I took many captives from Jerusalem and from the rest of Judea and Samaria and resettled them in Egypt. Other accounts maintain that the Ptolemies were tolerant of the Jewish concept of G-d and of the Jewish societal model. For a century and a half, the Jews and the Egyptian Greeks lived in harmony, trading with each other and benefiting by the international contacts that the Jews had established with their fellow Jews. In fact, according to these other historians, Ptolemy I was so kind to the Jews that many went voluntarily to live in Egypt, including the respected High Priest Hezekiah.

Under the Ptolemaic dynasty, with its political seat in Alexandria, local Egyptian officials taxed residents in Israel. It is during this period that the High Priest became the most influential figure in Jewish life. In the year 280 BCE, two powerful dynasties fought for control of the Middle East: the Ptolemies who controlled Egypt, Palestine, and Phoenicia, and the Seleucids who controlled Asia Minor, Syria, and Mesopotamia. The Seleucids desperately wanted to control Palestine and Phoenicia, areas that included important seaports. Numerous battles ensued between the Syrian kingdom and the Egyptian Ptolemies. The resulting clashes increased the sufferings of the Jews, who favored the Egyptians because they were generally kind and tolerant of the Jews.

198–167 BCE

After numerous attempts to capture Phoenicia and Palestine, Antiochus III ("the Great") defeated Ptolemy's General Scopas, initiating the

---

39   One of Alexander's surviving generals and heirs to the Hellenistic empire.

rule of the Syrian Seleucids in 198 BCE. Antiochus III granted the Jews of Jerusalem religious freedom to observe their ancestral laws. His son, Antiochus IV, didn't continue this policy of tolerance.

190 BCE

Antiochus III the Great ruled between 222 and 187 BCE. Josephus depicts him as welcoming towards the Jews and mindful of their loyalty to him.[40] It was his son, Antiochus IV Epiphanus, who subjugated Judea and was defied by the Maccabees in the story of Chanukah. The contrast between father and son was, as Josephus puts it, "according to the law of their forefathers." Antiochus III the Great was defeated by the Romans and lost control of Asia Minor. The Romans took his son (who would later become Antiochus IV Epiphanus) hostage, forcing him to pay heavy tribute to the Romans. Three years later, Antiochus III the Great died while trying to loot a Roman Temple. The seizure of power in 175 BCE by his son Antiochus IV Epiphanus from Seleucus IV Philopater brought about the first organized harassment of the Jews.

Antiochus IV appointed Jason,[41] brother of Onias III, who accelerated Hellenization in Palestine, eager to make Jerusalem a Greek city-state by force.[42] From this point on, the office of High Priest became a political appointment. The people, however, rejected political appointees as High Priests, and their struggle began as the appointee sought to retain power by force. The book of Maccabees describes how, in 170–169 BCE, Antiochus looted the Temple treasury.[43]

169–167 BCE

Forced Hellenization emerged when Antiochus Epiphanus assumed office. Prior to that time, Jews in Judea enjoyed relative freedom and, as a result, many Jews chose to assimilate.

---

40   see Antiquities, chapter 3, sections 3-4

41   The Seleucid Empire controlled Jerusalem during the tenure of Onias III and Seleucus IV Philopater. Both were friendly to the Jews and paid all expenses connected with the *Beit haMikdash*. According to 2 Maccabees, Simon, a Hellenizer and also an official of the Temple who was a member of the Tribe of Benjamin, persuaded Seleucus IV Philapater to loot the Temple. The effort failed and the court never absolved the High Priest.

42   Daniel 11:28; 1 Maccabees 1:20-23

43   ibid

Antiochus returned from a failed attempt to attack Egypt and encountered a popular Jewish rebellion in Jerusalem against his appointees Jason and Menelaus. The decisive moment came when Jason's successor as High Priest, Menelaus, permitted Antiochus to plunder the Temple. The rebellion enraged Antiochus, who ordered his troops to attack and seize the city. With the rebellion under control, Menelaus was reinstated in office.

Once again, the Jews rebelled. This time, Antiochus sent in a strong force, suppressing the rebellion and establishing a garrison in the city. Determined to teach the Jews a lesson, Antiochus issued one edict after another as he sought to abolish the Jewish religion throughout Judea. The Temple rituals in Jerusalem were purged and the Temple was turned into a pagan temple for Zeus. The worship of pagan gods became obligatory and enforced. Possession of a Torah scroll was illegal. Sacrificial offerings to HaShem were forbidden, as was circumcision. Sabbath and festival observance was also forbidden. Anyone practicing Judaism or refusing to participate in pagan rituals was tortured. On December 25, 167 BCE, Antiochus defiled the Holy Temple by offering pigs as a sacrifice to Zeus.

Those loyal to HaShem and to Torah observance were called *Chasidim* — the pious ones. They united to preserve Judaism.

167-63 BCE

The suppression of Jewish religious observance, the defilement of the Holy Temple, and the forced imposition of Hellenistic practices by Antiochus Epiphanes led to the Maccabean revolt, which began in the year 165 BCE and continued until 164 BCE, when Judah the Maccabee recaptured Jerusalem and restored the Temple.

The independent Hasmonean Kingdom of Israel survived until the year 63 BCE when Roman general Pompey captured Jerusalem.[44]

63 BCE

The Roman Period, which began in the year 63 BCE, lasted for hundreds of years. It was then, eighty-two years before I was born, in the year 63 BCE

---

44   Even then, the Hasmonean rule continued until 37 BCE, but only under the protection of Rome. In the year 40 BCE, Rome appointed Herod as King of Judea. Jewish independence under the Hasmonean monarchs lasted but a century.

that General Pompey subdued Judea and captured Jerusalem, after which it became a client kingdom. The Hasmonean rule was now submissive to Rome. Jewish self-governance ended with the fall of the Hasmonean Kingdom. Still, despite some semblance of semi-independence under Roman rule, the craving for Jewish nationalism ignited a series of Jewish-Roman wars in the first two centuries of the Common Era, including the Great Revolt (66–73 CE), the Kitos War (115–117 CE), and Bar Kochba's revolt (132–135 CE).

The success of any victory was short-term. The Jewish rebels were no match for the powerful Roman legions, who plundered and burned the reconstructed Second Temple, razed Jewish strongholds (Gamla and Yodfat in 67 CE and Masada in 73CE), and slaughtered thousands of Jews. Many of those who were not slaughtered were taken captive to Rome as slaves. In fact, a major factor in the dispersal of Jews throughout the world was their sale as slaves throughout the empire. With the passage of time, Jews who survived the onslaught and were not enslaved initiated commerce with others in the Roman Empire. Jews would come to Rome on political and business missions as commercial trade developed. Even prior to 63 BCE, when General Pompey conquered Judea and captured Jerusalem, there was a sizeable Jewish presence in Rome dating back to 161 BCE.[45]

37 BCE

Herod's rule began in the year 37 BCE with the capture of Jerusalem. He was the pro-Roman king of a small Jewish state. Considered a puppet of Rome, he had considerable leeway in establishing a domestic policy of his own. Although he tried to defer to the religious sensitivities of the Jews, many were not happy with his rule. His appointment caused a lot of bitterness among the Jews. Although Herod observed Jewish practice, his mother was not Jewish, hence he was not considered Jewish by the dominant Pharisaic tradition (i.e., not *halachically* Jewish).[46] Herod may have deemed himself to be Jewish, but he was not considered Jewish by

---

45   When Jason ben Eleazar and Eupolemus ben Johanan came as envoys of Judah Maccabee. https://www.jewishvirtuallibrary.org/jsource/vjw/Rome.html1

46   "Herod I". Encyclopaedia Judaica (CD-ROM Edition Version 1.0). Ed. Cecil Roth. Keter Publishing House.

the observant Jews of Judea,[47] who yearned to achieve political independence. These proud Jews, fiercely loyal and devoted to a Torah nation, sought to throw off the yoke of foreign control and to assert their separate identity and culture. Despite this resentment, the new king started an extensive building program. He expanded the Temple Mount area, which resulted in an enlarged platform.

19 BCE — The Year I was Born

You might say that I was "born" in the year 19 BCE when Herod renovated the Temple and the surrounding platform. The Second Temple was repaired and restored by Herod the Great in the year 20 BCE.[48] That is how it became known as Herod's Temple. Herod undertook an immense project on the Temple Mount, greatly expanding the area of the Mount.[49]

Today's Western Wall formed part of the retaining perimeter wall of this platform. I am one of the huge lower stones called *ashlars*[50] that, together with the stone courses that are underground, are the original stones from the time of Herod. The stones that are higher up date from later Muslim times. If you look very carefully, you can distinguish between the original Western Wall stones and the others by their size and by how they were chiseled. Every one of us original stones has a chiseled outer edge on all four sides. Most of those added later lack this framed-edge feature. (See Chapter VI to learn how the stones were quarried, transported, and then erected to form the Western Wall.)

Note: The chronological timeline continues in Chapter VII.

---

47   Antiquities of the Jews, 14.15.2

48   "In the eighteenth year (20-19 BCE) of his reign, Herod rebuilt the Temple on a more magnificent scale," Source: http://www.jewishencyclopedia.com/articles/14304-Temple-of-herod

49   Herod expanded the Temple Mount area by enclosing the outer limits with massive retaining walls. The space between the retaining walls and the original ramp was filled with a series of domed vault structures. The vaults were covered with earth, creating a level platform. The Western Wall was the longest of the retaining walls, measuring 1,580 feet (485 meters) from north to south. The segment of the wall venerated today is 195 ft. (60m.) long located toward the southern end.

50   The wall that Herod's artisans built with me is called a *Coursed Ashlar Wall*. It simply means that they positioned cut, rectangular stone in rows that fit together with precision. *Ashlars* are dressed stones. Every one of us original stones has a chiseled outer edge on all four sides. See http://www.biblicalarchaeology.org/

CHAPTER VI

How I Came to be a Part of The Western Wall

Most of us stones are quite ancient, having been carved out from a nearby stone quarry some just over 2,000 years ago. Just a few years ago (2007), archaeologists discovered a quarry compound that may have provided King Herod with the stones for Herod's Temple. Israeli newspapers reported that "coins, pottery and an iron stake found indicated the date of the quarrying to be about 19 BCE. Findings included 'cut stone blocks that match the size of the ones used in the construction of the Temple Walls.'" The archaeologists suggest that Herod must have trained 10,000 workers in order to complete the work.[51]

You should have been here when they tried to separate me from the bedrock. The stonecutters used hammers, chisels, and metal wedges as they struggled to extract me. While I was not the heaviest stone, I was not a lightweight either. Giving birth to a stone is quite different from giving birth to a human baby. Those working to extract me from the quarry were quite a team. Remember that I was born before the invention of hydraulic stone splitters, cutting saws, pneumatic machines, surfacing tools, or sandblasting nozzles. These artisans had rudimentary tools such as chisels, mallets, and wooden beams. They may have lived long ago, but they had a keen knowledge of design techniques and principles involved in extracting huge stones from a mountain. They may not have had precise technical plans or blueprints, but they did have simple drawings and

---

51   From *Ha'Aretz* article dated September 25, 2007, describing the find by Yuval Baruch, archaeologist with the Israeli Antiquities Authority.

handwritten specifications. They had a working knowledge of arithmetic, algebra, and classical geometry based on Greek, Egyptian, and Babylonian sources.

I was impressed with their preliminary deliberations and relieved that they did not just start chopping. The work crew was giving full attention to what the supervisor was saying. He demanded their full attention, making sure that they all understood the points that were being made. A few had questions, which were answered patiently. After all, this was a holy assignment. Careless mistakes would have ruined the stone, possibly causing injuries. As I waited patiently for the first chisel strike, I could sense the critical thinking going on. This was a top-flight team. The team used logic and reasoning to identify the strengths and weaknesses of alternate solutions to the quarrying task.

My six faces have been carved with such exactness that they lie flawlessly aligned with and on top of each other, without mortar.[52] Now, 2,000 years of erosion have wiped out any evidence of the superior lines and borders of many of the monumental stones. We all get old; humans, animals, plant life and yes, even stones like me who are classified as mineral life. You need not look any further than our windswept weather-beaten faces for proof.

"Ouch! That hurt!"

Obviously, this stonecutter's hand and arm were not steady. I guess they give beginners the initial task. Gradually, as these beginners develop greater manual dexterity, they go on to assignments that are more precise. Without recourse to aspirin or other painkillers, I had no choice but to bear the pain of each cut. Now, a more experienced stonecutter took over. Boy, you should have seen him at work. This person had the ability to bend, stretch, twist, and reach with every part of his body, his arms, and his legs as he continued chiseling into the stone. This guy had powerful abdominal and lower back muscles that supported his body repeatedly

---

52   It would seem that the rear of each stone was also "faced" in order to bear up against the soil pressure of the filling behind the Wall. The rows terraced, with each row being set back a fraction of an inch in relation to the one below. This setback creates an eastward gradient that, given the weight of the stones, explains the extraordinary solidity of the Western Wall. See http://mosaic.lk.net/g-Wall.html.

as his hammer repeatedly struck the chisel-head. Every five minutes or so he paused to wipe the fine stone-dust from his face, sip from the water jug, and review the progress. As he rested, he spoke to the others explaining how to next proceed. Extracting me from the quarry took almost a week. Nevertheless, I survived and am here to continue my story. Remember, too, that this was thousands of years before stonemasons would have such common protective or safety equipment such as safety shoes, plastic glasses, gloves, hearing protection, and hard hats. Every one of the workers understood the need for precaution against accidental injuries.

Standing in Awe and Respect

One thing is certain. All who look at the Wall stand in awe and respect because this site is so holy. For people of faith, the Kotel represents the last recognized and accessible vestige of our Holy Temple complex. For others, their mere presence here makes them more receptive to their ancient tradition.

Over the centuries, I have watched first-time visitors to the Kotel. I study their facial expressions. Some scan the Wall with wonder. Others gaze with admiration and amazement at the remarkable technological and artistic accomplishment. Even today, first-time visitors marvel as they study and photograph the Western Wall with its massive courses of stone. Children ask their parents and parents ask themselves: "How those did engineers of 2,000 years ago erect such a massive and imposing structure? What tools did they use to cut the giant stones? How did they transport them? How did they lift them to such a height?" Scientists can only speculate because, truthfully, they still have not worked out all the techniques that were used. Archaeologists base their thinking on ancient professional writings, sketches and drawings, and the techniques used by pre-technological societies.

I wish they would ask me. I was here from the start. I can tell them exactly how things were done.

Next time you come to visit the Western Wall, come over to me and I will direct you to the Western Wall Tunnels. In these tunnels, you can see a row of huge stones in the tunnels, called the "Master Course." These stones are by far the biggest building stones ever found in Israel.

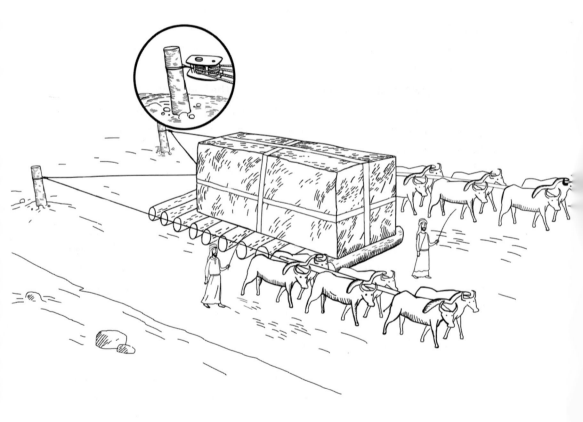

Transporting the Stones[53]

Go ahead and ask: "How was it possible to move such a massive rock?" Considering the absence of modern techniques and equipment, the very thought is mind-boggling.

It's a good question, which I'll try to answer based on my experience and observation. First, they had to separate the stones from the bedrock. Remember: 2,000 years ago they did not have blasting materials. Alfred Nobel did not invent dynamite until 1867! Quarrying, or extracting the stone from the bedrock, was done by stonecutters using hammers, chisels, and metal wedges. We've discussed this above.

Next was moving the stones. That was a challenge. They needed a lot of muscle power, skill, and creativity to move and lift these enormous stones. They built a device that was a combination hoist-derrick-winch to elevate the huge stones. These were then positioned onto log rollers and pulled along by oxen or other beasts of burden. That is how we were transported to our present site. The smaller stones were heaved unto wagons that were hitched to oxen.

The biggest challenge came in transporting the huge stones that had been carved out of the bedrock. Stones that were too heavy for wagons required greater creativity. Huge wooden wheels were constructed with a square cutout. Each end of the stone was positioned in the center of the huge wooden wheels. In many cases, the massive wooden wheels, some measuring twenty feet or more in diameter, were constructed around the exposed end of the stone. The stone acted as an axle, essentially a shaft on which the set of wheels revolved. All that was required now was to roll the wheels. In fact, the two wheels and stone axle were hitched to a team of oxen and rolled forward to its destination. This technique was probably learned from a Greek architect living in the fifth century BCE who conceived a method whereby two huge wheels were built or connected on either side of a stone.

Rollers and Levers

The technical capabilities of the ancient Jews were quite incredible and included the use of rollers and levers to move huge stones my size. Picture

---

53 See the animation and explanation at: http://english.thekotel.org/content.asp?back=1&id=97

me: a massive block of stone, on log rollers. The builders were quite familiar with methods of mechanical advantage such as levers, inclined planes, pulleys, etc., to do the job. Moving the massive stones involved hundreds of strong men who pivoted, tilted, and rocked the heavy load into position. Once positioned, their combined muscle-power pushed from behind as a team of oxen pulled from the front. As the oxen would pull, the stone would roll across the logs like a conveyor belt. As each log was exposed in the rear, a team of men would carry it forward and position it in front of the heavy load in the desired direction to keep the stone rolling along.

At times, a different technique was used. Two sturdy stakes would be driven into the ground five or ten meters ahead of the stone, one on either side of the stone. A team of six oxen on either side of the stone and facing in the opposite direction of transport would be harnessed by means of a set of pulleys to these wooden stakes. As the oxen pulled, the stone would progress slowly in the direction of travel rolling across the logs. Then, a crew of workers would place the log rollers ahead of the stone in the direction of the transport to keep the stone rolling along. Quite ingenious — and it worked.

Of course, the terrain had to be prepared. Where a natural smooth path did not exist, a special advance team would create a relatively smooth path of earth with a mud-mixture of sand and smaller stones. Picture it as a human "work train" that accompanied the huge stone in motion. At times during transportation, ramps, platforms, or fillers were required. These were constructed with this mud-mixture material, and then broken up and reused as the process was repeated. It was very similar to the methods we use today, which include scaffolding, wall forms, blocking, etc. This eased the task of movement.

Unfortunately, there were accidents when a stone would slide off the rollers. Sometimes the rollers were of little use and the workers had to resort to sliding. This was not easy because of the ground slope and the surface smoothness of the path. Large diameter rollers work very well on smooth surfaces. On rough surfaces, they had to use smaller diameter rollers involving lubricated sliding. Sliding worked best, but in my case, it was a combination of rolling and sliding to get me from the quarry to where I now stand. A number of the very, very large stones were actually rounded at the quarry, rolled to their final destination, and then chiseled down to the end product. In a number of cases, the sides of the stone were chiseled to form a lip onto which a rope would be attached for easier dragging. Sometimes, they would use different types of liquid lubricants in order to facilitate movement of the large stones.

Erecting the Wall

To erect the wall, they experimented with a number of techniques. One such method was to use a wooden ramp and log-rollers. Ropes were used to pull the stone up the wooden backdrop with the help of the same log-rollers. This was the system they used in Egypt to erect obelisks. We can only theorize as to how these huge blocks were raised. Most probably, a fulcrum was created from a mound of smaller stones. A long wooden tree trunk was then used as leverage to raise each block incrementally.[54]

---

54 Here is how the Egyptians raised their blocks to erect the pyramids: Stone blocks with special grooves would be installed on the extension as fulcrums over which long wooden tree trunks would be placed. These timbers would have diameters of one-half to one foot and would be twenty to twenty-five feet in length. The short arm of a timber would be attached

At one time, the above-ground portion of the Western Wall of the Temple Mount measured 1,592 feet in length. Sections of the wall were devastated by the many wars. When Jews shifted their central place of worship from the Mount of Olives to the Western Wall 750 years ago, they settled on a section measuring 65 feet long and 49 feet high. That segment consisted of five of the original layers of stone running horizontally in the Wall. The four layers added on top of the five original layers are large undressed stones that were added by Muslim builders in the 7th century. On top of these, another sixteen layers of small stones were added some time later. Not too long ago, the Muslim *Wakf* added several new rows, ostensibly as a maintenance effort.

Statistics

I recall how, starting with the early 8th century, Muslims built their houses right up against the wall, concealing most of its span. As to its height, the Western Wall now rises to about sixty feet from the paved area to its peak.

Let me share with you an astounding statistic. Most tourists, and many Israelis, are simply not aware of the fact that the total height of the wall, from its foundation to its top, is 98–105 feet. What you see from where you are standing is just the exposed section — a 62-foot-tall wall. The Wall was constructed with forty-five layers of stone, twenty-eight of them above the current paved level of the plaza and seventeen below the current paved level of the plaza. The first five layers of stone, erected about the same time as I was brought to the Kotel, were enormous meleke limestones quarried from either Zedekiah's Cave, located under the Muslim Quarter of the Old City, or, some say, from Ramat Shlomo, some two-and-a-half miles northwest of the Old City.

---

to a block, while the longer arm would have a net-basket attached to it. Weights would be incrementally added to this end, thus raising the block. The traditional view of Egyptologists is that the builders used some sort of ramp to raise the blocks. Evidence for the use of ramps includes paintings of construction ramps, a ramp found at an unfinished temple, and the remains of ramps present at a couple of pyramid sites. http://www.ling.upenn.edu/~jason2/papers/pyramid.htm

Mind-boggling, Isn't It? Well, here's More:

Is that thirty-pound backpack weighing you down? Think of the mammoth-sized stones in front of you. Most of these original stones weigh between two and eight tons each. That is between 4,000 to 16,000 pounds! But wait, the weight of these huge stones is dwarfed by some others that weigh even more. There is one astonishing gigantic stone to be found in the northern section of Wilson's Arch that measures more than forty-two feet and weighs an estimated 570 tons, or more than a million pounds! That certainly qualifies as one of the heaviest items ever hauled up by man without power-driven equipment. Most of the enormous stones making up the wall weigh between two and eight tons, but some exceed forty tons.

To describe that stone as my big brother would be an understatement. The comparison is my restrained way of expressing the contrast in size. It is indeed a lesson in humility. Any thought that my immense girth and weight would justify an air of superiority is quickly deflated when I consider my big brother's gargantuan mass.

Let me share with you a lesson that I have learned. I told you at the beginning of this book that we stones have feelings and emotions. The true humility of a Kotel stone becomes apparent when he has an open eye and a soft spot for Jews whose fate has brought them to the Kotel for the first time. Many visitors know very little about our rich tradition, usually through no fault of their own.

I have cultivated a kind of humility over the centuries, which enables me to view each person as worthy of my attention. A little humility, however, may be just what we need. Why not draw on our vast and rich Torah tradition to improve our character and become more ethical, moral, and righteous? *Anava* (humility) is followed by fear of G-d, wealth, honor, and life.[55] If we could only truly grasp the significance of humility and emulate its courage, sincerity, and deep substance, it would not only lead to more wholesome lives, but also perhaps contribute to the solution of many conflicts previously deemed irresolvable.

By the way, even though English is not my primary language, I find it interesting to note the etymological root of the word *humility*. It comes from the Latin word *humilis* meaning "low," which, in turn, comes from the Latin *humus* which means "earth" or "dirt" or "soil."

---

55   Proverbs 22:4

I have personally witnessed the transformation in people's lives who have embraced the Torah teachings on humility. It isn't necessary to forfeit your self-esteem. Trust me, you will gradually be able to find a balance between humility and self-esteem. Try judging other people fairly. Give the other fellow the benefit of the doubt. Learn when forgiveness is mandatory, discretionary, or prohibited. Words can hurt, so avoid talk that hurts or shames others. Control your inclinations. Don't let hatred, retribution, jealousy or resentment dictate your behavior.

As former Chief Rabbi of Great Britain Jonathan Sacks has written:[56]

> What glorious revelation humility is of the human spirit. Humility is more than just a virtue: it is a perception, a language in which the "I" is silent so that I can hear the "Thou," the unspoken call beneath human speech, the Divine whisper within all that moves, the voice that calls me to redeem its loneliness with the touch of love. Humility opens us to the world. And does it matter that it no longer fits the confines of our age? The truth is that moral beauty, like music, always moves those who can hear beneath the noise. Virtues may be out of fashion, but they are never out of date. The things that call attention to themselves are never interesting for long, which is why our attention span is so short. Humility — the polar opposite of "advertisements for myself" — never fails to leave its afterglow.

---

56   http://www.chabad.org/library/article_cdo/aid/83807/jewish/On-Humility.htm

CHAPTER VII

(Chronological timeline continued from Chapter V)

4 BCE — King Herod Dies

The news came in bit by bit. Gradually, it became clear that King Herod was dead. Herod (Hordos in Hebrew) was appointed by Rome as king of Israel. I remember him for his massive building projects in Jerusalem, and am ever grateful to him for the rebuilding of the Second Temple in Jerusalem and, of course, for the walls surrounding the Temple Mount. Perhaps I would not be here were it not for Herod. However, there was another, darker facet to Herod's rule. Many who came to the Kotel described Herod as "a madman who murdered his own family and a great many rabbis."[57]

Savage Ferocity

26–36 CE

Pontius Pilate was the Roman governor of Judea from 26–36 CE. He was the judge at Jesus's trial and the man who authorized his crucifixion. The Christian Gospels portray Jesus as blameless in the numerous intrigues against Rome. Not only do the Christian teachings depict Pilate

---

57 http://www.aish.com/literacy/JewishHistory/Crash_Course_in_Jewish_History_Part_31_-_Herod3_the_Great.asp

as unenthusiastic about putting Jesus to death, but they point the accusatory finger at the Jewish priestly hierarchy.

And so it was, on the 14th of Nissan (April 25) in the year 31 CE, that Jesus was crucified. Pilate was described by the Jewish philosopher Philo of Alexandria: "Pilate was inflexible; he was stubborn, of cruel disposition. He executed troublemakers without a trial."[58] He refers to Pilate's "venality, his violence, thefts, assaults, abusive behavior, endless executions, endless savage ferocity."

The historian Josephus later recorded how Pilate continually ignited near-rebellions because of his lack of consideration for Jewish religious customs. Prior Roman governors showed consideration for Jewish sensitivities by removing all icons and images from their banners when entering Jerusalem. Pilate, however, allowed his soldiers to sneak them into the city at night. On the following day, hundreds of Jews gathered at the Kotel and elsewhere throughout Jerusalem, furious at Pilate's duplicity. The Jews appealed to Pilate to remove Caesar's image from the flags and banners. Not only did he rebuff their repeated requests but he ordered his soldiers to surround the demonstrators and to threaten them with death if they continued to protest. After five tense days, the offensive images were removed when Pilate realized that the Jews were prepared to die sooner than see their religious traditions trampled.

I want to tell you about another perfidious incident which I overheard from many of the worshippers who came to the Kotel. (Josephus confirms the veracity of this episode.) It seems that Pilate looted money from the Temple to build an aqueduct. When Jews remonstrated, Pilate arranged for his soldiers to indiscriminately assault the Jews, killing dozens in the process, hoping to suppress their protests.

39 CE

In the year 39 CE, the mad Roman Emperor, Caligula, proclaimed that he was a deity. He ordered that a statue of him be set up at every temple in the Roman Empire. This harsh declaration infuriated the Jews. They categorically refused to permit the statue to defile the *Beit haMikdash*.

---

58   Philo, On the Embassy of Gauis. Book XXXVIII 299-305
      See also: http://www2.educationalcoin.com/2013/11/15/the-coins-of-pontius-pilate/

A delegation of Jews traveled to Rome to try to pacify the emperor, but to no avail. He threatened not only to destroy the Temple but also to massacre all the Jews. Only the sudden violent death of Caligula saved the Jews and the Temple from immediate destruction. Caligula's threats brought about a more fundamental change in the attitude of many of the remaining (more moderate) Jews. They realized that there was no assurance that the next Roman ruler would not execute the plan to destroy the Holy Temple and bring about the end of Judaism.

The Jews were troubled. There was fear, anxiety, and apprehension. Simmering emotions gradually began to boil. Undeniably, this was a major topic of conversation as passions raged. Different groups advocated alternate courses of action. The more extreme groups were livid with anger. Others — more conservative than the first — cautioned against any rash action. A storm was brewing amidst commotion and disorder. Many came to the Wall seeking some sign from heaven. I don't know why they preferred coming to my Wall rather than to the *Beit haMikdash*. It was a time when Rome appointed the High Priest. Often they selected someone who the Jews distrusted, probably one who conspired with Rome. Additionally, the atmosphere was wrought with fear and suspicion. It was said that at times Roman soldiers exposed themselves in the Temple and burnt a Torah scroll there. Perhaps the Temple at that point in history was not conducive to prayer.

41–44 CE — The Third Wall

Herod's grandson, Agrippa I, first started building the "Third Wall" during his reign over the Land of Israel in the year 40 CE. This "Third Wall" of Jerusalem, so described by Josephus in his monumental work *The Jewish War*, was the northern-most boundary of the ancient city of Jerusalem. Herod built the first two walls but died before he could complete the remaining walls. It was Herod's great-grandson, King Agrippa II, who completed the construction of the Third Wall started by his father Agrippa I. The Jews loved Agrippa. He traced his lineage to the Hasmoneans; his grandmother had been Herod's wife Marianne (Miriam), a virtuous and devout Jew. Had the wall been finished, few would have believed that the Romans could ever breach it. Each of its bonded stones measured thirty feet long and fifteen feet high and was fifteen feet thick. The

Third Wall was designed to protect the northern boundary of the newly expanded city of Jerusalem. Construction was halted at the intrusion of the Roman governor of Syria, who was suspicious of Agrippa's motives. They feared that he meant to use it in a rebellion against Rome.

We started working on it again after the Great Revolt against the Romans began in 67 CE. Extraordinary effort on the part of the Jewish defenders succeeded in raising the height of the Third Wall. Massive fortified towers were built at strategic locations along the Wall. Still, despite its thickness and height, the Romans were able to penetrate the Wall with their battering rams and siege engines. In the year 70 CE, the Romans succeeded in breaking through, leading to the utter destruction of the city and the Temple.

Take a tip from me. Next time you come to the Kotel, take time afterward to view what remains of that third wall. Walk or drive to the Paz gas station in east Jerusalem. You will see a few large, dressed limestone blocks embedded in the pavement. I admit that it does not look like much now. However, to the Jewish defenders of Jerusalem, it bolstered their dream for independence from foreign subjugation.

66 CE — Revolt against the Romans

Did you hear the news? The Jews revolted against the Romans! This is serious business.

I knew it was coming. Who could blame the Jews for wanting to overthrow the Roman rule? The Romans first occupied our land sometime between 67 and 63 BCE. It was at the time of the Maccabean Revolt. It was not just a war against the Greeks. It was a civil war between those who were faithful to the Torah against Hellenized Jews who were backing the Greeks. Roman rule was oppressive. For the past sixty-six years, Judea was ruled by Roman procurators whose task was to collect taxes from the Jews and pass the sums collected to Rome. They were assigned a quota. Anything collected beyond the quota they could keep. This resulted in the imposition of confiscatory taxes. This alone was repressive and cruel. But what the Jews resented most was Rome's decision to usurp the appointment of the High Priest. The High Priests represented the Jews before G-d on their most sacred occasions. Only those priests who collaborated with Rome were appointed. Thus was born a group of anti-Roman rebels zealously agitating for political and religious liberty; this group instigated the Great Revolt.

I heard the stories about the flagrant and often vulgar humiliation of Judaism's religion and holy sites that were triggered by Caligula's death. I was horrified to hear that that the *Beit haMikdash* was disgraced by the disgusting behavior of some Roman soldiers, and that a Torah scroll was burned. I could feel the resentment as it turned into outrage. Jews, having poured out their hearts at the Temple, came to my Wall. Here, at a less ceremonial site, they could vent more freely. They told me about Rome's brazen scorn for Judaism, and the shameless preferential treatment given to gentiles living amongst the Jews.

I knew something was in the air when a group of worshippers came rushing towards the Kotel one day with the news that vast quantities of silver were stolen from the Temple by the Romans. This alone would suffice to bring about the revolt. What I didn't know, which I later learned from worshippers, was that at the beginning of this First Jewish-Roman War, a group of Jewish radicals managed somehow to overcome the Roman garrison at Masada. Herod the Great fortified this very site 100 years earlier as a refuge for himself in the event of a revolt.

The incensed Jews rampaged in retaliation against Rome. In their fury, they devastated the small Roman battalion stationed in Jerusalem. The larger force of soldiers sent from Syria to route the Jewish insurgents was also wiped out by the enraged Jews. While the victory was heartening, it triggered a great Roman response, which came just as expected as day follows night. More than 60,000 heavily armed and highly professional troops came to punish us. They began with the Galilee in the north. The Galilee was defeated, with more than 100,000 Jews either killed or sold into slavery. The refugees who escaped the Galilean massacres were resentful that the Jews of Jerusalem did not come to their aid.[59] They fled to Jerusalem and began systematically murdering anyone in the Jewish leadership who was not as radical as they were.[60] Fellow Jews from the north killed the moderate Jewish leadership of

---

59   "Throughout the Roman conquest of this territory, the Jewish leadership in Jerusalem did almost nothing to help their beleaguered brothers. They apparently had concluded — too late, unfortunately — that the revolt could not be won, and wanted to hold down Jewish deaths as much as possible." http://www.jewishvirtuallibrary.org/jsource/Judaism/revolt.html

60   Ibid.

Jerusalem. The Jews of Jerusalem were disillusioned and leaderless. Their predicament was clear to all but a few zealots.

67 CE — The Siege of Yodfat

Let me tell you about another siege, The Siege of Yodfat. Think about it as part of the Great Revolt. Remember the background. Let us picture the scene: The southern kingdom of Judea had been a problematic constituency during the first century CE, ripped apart between rival religious factions, stressed to obey the Roman rules while maintaining their obedience to G-d. As in Jerusalem, Masada, Gamla, and elsewhere, the Roman procurators were often corrupt and repressive. I've told you about the major rebellion that finally erupted last year with a rebel government established here in Jerusalem. The Roman forces besieged the Jewish town of Yodfat. The siege lasted for forty-seven days, ending with the destruction and ransacking of the town and the death of most of its residents. Those not killed were taken away as slaves. It was the second bloodiest battle of the revolt. Only the violent and gruesome sacking of Jerusalem by the bloodthirsty Romans exceeded the horrors of Yodfat.

67 CE — The Battle at Gamla

We at the Kotel could not believe what was happening. It was about the time of Rosh Hashanah and Yom Kippur, 67 CE, when the Roman generals Vespasian and Titus, laid siege to Gamla. Josephus, the rebel commander, told the story of the Battle at Gamla.[61] Gamla was an impenetrable stronghold, also called the "Masada of the North." It proved itself for its strong defense against the Romans in the Jewish Revolt in 66 CE. Bordered on all sides by steep ravines, it was accessible by only one trail from the northeast. Jewish rebels fortified this access point as protection against the Roman invaders. We, in Jerusalem, never thought it possible for the Romans to conquer Gamla. When we later heard of its defeat by the Romans, we were terrified. The fall of Gamla, with the loss of 9,000 Jewish lives, was a bad omen. Did it herald the conquest of the rest of Judea?

---

61   Josephus, War, 1-82

70 CE — A Malicious Strategy

The festival of Passover was just a week away. I was delighted to see so many pilgrims coming to Jerusalem. Yet I was troubled and concerned. Had the Romans decided to stop their oppression of the Jews? Or was there some other sinister reason? While I welcome the participation of so many Jews coming to Jerusalem, the average worshipper did not seem to be disturbed. Nowhere were there any ominous signs. The Roman legions apparently publicized throughout the country their decision to permit holiday pilgrims to enter Jerusalem for the festival of Passover. With the holiday over, the malicious Roman strategy was exposed. They purposely prevented the pilgrims from leaving Jerusalem, creating a strain on the supply of food and water for the city's inhabitants. Negotiations between the Romans and the city's defenders were fruitless. I remember well how frightened worshippers came to the Kotel with news that the Romans had breached the walls of Jerusalem, setting off street-fighting with the zealots. Weakened and emaciated from lack of food and water, a few who came to the Kotel told me about a new type of siege engine. I had heard about battering rams in the past. The battering ram of old was a large, heavy log carried by several people and propelled with force against a fortified wall. They had to use a massive enough log and move it quickly enough to create sufficient momentum to damage the wall. However, this new type of siege engine was more sophisticated in design. Its battering ram hung from a support structure mounted on a wagon. The massive ram itself, suspended by ropes, could move back and forth freely as it was thrust against the wall of the city. The attacking tip of the ram was bolstered with a metal head.

We had no newspapers, radios, or cell phones in those days. News came to us from visitors to the Kotel.[62] This morning, I was horrified to learn that Roman troops had besieged Jerusalem. All around us within the city, Jews were blaming each other for the revolt's failure. Fear spread throughout. It was obvious to all that Roman military superiority would wreak death and devastation on the Jews in Jerusalem. Hundreds of

---

62   Why to the Kotel and not to the *Beit haMikdash*? I can only theorize that due to tensions with the Romans, some Jews opted to pray at the Mount of Olives and others at the Western Wall. Following the destruction of the Second Temple in 70 CE, the Western Wall was especially cherished as it is the spot closest to the Holy of Holies.

years from now, the rabbis would conclude that the revolt's failure was due less to the might of the Roman army but more to the baseless hatred (*sinat chinam*) among the Jews.[63] True, the zealots initially repelled the Roman sieges, but the chaos and disarray indicated just how poorly prepared they were for the forthcoming battles. Rabbi Yochanan ben Zakkai, always even-tempered, did his very best to avoid internal strife.

Anticipating a Roman siege, the Jews built up stocks of dry food sufficient to feed the city for many years. I was sickened to learn this afternoon from one of the regulars at the Minchah services that the zealots burned the entire supply of dry food that had been stockpiled for the express purpose of feeding the entire city in the event of a siege. This half-crazed action set off mass starvation, in the misguided belief that wiping out this anti-siege food supply would oblige all factions to take part in the revolt. The resulting starvation created unnecessary anguish, distress, and despair.

Smuggled Out of Jerusalem

On the heels of this news, I learned that the zealots' leader had ordered the execution of anyone advocating surrender to Rome. Some eminent sages opposed the revolt, most conspicuously Rabbi Yochanan ben Zakkai. I was concerned for his safety.

Providentially, I was told that Rabbi Yochanan ben Zakkai was smuggled out of Jerusalem by his disciples, camouflaged as a corpse. Once safely outside Jerusalem's walls, he surrendered to the Roman general Vespasian and correctly prophesied that Vespasian will be named emperor, and was accorded extraordinary leniency. He then asked Vespasian to grant him a site in Yavneh where he could establish a *yeshiva* and study Torah in peace. Vespasian pledged that if the prophesy came true, he would honor Rabbi ben Zakkai's appeal. Following this, Vespasian became emperor and granted a space in Yavneh for Torah learning. That *yeshiva* developed into the focal point of Torah learning for centuries to come, supplanting Jerusalem as the location of the *Sanhedrin*. Later generations would benefit from this decision. His *yeshiva* would become a starting place for the *Mishnah* and subsequent *Talmud*.[64]

---

63 *Yoma* 9b

64 "We do know that some great figures of ancient Israel opposed the revolt, most notably

According to the *Midrash*,[65] after Vespasian conquered the city of Jerusalem, he directed four generals to destroy the walls surrounding the Temple Mount. Three generals followed orders and destroyed their walls. I could never fathom why the general assigned to destroy my wall (the Western Wall) never even attempted to destroy it. Clearly, HaShem so decreed, perhaps since the *Shechinah* dwells in the west. When asked by Vespasian why he failed to destroy the Western Wall, the general replied, "By your life, I acted so for the honor of your empire; for if I had demolished it, nobody would know (in the time to come) what it was [that] you destroyed; but when people [will] look at the Western Wall, they will exclaim, 'Behold the might of Vespasian from what he didn't destroy!'"[66]

The Summer of 70 CE

The Romans finally succeeded in overpowering the dozing zealot guards and capturing Antonio's Fortress. The Fortress, built by Herod the Great, is located on the Northern Wall of the Temple Mount. From that vantage point, the Romans, now garrisoned there, could not only look right over into the Temple Mount area but could launch an attack on the Temple itself. It was a black day for us and for all of Judaism when the Romans breached the walls of Jerusalem. What followed next is beyond description. The fury of the most powerful empire in the world was unleashed against the half-starved citizenry of Jerusalem. The sadism and brutality of the Romans was evident everywhere.

A few weeks later, while we were still reeling from the desolation and the carnage, we received another shock. We heard, felt, and smelled the devastation being wrought on the Temple Mount. The Romans had destroyed the Second Temple! We were stunned. We stones, and the few remaining Jews of Judea, were frightened and distressed. This final blow was so devastating to a people supposedly hardened by a history of past repression.

Rabbi Yochanan ben Zakkai. Since the zealot leaders ordered the execution of anyone advocating surrender to Rome, Rabbi Yochanan arranged for his disciples to smuggle him out of Jerusalem, disguised as a corpse. Once safe, he personally surrendered to the Roman general Vespasian, who granted him concessions that allowed Jewish communal life to continue." http://www.jewishvirtuallibrary.org/jsource/Judaism/revolt.html

65 *Midrash Rabba*, Lamentations 1:31

66 From the Discovery Seminar Sourcebook

Josephus, the Roman historian, wrote that 1,100,000 people were killed during the revolt, siege and destruction, most of whom were Jewish, and that 97,000 Jews were taken prisoner and enslaved, including Shimon Bar Giora, a Jewish hero who was a leader of the Jewish revolt against Rome. Bar Giora was put to death in the year 71 CE as the symbol of the Jewish defeat, after the triumph of Vespasian and the overthrow of Jerusalem. Those who could flee escaped to surrounding lands.

Rumor had it that Titus, the Roman emperor, did not want to destroy the Temple. Rather he wanted to take possession of it and convert it into a Roman temple dedicated to him and to all Roman deities. That aspiration quickly faded when one of the Roman soldiers threw a burning stick onto one of the Temple's walls. The speed with which the fire spread and its intensity was staggering. It was the end of August, the height of the dry season. The date was the ninth of the Hebrew month of Av. The fire, now out of control, continued to burn violently, destroying the Holy Temple on the 10th of Av. People fled as the fire spread into the inhabited neighborhoods of Jerusalem. This, the saddest day in Jewish history, will be marked for generations to come as a fast day. For on this day in the year 586 BCE, the First Temple was destroyed. This day also commemorates the return of the twelve scouts sent by Moses to observe the land of Canaan, as well as many other Jewish tragedies in the past — and future. The destruction of Jerusalem was Rome's way of punishing the Jews for the Great Revolt.

For days and weeks, virtually no one came close to the Temple Mount. With the passage of time, a few survivors risked coming to the Kotel, now the only remnant of the Temple complex. Desperate and despondent, they came seeking solace and pleading for salvation from G-d.

I can still recall the torrent of images from that time. I felt the heat of the blazing fire, its blistering intensity searing the faces of the Kotel stones. The raging inferno burned everything in its path — including the grass that grew out of the upper cracks. The traumatic images have been indelibly etched in my memory. Over the many centuries since then, I have seen and felt many man-made disasters from wars and from man's inhumanity. These emotions are reignited every year as Tisha b'Av approaches. That sad day of fasting provides the catalyst for a torrent of visual memories and nightmarish narratives to emerge.

On that day, my Wall was truly a Wailing Wall. Tens of thousands of Jews in every generation throughout the centuries bewailed the downfall of our Holy City. Here they kiss the stone wall and water it with their tears. I cry with them as they recite prayers and Lamentations, which were composed by the prophet Jeremiah. The Book of Lamentations, written in 586 BCE after the destruction of the First Temple, so vividly touches on the cataclysmic events of the destruction of our Holy Temple. I, nothing more than an inert stone, join them in grieving over the terrible destruction that even now lingers immediately before my eyes, refusing to be erased from memory. On Tisha b'Av, Jews throughout the world mourn the destruction of the Temple. But only at the Kotel itself will the events of 2,000 years ago be experienced as vividly as if they had happened yesterday. Standing at the Kotel, the Jew cannot disconnect himself from the pain, torment, and misery of those traumatic events two millennia ago.

After the Romans destroyed the Temple and reduced the rest of the city to rubble, I remember seeing how they were laying wide stone roads over the fragments of broken buildings. So intent were the Romans to wipe out the memory of the Jewish nation that they changed the name of the city to *Aelia Capotalina* and rebuilt it in a vastly different layout, obliterating any vestige of its Jewish past. Take a walk over on the western side of the plaza just before the Western Wall. As you look into the large pit, notice some of these very same paving stones along with large pillars. In fact, archaeologists digging underneath parts of the road found some rare ancient Hebrew seals called "bullas"[67] used by officials in the First Temple, and uncovered remnants of homes from the First Temple period dating almost 3,000 years ago.

72–74 CE — Masada

According to Josephus, Masada was first constructed by the Hasmoneans. Between 37 and 31 BCE, Herod the Great fortified it as a refuge for himself in

---

67   "A bulla is a very small seal impression made of clay. They were used by officials sealing documents. They would roll up a papyrus document, tie it with string, and then put a bit of soft clay on top of the string and stamp it with a seal. This kept the document secret, because the seal would be broken if it was opened. http://www.pbs.org/wgbh/nova/ancient/palace-king-david.html

the event of a revolt. Masada , that ancient "fortress" overlooking the Dead Sea, was guarded by a Roman garrison. We at the Wall were well-aware of the rivalry between the main group of zealots and an extremist splinter group. Both opposed Roman rule of Judea, yet the hostility and bitterness between the two groups precluded any possibility of cooperation in opposing the Romans. Frankly, I was afraid of the Civil War between them.

100 CE — Trajan, a Friend of the Jews

In the year 100 CE, Trajan became emperor. He was also a very great friend to the Jews and he gave them, at the time of Rabbi Joshua Ben Chananiah, permission to rebuild the Temple. Regrettably, they neither could — nor would – take advantage of this opportunity.[68]

115–116 CE — Forced Hellenization

Although initially Trajan was a very great friend to the Jews,[69] the atmosphere soured after Bar Kochba rebelled against the Romans. For reasons that are not clear, the Jews arose in Egypt and in Cyprus "as though carried away by some wild and riotous spirit."

In an attempt to pacify the eastern borders of his empire, Trajan successfully attacked Armenia and the kingdom of the Parthians. He began to carve out new provinces in Mesopotamia and Assyria. Among the rebels fighting him were the Jews of Egypt, Cyprus, and (what is now) Libya.

Under Roman rule, Cyprus remained in peace for over three hundred years, until a Jew named Atermion started a revolt against Rome in 115 CE. Trajan quelled the rebellion at a cost of 24,000 Jewish lives.

The newly conquered region of Mesopotamia was restless and ready to explode. The revolt started in the Greek island-town Cyrene. Though the Jews were fighting against Trajan, they were nevertheless ordered to attack and destroy the pagan temples of Apollo, Artemis, Hecate, Demeter, Isis, and Pluto, and to assail the worshippers. The pagans fled to Alexandria in Egypt, which was Judaism's largest city. There the pagans captured and killed many Jews.

---

68 See *Bereshit Rabbah* 64, as quoted in http://www.jewish-history.com/palestine/period1.html

69 http://www.jewish-history.com/palestine/period1.html

In 116 CE, the Jews retaliated by destroying the temples of pagan gods and destroying the tomb of Pompey, the Roman general who had captured Jerusalem two hundred years earlier. The Romans were quick to strike back, sending superior forces to Alexandria, where they defeated the Jews and killed thousands of their enemies throughout the empire in a successful suppression of the revolt. Trajan and his successor Hadrian confiscated Jewish property to pay for the reconstruction of the destroyed pagan temples.

Meanwhile Trajan, fearful that the revolt would widen to the Jews in the unruly eastern provinces, ordered his commander to crack down on the Jews and to expel them from these regions. That order culminated in the murder of many Cypriote, Mesopotamian and Syrian Jews. So successful was this Roman commander in cleansing these eastern provinces of Jews that he was appointed governor of Judea and initiated a policy of forced Hellenization.

118 CE

Hadrian allowed the Jews to return to Jerusalem and granted permission for the rebuilding of their Holy Temple, but soon reneged.

130 CE

The Jews may have been physically removed from Jerusalem, but they never abandoned hope of restoring the Temple or of establishing Jerusalem as the capital of the Jewish nation. Indeed, it was to remain the heart and focus of Jewish national and spiritual aspirations to this very day.

For six decades, the Romans continued to suppress the mutinous province. Fearing another rebellion, the Romans designated a governor backed by an entire army legion for the region. The Jews were chafing under the bit of Roman domination. However, this feeling of irritation, annoyance, or impatience was curbed by the realization that Rome possessed crushing power and from the memory of the previous failed revolts. I sensed and felt their annoyance and irritation, and secretly prayed that they would not act impulsively.

132–135 CE — Bar Kochba Revolt

Still, considering the Roman oppression, it was no surprise to me when I heard the news of the Bar Kochba revolt. By some accounts, it was the third rebellion by the Jews of Judea, and the last of the Jewish-Roman Wars.

I had known Simon bar Kochba, the commander of the revolt, from his occasional visits to the Wall. Many hailed him as a Messiah, one who was capable of restoring the Jewish commonwealth. I must admit that I was amazed at his success. The outcome of his triumphant revolt was to reestablish an independent State of Israel over parts of Judea. Regrettably, after only two years, the Romans crushed the reborn state. The Jews fought doggedly and valiantly, but could not prevail against the twelve legions of the Roman army.

I cried along with many others. The furious Romans barred Jews from residing in or visiting Jerusalem. Even the early Christians, who at the time were still considered Jews, were also barred from Jerusalem. The Bar Kochba revolt, coming after the Great Revolt of 66-70 CE, was one of the worst calamities in Jewish history prior to the *Shoah*. The upshot of these failed rebellions was more than one million slaughtered Jews and the end of Jewish sovereignty over the Land of Israel for almost two thousand years.

This loss in itself exacerbated the magnitude of later Jewish catastrophes, since it prevented the Land of Israel from serving as a refuge for the large numbers of Jews fleeing persecutions elsewhere. Following the destruction of the second *Beit haMikdash* (70 CE) and the later Jewish Revolt (135 CE), Jerusalem fell under Roman rule. Hadrian rebuilt the city as a pagan shrine called *Aelia Capitolina*. Jews were officially forbidden to live there.

135 CE — Hadrian's Visit to Jerusalem

News of Emperor Hadrian's upcoming visit to see the ruins of Jerusalem firsthand was on the minds of many who came to the Kotel. It was rumored that the Emperor was compassionate and sensitive toward the Jews. After all, he had promised to rebuild the city. Their hopes quickly vanished when they learned that his intention was to rebuild the Holy

City as a Roman metropolis and that he would erect a new pagan temple dedicated to Jupiter upon the ruins of the Second Temple. Possibly suspecting another rebellion, the Emperor ordered an additional legion to be stationed in Judea. If there was any attempt at cooperation with the Romans, it quickly evaporated when the Jews discovered that Roman soldiers were plowing up the Temple. When Hadrian outlawed circumcision, relations between Rome and the Jews deteriorated rapidly, and the Hadrian era was overall horrible for the Jews.

212 CE

Living under Roman rule was often very difficult. Yet, every so often we heard some good news. One such decree was the granting of Roman citizenship to all freemen throughout the Roman Empire, including Jews, by Emperor Caracall.

312 CE — Progressive Deterioration of Jewish Rights

Not long after the Byzantine conquest of the Roman Empire in 312 CE,[70] Christianity became the official religion of the Roman Empire under Constantine the Great. He rebuilt Jerusalem as a hub of Christian worship and built the Church of the Holy Sepulcher in 335 CE. Conditions for the Jews turned from bad to worse. We groaned under the increased persecution. Under the influence of Christianity that grew in power throughout the Roman Empire, many laws were issued — each of which further curtailed Jewish rights. The progressive deterioration of Jewish rights confirmed the second-class status of the Jew. Henceforth, the Jew in the medieval world would suffer not only political decline, but would be subject to church-sanctioned disabilities further downgrading the Jew to even lower levels.

All sorts of prohibitions, injunctions, and sanctions constantly bombarded us. We were forbidden to proselytize, to intermarry (not that we wanted to), or to testify against Christians in court. Jews were barred from holding any valued position in the Roman state. The most troubling was the

---

70   The Center for Online Judaic Studies confirms that the Byzantine Period ranged from 312–632 CE. http://cojs.org/cojswiki/Byzantine_Period,_312-632_CE

ban on building new synagogues and owning slaves. Slave labor was very common throughout the medieval world. This adversely affected the economic life of the Jews. Once a year, on Tisha b'Av, Jews were permitted to visit Jerusalem and to worship on the Mount of Olives and sometimes on the Temple Mount itself. Such permission to enter Jerusalem and to mourn the destruction of the Temple was granted upon payment of a stiff fee to the Romans. Year in and year out, I witnessed how the Jews came that one time a year on Tisha b'Av. They would rend their garments and grieve over the destruction of the Holy Temple. The scene was pitiable, and yet at the same time they had not given up. We stones cried. Our precious Jews were still barred from their own city, except for that one day a year. Jews would not be permitted freedom of entry into Jerusalem until 614–629 CE when the city would come under Persian rule.

361–363 CE — Julian's Tolerance of Judaism

Closely following his accession to the throne, Julian declared freedom and equal rights to all — Jewish, pagan, and Christian. Julian's open hostility to Christianity was in stark contrast to his tolerance of Judaism. His respect and kindness for the Jews was like a breath of fresh air. During his brief reign, I could see the gloom and despair disappear from the faces of the many that came to the Kotel to give thanks to HaShem. From the conversations and prayers of the pious Jews who now thronged to the Kotel, I learned that Emperor Julian's knowledge of Jewish affairs was extensive. He wrote extensively, setting forth his mostly favorable views on Judaism in contrast to his passionate, strongly worded arguments against Christianity. While he rated Hellenism as the best system for his empire, Christianity, he declared, was inferior to Judaism. We literally danced with joy when we heard the news that the Emperor Julian permitted Jews to settle in the city of Jerusalem and promised to rebuild the Temple. He was dubbed "the Apostate" by the Christians because he refused to accept Christianity, which he regarded as a harmful influence and sought to uproot it. He scoffed at Christianity's claim that it replaces Judaism. His letter to the Jews was widely circulated. It read, in part:

> I too shall build and populate, by my efforts,
> after I successfully conclude my war against the

Persians, the Holy City of Jerusalem, which for
many years you have yearned to see settled by
yourselves, and together with you I shall give
glory to the very great G-d.

What great news! We at the Kotel were euphoric! After centuries of
abuse, finally our prayers were answered. Julian's letter addressed to the
"Community of the Jews," (363 CE) refers to his ending the collection of
onerous taxes that had been imposed upon the Jews for centuries. It was
clear from his dreamlike statement that he intended to treat Jews amica-
bly. It was like an intense dazzling light, brilliantly shining on the Kotel.

Amidst this euphoria, there was a sense of ambivalence. The restoration was supposed to have come with the appearance of the *Mashiach*.
Surely, this compassionate Roman Emperor could not possibly be considered the *Mashiach*! Furthermore, how could the Third Temple be rebuilt
without the missing elements:[71] the Holy Fire, the Ark, *Urim* and *Tumim*,
the anointing-oil, *Ruach HaKodesh* (the spirit of prophecy) and the *Shechinah*? True, these were missing from the Second Temple as well, but wasn't
the Third Temple supposed to be complete, perfect, and final? Or, might
it be built even without these?[72]

Julian's support of Jews was a longed-for respite, coming as it did after centuries of antagonism and aggression. Unfortunately, the prospect
of a rebuilt Temple was dashed when fire broke out at the site just as work
began. Frightful balls of fire erupted next to the foundations. The bizarre
and unrelenting assault forced the now-scorched workmen to back away
and discontinue work. Some attributed the fire bolts to the Galilee earth-
quake of 363 CE. Others blame the Jews themselves for their ambivalence
about the project. Still, others suspected sabotage. Christians cheered,
claiming divine intervention. Shortly thereafter, Julian was killed in battle in Persia, effectively ending his plans for the rebuilding of the Temple.

---

71   *Yoma* 21b

72   *Yer. Ta'anit* 65a

Permission to Resettle Jerusalem

425–438 CE

In the 4th century, Jews had difficulty getting the right to pray near the Western Wall, even for Tisha b'Av. It was not until the year 425 CE that the Jews of the Galilee received permission from the Byzantine Empress Augusta Aelia Eudocia to pray by the ruins of the Temple. Permission was also granted to Jews to resettle in Jerusalem. Eudocia was the wife of Theodosius II, East Roman emperor. Although a Christian, she used her substantial influence to protect Jews and pagans alike. (From that time until the onset of Muslim rule, Jews were officially permitted to pray at the Western Wall.)

I remember when I heard from a number of visitors that the Jews of the Galilee and its surroundings petitioned the Empress Eudocia for permission to pray in the ruins of the Temple. While they had permission to pray on the Temple Mount on Tisha b'Av, they sought her consent to pray on the Temple Mount on holy days other than the ninth of Av. When news of her consent reached us at the Kotel we were ecstatic. I heard plans being made to invite Jews of Persia and the other cities in Byzantium to gather in Jerusalem for the Succot festival. That year, more than 100,000 gathered in Jerusalem for what is also called the Feast of the Tabernacle. Many came prior to the day of the festival. Men and women assembled, all dressed in black, rending their garments into pieces and putting ash on their heads as a sign of mourning for the destruction of the Temple. As I scanned the multitude on the festival day itself, I witnessed a barrage of stones thrown at them. Some were killed and many were injured, some seriously. Later I learned that a fanatical Syrian monk, Bar Sauma, known for his hostility against Jews, galvanized his disciples to stone the Jewish procession around the Temple Mount. Many Jews died. Jewish survivors detained eighteen of his disciples and appealed to Empress Eudocia for justice. Syrian monks then threatened to burn the Empress if she sided with the Jews. An investigation by the Roman governor whitewashed the entire incident, publicly announcing that the Jewish victims died of natural causes.

Too often, when Jews sought justice from the authorities, they were rewarded with a perfunctory investigation or through a biased presentation of facts. Whether under pressure from anti-Semites or for other reasons, governments invariably glossed over or covered up vices, crimes or scandals, exonerating those who have attacked the Jews.

443 CE

The best news I heard that year was the consent given by the Byzantine Empress Eudocia for the rebuilding of the Temple. Regrettably, the endeavor was unsuccessful.

584 CE

Emperor Maurice Tiberius was a good and kindly prince. Throughout history, our land experienced a number of violent earthquakes because it lies along the Syrio-African Rift Valley.[73] One of these earthquakes seriously damaged the reconstruction effort on the Temple that was started by Julian. The caring Maurice sent Jewish builders from Constantinople to Jerusalem to repair Julian's structure on the Temple Mount.

614 CE —The Final Collision

Do not ask me to explain the next twenty-four years. It is too complex and confusing for humans, let alone a huge stone like me. Okay, I sense that you want some explanation. Since you insist, I will try to make some sense of what has been going on.

From the year 614 CE until 638 CE, our land changed hands three times. Do you remember that I told you about the war between the Romans and the Persians? For 400 years, the Byzantine army of Rome and the Sassanid army of Persia fought for control of this land. At times victorious and at other times defeated, the two factions grew weaker from the protracted warfare. The Siege of Jerusalem in 614 CE marked the turning point and the beginning of the final collision between these two behemoths.

I could hear the buzz of those who came to the Kotel. News of the Persian army's advance was hailed by the Jewish communities, who rose in

---

73   Dead Sea Rift — a geological fault line

revolt against the Christian (Byzantine) rulers who had been oppressing the Jews mercilessly.

Understandably, the Jews of Palestine sided with and helped the Persians in their battle. The Persian forces captured Jerusalem — then the Christian Empire's most holy city.

Repressive Roman Rule Coming to an End

First a bit of background: Remember that in those days we did not have a census. Nevertheless, I heard stories and reports that there were approximately six million Jews living throughout the Roman Empire, and another two million who lived under the Persian Empire. The Jews of the Persian Empire were more affluent and had a measure of self-rule, including tax collection and maintaining their own militia. The Roman government was more devious than the Persian rulers were toward its Jews. With 10 percent of the Roman population being Jews or Judaizers,[74] its government schemed to sway its Jewish population against the Persians. During its wars with Persia, Rome manipulated the Jews, pledging that they would permit the restoration of the Temple — promises that were repeatedly broken.[75]

It was the summer of 614 CE. Persian troops penetrated Jerusalem, systematically demolishing all the churches. Many of its Christian inhabitants were slaughtered. The 37,000 Christians who survived were exiled to Persia. Christian revisionist historians accuse the Jews of complicity with the Persians in the massacre of the Christians and the destruction of the churches.

I can attest to the fact that the Jews were not involved in any of the killings or in the destruction of the churches. Once again, the Jews were scapegoats. The innocent Jews were again blamed and punished for the sins, crimes, or sufferings of the Christians. This was a useful tactic to distract attention from the real causes. For most of its 2,000 years, Christianity actively sought to scapegoat Jews. Attacking Jews was an

---

74   Gentile Christians adhering to the Torah Laws originally given to the Israelites.

75   "The Persian conquest of Jerusalem in 614 CE compared with Islamic conquest of 638 CE."– *Its Messianic nature and the role of the Jewish Exilarch.* Ben Abrahamson and Joseph Katz. http://www.eretzyisroel.org/~jkatz/The%20Persian%20conquest%20of%20Jerusalem%20 in%20614CE%20compared%20with%20Islamic%20conquest%20of%20638CE.pdf

excellent scheme to divert attention from their real troubles and a means for venting their aggression. When problems occur in the non-Jewish world people do not like to blame themselves. Jews, on the other hand, look within themselves to see what sins they may have committed that may have brought about the problems.

The yoke of repressive Roman rule was ending. With the conquest of Jerusalem, the city and its government passed into the hands of the Jews for three years.[76] We celebrated and thanked HaShem.

Black Day in the History of Jerusalem

617 CE

In the months following the Persian conquest of Jerusalem, I already began to hear signals that all was not well. The euphoria of 614 CE began to evaporate. The state of affairs of the Jewish population began to worsen. None of us really knew what prompted the decline. Perhaps the Persians realized that the tiny Jewish community was no longer a strategic asset for them. In any case, the year 617 CE marked a black day in the history of Jerusalem's Jewish community. A riot occurred in Jerusalem, in which a gang of young Christians (or Persians) killed the Jewish governor, Nehemiah ben Hushi'el, together with his "council of the righteous."[77] Before long, the episode spiraled into a

---

76 "Although having a sort of autonomy in the Galilee until the 4th century, such as the School of Iamnia (Yavne) and later a limited success in establishing the short-lived Sassanid Jewish Commonwealth in 614-17 CE, Jewish dominance in parts of the Southern Levant was regained only in the mid-20th century, with the founding of the State of Israel in 1948." http://en.wikipedia.org/wiki/Jewish%E2%80%93Roman_wars.

77 "Five years after his appointment to lead the conquest of Israel, and the 'ingathering of the Jewish nation,' the Exilarch Nehemiah was made ruler of Jerusalem... and began the work of making arrangements of the rebuilding of the Temple and sorting out genealogies to established a new High Priesthood. The Jews were exuberant, but an uneasy, explosive tension was in the air. A mob of young Christians united and killed Nehemiah ben Hushi'el and his 'council of the righteous.' They dragged their bodies through the street and dumped them over the city wall. Then, the whole Christian population rebelled from Persian service. After this, a battle took place among the inhabitants of the city of Jerusalem, Jew and Christian. The multitude of the Christians grew stronger and struck at and killed many of the Jews. The remainder of the Jews jumped from the walls, and went to the Persian army in Caesarea." From: The Conquest of Jerusalem 614 CE, a historical reconstruction based on Sebeos.

full-blown Christian uprising with Jews and Christians clashing with each other within Jerusalem.[78]

629 CE — Massacre and Forced Baptism

The year 629 CE marked another heartrending cycle of oppression. Jerusalem was captured by the Byzantine Christian Emperor Heraclius, who massacred or expelled all of its Jewish inhabitants. He reinstated the past decrees of Hadrian and Constantine that banned Jews from the city. For the next few years, my fellow stones and I longed to feel the warmth of a Jew, but to no avail. Only years later did we learn of the terrible decree issued in 632 CE to impose forced baptism of Jews throughout the Byzantine Empire. This was the incubator period of Christian anti-Semitism.

634–638 CE — Rise of Islam

The Christian restoration of the Holy Land was also short-lived. Four centuries of warfare between Rome and Persia exhausted the great powers and paved the way for a new power — Islam. Among the many rumors floating around the Kotel was that the Jews made an alliance in 614 CE with Persia, and later in 638 CE with the Muslims in an attempt to restore the Temple. One story I heard was that the Babylonian Jewish Exilarch Nechemiah ben Hushi'el, his brother Shallum (Salmaan Farsi), and nephew Yakov (Ka'b Al-Ahbar) combined forces with the Muslims to conquer Jerusalem. It seems that twelve Jewish refugees went from Edessa by way of Medina to Mecca to meet with the Prophet Mohammed. Others suggested that they were Jews from Medina. In 634 CE, Muslim military forces invaded the land from the south, laying siege to Gaza. Two years later, they defeated the Byzantines at the Yarmuk River, capturing Jerusalem. We knew very little about this new monotheistic faith that was fated to affect the make-up and temperament, not only of Jerusalem, but of the entire Middle East for many centuries to come.

---

78 Note: The Book of Zerubbabel states that Nehemiah ben Hushi'el was executed by the Persians (not Christians). Haim Hillel Ben-Sasson (1976). *A History of the Jewish People.* Harvard University Press. p. 362. Retrieved January 19, 2014.

638-644 — Raised Hopes Crushed

The Muslim conquest was a relief! Christian control of Jerusalem, with its oppression of the Jews, had ended. We were encouraged by what we heard about the caliph, Umar. Not only was he tolerant of our Jewish religious practices but he promised to restore some of our sites. The upper levels of smaller stones were added following the conquest of Jerusalem by the Muslims. Frankly, I was not sure that my shoulders could support the weight of the additional layers, but we stones from the Jerusalem quarries were made of rugged stock. I hardly felt any additional pressure as the new stones were added.

Now, not only did Jews and Christians claim Jerusalem as their sacred city, but also followers of Islam fixed their entitlement to the Holy City. The empire of the Umayyads extended from the borders of France to the borders of India. It was the year 638 CE when excited worshippers brought me the news that the Christians capitulated to the Muslims. I had no idea what would happen next.

A few days later, I heard some astonishing news. It seems that the conquering caliph, Umar, acknowledging Islam's Judaic roots, decided to visit the Temple Mount. I was told that the caliph was sickened on seeing how spiteful the Christians were toward the Jews. To underline their disrespect toward the Jewish faith, the Christians had piled garbage on the hallowed area of the Temple Mount. Umar was horrified. Out of respect for the Jews, he directed that the sacred enclosure be cleared of all the rubbish. Our hopes were further raised when Umar turned down the Church's call to maintain the long-standing ban against Jews living in Jerusalem. To emphasize to the Christians that he was in charge, he invited Jews to come back and live in Jerusalem.[79] Seventy Jewish families settled in a quarter adjoining the Western Wall. With the passage of time more Jews were allowed back into Jerusalem. For the first time in 500 years, Jerusalem was open to Jewish residence. I can just picture how happy Solomon and David would have been to see Jews living in Jerusalem and worshipping in their Holy City! Once again, we rejoiced as Jews streamed to the Kotel to give thanks to HaShem. Because of the Judeo-Muslim alliance that liberated Jerusalem, we

---

79   Note that Christians and their holy sites were also promised protection under Muslim rule.

Jews were now permitted to begin the building of a wooden Temple on the Temple Mount.

Unfortunately, once again, our joy was short-lived. The stab in the back penetrated to our innermost souls as news surfaced that the Muslims were preparing to build a mosque over the ruins of the Jewish Temple. The first such mosque, as told to me by a middle-aged Jew, was a huge rectangular wooden structure.

692 CE — Mosque Built Over Ruins of the Jewish Temple

The decision by the Umayyad caliph Abd al-Malik to build the Dome of the Rock, an Islamic shrine encompassing the Foundation Stone, came as a further blow to us and to the Jewish community. We were powerless to stop the Islamic rulers from building on top of the holiest spot in Judaism: the Temple Mount. Situating the Dome of the Rock on the site formerly occupied by the Temple itself was an affront to the Jews. This Muslim shrine was built over the outcropping of limestone rock where our forefather Abraham prepared to sacrifice Isaac. In the eyes of the Muslims, the Dome of the Rock was a symbol of Islamic triumph over the religions of the Jews and the Christians.

The grief that for centuries engulfed our people, especially on Tisha b'Av, intensified tenfold following the construction of the Dome of the Rock. The recurring tragedies that befell our people and caused so much suffering could not possibly compare to the disaster taking place so very close to me and my fellow stones. The mere presence of an Islamic shrine atop our holiest site created the strongest of feelings in the hearts of everyone coming to pray at the Kotel. I saw and felt the mood of all those who came — some with tears and others with thoughts too deep for tears. I had the feeling that HaShem was once again directing an inexplicable drama of our history as a people. And we've been weeping ever since — old and young, men and women — shedding tears of sadness and tears of hope. I have seen Jews coming to Jerusalem at great expense and danger just to have the chance to pray at the Kotel. Once here, they would pour their hearts out to HaShem, pleading with Him to redeem His people and to rebuild the Temple. I can tell you many heartrending stories about how unabashedly these crestfallen petitioners melted me and my fellow stones with their kisses; how these despondent and mournful Jews watered the Wall with their tears.

As bitter as my fellow stones and I felt about the Dome of the Rock, we took solace in the tolerant atmosphere that prevailed during the rule of the Umayyad Muslims. They allowed Christian and Jewish pilgrims to freely visit the Holy City. Some Jews from Medina who came to the Kotel told me a startling fact: it seems that Muslims (like the Jews of Arabia) faced Jerusalem when praying. When the Jews living in Medina resisted Mohammed's prophetic claims, Muslims shifted the center of prayer to Mecca.

750–974 CE — Umayyads and Abbasids

The Muslim Period (638-1099 CE) began with the conquest of Jerusalem around 638 CE by the (generally tolerant) Umayyad Arabs.[80]

The Abbasids, who ruled from 750–974 CE, were not at all tolerant. The Abbasids were composed of non-Arabic Muslims and Shiites, who went up against the mostly secular Umayyad caliphs. The Umayyads were a wealthy class in Mecca who had initially opposed Mohammed and were never fully accepted by the Muslims. The Abbasid seizure of the caliphate from the Umayyad could not have succeeded without reliance on foreigners who had converted to Islam. These foreigners, mostly Iranian, were for the most part second-class citizens who were clients of the Abbasids and utterly dependent on them for protection. The Abbasid caliphate brutally secured control and began a series of administrative moves that would ensure its supremacy for hundreds of years.

969 CE — An Intolerant Shiite Sect Comes To Power

The Umayyad (and, to some extent, the Abbasid) Period, in which peoples of different faiths lived peacefully with each other, came to an end in 969 CE. That was when the Fatimid caliphs of Egypt (an intolerant Shiite sect) came to power. They destroyed all synagogues and churches. With the destruction of each synagogue, despondency saturated the air around the Kotel. Brokenhearted Jews burdened with the weight of sorrow came

---

80   Throughout this book, we sometimes use the term Muslim to mean Arab. At times, the term Arab is a more precise designation.

to beseech G-d to stop the devastation. It was not the first time that I had witnessed the demolition of houses of worship and houses of study unleashed by these fanatic and militant Muslims.

Exactly who were these Fatimids? About this time, Muslim rule extended from Iraq in the east, which was the geopolitical focus of the Abbasid caliphs, to Spain in the west. With the central area (Syria and Palestine) now partially neglected by the Abbasids, Egypt emerged (after 868 CE) as the commanding power in Palestine. After years of turmoil, during which differing Muslim powers ruled, the Holy City of Jerusalem came under the control of the Fatimids (969-1161 CE).

1165 CE — The Rambam at the Kotel

I remember it well. It was the year 1165 CE when the famous Torah scholar (and physician), Rabbi Moshe ben Maimon (known as the Rambam, or Maimonides) arrived in Jerusalem and honored us with his prayers at the Kotel.

Most of you are familiar with Rambam. Born in Spain, he and his parents fled from persecution to North Africa and eventually settled in Egypt. I was privileged to see him during his brief visit to Israel. His masterful commentaries and writings on Jewish Law and Philosophy include the *Mishnah Torah* and *Guide to the Perplexed*. His visit on the 6th of the Hebrew month of Cheshvan 4296[81] is marked with special prayers at the Kotel.

1071 CE — The Seljuk Turks: Cruel and Utterly Intolerant

News travels fast. I heard the commotion following the morning prayer services. The days and weeks that followed that initial commotion turned into instability, uproar, and chaos. It appeared that the Seljuk Turks conquered the Byzantines and took control of Jerusalem.

Who were these Seljuk Turks? The Seljuks were a tribe of Tatars from Central Asia who established a powerful empire in Persia from 1060 CE to

---

81   No one is sure of the date, but I found reference to it on the following site, where it is suggested that Rambam went up to the Temple in 1165 CE (4296 in our calendar). http://www.jewishmag.com/169mag/rambam_Temple_mount/rambam_Temple_mount.htm

1307 CE. They ousted the Egyptian rulers of Palestine and closed Christian pilgrimage routes that had existed since the time of Constantine. Even during previous Muslim rule, Jews and Christians were allowed to visit the city. All this changed. The Seljuk Turks were ruthless and very intolerant of other faiths. For centuries, we stones of the Wall welcomed the *Avelei Zion* ("Mourners of Zion"). These were groups of Jews dedicated to mourning the destruction of the Temple in Jerusalem. I cried along with these faithful, sincere Jews, unswerving in their dedication to the restoration of the *Beit haMikdash*. With the conquest of Palestine by the Seljuk Turks in 1071 CE, the *Avelei Zion* disappeared from Jerusalem.

1095–99 CE — Harassment of the Jews

Fatimid Caliph al-Hakim kindled the spark that inflamed European Christendom. He callously reinstituted long-forgotten harassment of Jews and Christians, displaying contempt for non-Muslims. The rumors of wholesale destruction of churches and synagogues were later confirmed as more and more eyewitnesses made their way to the Kotel. Some say that a thousand churches throughout the Islamic Empire were destroyed, including the Church of the Holy Sepulcher in 1099 CE.

CHILDREN AT THE KOTEL—(CIRCA 1890)
courtesy American Colony Photos-Library of Congress; Govern-
ress Office] [Code: D 220-018]
he garbage and other debris strewn around the narrow
·ay between the Kotel and the Moroccan houses built
* ten yards from the Western Wall. Note also the messy*
·glected vegetation.

1099 CE — The Crusades

Incensed, Christian (Western) Europe launched the Crusades — a series of holy wars that ended in the capture of Jerusalem in 1099 CE. Lacking unified command, the First Crusade was an impressive and ambitious undertaking. The army, which rallied to the cause, consisted of 20,000 fighting men, one quarter of whom were knights, along with 15,000 pilgrims, both men and women. They set out on their march to Jerusalem to free the Holy City from the rule of the infidel Muslims, 1,200 miles away, at the height of summer and across unfamiliar lands.

As this blundering army marched through France and parts of Germany, they spent most of their time foraging for food and supplies. Sporadic battles along the way further weakened the bedraggled foot soldiers. With most of the horses dead, battles were fought on foot. As more and more of the pack animals died, a band of followers had to carry the baggage themselves. At least one-third (and possibly more) of the foot soldiers and followers died en route.

Baptism or Death!

Church sermons advocating the First Crusade inflamed already existing anti-Semitism. For centuries, Jews in both France and Germany were regarded as non-believers who were responsible for the Crucifixion. There were practical motivations for anti-Semitism as well: many Crusaders borrowed heavily from Jewish moneylenders to purchase weaponry and equipment for the expedition. Historically, killing Jewish creditors was a great way to avoid repaying loans. How well I remember hearing stories of forced conversions and mass expulsions against Jews in Christian Europe during the seventh century. While there have been sporadic anti-Jewish persecutions since then, particularly in Metz in 888 CE, a conspiracy against Jews in Limoges in 992 CE, and one in Treves in 1066 CE, these were unlike the unrestrained widespread acts of violence that marked the First Crusade.

Drenched in Tears…

One survivor who reached the Kotel read the following letter to his brethren at the Kotel:

"At the time the [Jewish] communities in France heard [about these things], trembling… seized them. They wrote letters and sent messengers to all the communities around about the River Rhine, [to the effect] that they should fast… and seek mercy from Him Who dwells on high, that He might save them from their hands. When the letter reached the holy ones in the land [of the Rhine], namely the men of renown…in Mainz, they responded [to their brethren in] France as follows: 'The communities have decreed a fast. We have done that which was ours [to do]. May the L-rd save us and may He save you from all sorrow and oppression [which might come] upon you. We are in great fear.'"[82]

Oh! How we cried when we heard about the attacks on Jews in the Rhineland. News of the violence began filtering in as a small number of the escapees managed somehow to reach Jerusalem with the Kotel as their destination. Between fits of crying, rending their garments, each told his story. I, an inert stone, broke down and cried. It was an awful scene. Those who came to the Kotel after such a difficult journey could not contain themselves. See that one wringing his hands, or his fellow beating his breast, or that one rolling on the ground crying his eyes out. I have seen much these past centuries, yet nothing moved me as much to join in the mourning, grieving, and wailing of these pathetic Jews who have probably lost family members, not to say anything about their worldly possessions. The entire area in front of the Kotel was drenched in tears. As I pieced together the grim story of the brutality and sadism that accompanied that First Crusade, I was seized with anger. My innermost being was racked with agony. I could see on the harrowed faces of these petitioners the signs of physical suffering. What I could not see, but which was far more important, was the severe psychological trauma that had engulfed them.

Speaking in a mixture of *Laaz* and Yiddish,[83] one middle-aged man told me about the bloodshed, the carnage, and the ferocity of the attacks

---

82   Quoted by Norman Golb (1998). *The Jews in Medieval Normandy: A Social and Intellectual History*. Cambridge: Cambridge University Press.

83   Yiddish usage began in the 10th century as Jews from France and Northern Italy began to drift to Germany to escape maltreatment. They spoke a Jewish-French dialect known as *Laaz*. These new immigrants incorporated into their daily speech terminology and idioms from *Laaz*. What emerged was a form of medieval German called Yiddish that integrated elements of *Laaz*, Biblical and Mishnaic Hebrew, and Aramaic. As Jews later migrated to Poland, Russia and other Slavic lands, Yiddish absorbed lexicon from those languages as well.

against the innocent Jews. Of course, this poor tormented man was not talking to me but to HaShem. Yet it was against me that he leaned with his arm, resting on me as a flood of tears washed my stone face and the stones below me. He had come to pray, but it was clear that he was demanding an answer from HaShem. He did not deny the existence of G-d. His innermost being was a cry, pressing G-d for some explanation. Why did G-d permit these Christian mobs to slaughter his entire family, along with the holy community that had been so faithful to G-d for centuries?

Atrocities Committed Against the Jews

Another petitioner who somehow escaped the fury of the mob and reached the Kotel told me more about the atrocities committed against the Jews. While many local bishops in Europe opposed the carnage against the Jews, they were helpless to stop it. The declared aim of the Crusades was not directed against the Jews. Yet Jewish communities in France and Germany were nonetheless hit especially hard. The Jewish community of Mainz was destroyed. With each coming week, I learned more horrifying details. Especially painful was the tragic news of the massacre of Kalonymus ben MeShullam, the Chief Rabbi of Mainz.

We heard how the Bishop of Speyer prevented a massacre by giving local Jews refuge in his palace. When the Bishop of Salt tried to give Jews refuge in his palace, the Crusaders forced their way in and killed everyone. Yes, there were righteous gentiles even in those days. While most of the Crusaders passed through the Jewish communities without attacking them, mob action came easily at the slightest encouragement from the Crusade leaders. Some of these leaders attracted the worst elements of the population as they passed through the cities. The standard demand, refined and repeated as they progressed toward Palestine, was that the Jews be baptized or be killed. This rampaging mob manipulated religion to kill Jews and seize their possessions.

Then I heard reports from a number of sources that one Jewish woman in the city of Mainz killed her children rather than see them killed.[84] What excruciating agony, torment, and sense of hopelessness must have seized this frightened woman! Oh, how we moan for her! Oh, how we grieve for her lifeless children! No sackcloth and ashes in the world will

---

84   *G-d's War: A New History of the Crusades.* Christopher Tyerman, p.102

suffice to lament what is happening to our fellow Jews in France and Germany. We weep. We sob. We wring our hands; we tear our hair, gnash our teeth and beat our breasts as we beseech HaShem:

> Dear G-d, I am but a stone, a vestige of the Wall, that surrounded the platform on which the Holy of Holies once stood. Yet I must speak! We have internalized Your prophet's (Yirmiyahu) message. Why the repeat of past disasters? Why have You decreed the deaths of so many innocents who have been faithful to Your Torah? Have they broken Your covenant? Have these holy souls been worshipping idols? Have they forsaken You and served foreign gods?
>
> I feel Your fire in my innermost being, yet I am but stone. How much more do those created in Your image feel Your wrath. *"Are not all my words as fire, sayeth the Lor-d, and a hammer that shatters rock"* (Jeremiah 23:29)

Why Were Jews So Hated?

You ask why Jews were hated so much, what triggered the centuries of persecution, of programs, of discrimination? I may be smart, but I really do not have all the answers. In medieval Europe, bishops and emperors encouraged Jews to settle in their towns. The Jews brought with them experience in commerce, something sorely lacking amongst the native populace. The non-Jews viewed the Jews as outsiders, strangers within the small communities that made up medieval towns. Restricted from agriculture and trade, Jews relied on one of the few permissible occupations: money lending — the one occupation that gave gentiles convenient excuses for hating Jews.

Jewish religious and cultural traditions kept them apart from their non-Jewish neighbors. Officially, Jews were assured of legal protection by local authorities. The reality was quite different. Defenseless, the Jews were highly vulnerable to sporadic mob action. The keyed-up atmosphere preceding the First Crusade was potentially violent. The mob was the tinderbox. The match was the lure of looting a Jewish community under the excuse of attacking the enemies of the Christian savior.

The quarreling Muslim chieftains posed no serious resistance to the massive waves of armed Crusaders determined to unshackle the Muslim hold on Jerusalem.[85] The frenzied mobs attacked, looted, and destroyed. I was helpless as they massacred practically all of the Jews and Muslims in Jerusalem. Innocent Jews, young and old, men and women, deep in prayer and supplication, met violent death by the sharp blades of Crusader swords.

Christianity now ruled Palestine. The Crusaders built churches and monasteries, hostels for pilgrims, and quarters for various religious orders. The Dome of the Rock was converted into a church and the Al-Aqsa Mosque was converted into a residence for the Christian king. During this period, Muslims and Jews were banned from living in Jerusalem. The Crusader conquest changed the character and composition of Jerusalem. The city became the hub of Christendom and the capital of the independent Latin Kingdom. The Christian sovereignty of Jerusalem lasted only eighty-eight years until the start of the Ayyubid Period (1187-1516 CE).

1187–1516 CE — The Beginning of 700 Years of Arab Rule

Following his successful takeover of Egypt in 1187 CE, Saladin launched a military assault against the Crusaders and recaptured the city of Jerusalem, thus marking the beginning of 700 years of Arab rule over Jerusalem. Unlike previous Abbasid rulers, Saladin refrained from harming the mostly Christian civilian population. Still, although churches were not destroyed, all signs of Crusader occupation were removed.

Mosques that had been converted to churches under the Crusaders were now restored to their original use. Crusader buildings, on the other hand, were converted into Muslim edifices. Fearing another Crusade, Saladin began to reconstruct the walls of Jerusalem.

---

85   In his *History of Islam - An encyclopedia of Islamic history*, Prof. Dr. Nazeer Ahmed states: "One of the astonishing facts about the Crusades is the small resistance offered by the Turks and the Arabs to the Crusader advance."
     As quoted in http://historyofislam.com/contents/the-classical-period/jerusalem-the-crusades/

Inexplicably, in 1219 CE, Saladin's successor began to dismantle the walls, leaving the city defenseless. Most of the frightened population of Jerusalem abandoned the defenseless city. It was not until Ottoman control of Jerusalem in 1539 CE, that the city's walls were rebuilt.

In 1193 CE, Saladin's son and successor, al-Hakam, conquered Jerusalem. He permitted Muslim Moroccan settlers to build houses only twelve feet away from the Kotel.

1260–1300 CE — The Mongols

The Mongols (whose religion was Shamanism)[86] made repeated attempts to expand into Syria and Palestine. Their horsemen — under the grandson of Genghis Khan — succeeded in capturing Aleppo and Damascus in Syria. Unlike Genghis Khan himself, who was very tolerant, his grandson's soldiers proceeded to loot, kill, and destroy. Many of these raids, which finally reached Gaza, were conducted towards the end of the Crusader period.

Still, this success was short-lived as the Egyptian Mamluks forced them to retreat. Still, the damage was done; the massacres perpetrated by the Mongol assault emptied Jerusalem of most of its inhabitants. For a number of months, not a single Jew came to the Kotel. The frightened survivors fled for their very lives. Only after the Mamluks restored law and order did some of its previous inhabitants begin to trickle back into the city. Over time, the stability created by the observance and enforcement of the law was sufficient to attract more Jews to settle in Jerusalem.

How I, a mere stone in the Wall, longed to see even a single Jew at the Kotel! When the first Jew eventually risked his life to come to the Kotel, I felt like holding him in my arms (so to speak), to squeeze and hug him. So happy was I to welcome him. Would more come? Gradually, over a period of time more and more Jews ventured to the Kotel. The depressive feeling following the slaughter and the flight from Jerusalem turned into joy. These Jews told me about the battle of Ain Jalut, which took place on

---

86 Shamanism is a religion practiced by certain tribal societies that is distinguished by faith in a concealed world of supernatural beings, devils, and ancestral apparitions reacting favorably only to the shamans. A shaman is a person who is believed in this indigenous culture to use magic and sorcery to cure the sick, divine the hidden, and to control events. He acts as a medium between the visible world and an invisible spirit world.

September 3, 1260 CE, between Muslim Mamluks and the Mongols in the southeastern Galilee, in the Jezreel Valley. The Mamluk Egyptians used explosive hand cannons in order to terrify the Mongol soldiers, who were only trained to fight on horseback. It was the first time since my birth that explosives were used in battle.

1267 CE — The Ramban at the Kotel

Could that be the famous Rabbi Moses ben Nachman Girondi approaching the Kotel? *Hodu La'Shem ki tov* (Thank G-d, for it is good)! I simply couldn't believe my eyes!

That illustrious rabbi (known by his name, Nachmanides, and by his acronym, Ramban) had indeed come to the Land of Israel.

If I could have, I would have stood up out of respect to the seventy-three-year-old Catalan rabbi, philosopher, physician, kabbalist, and Biblical commentator. I heard many stories about how he left his city of birth, settling for three years in southern France prior to settling in Jerusalem in 1267, seeking refuge in Muslim lands from Christian persecution. He was born in Girona, a city in the northeast of Catalonia, Spain, where he served as the Chief Rabbi of Catalonia.[87] In a letter to his son in Spain, written shortly after his arrival in Jerusalem, Ramban bemoaned the emptiness and the bleakness of the Holy City, noting that there were only two Jewish inhabitants in the entire city. When Jews learned of Ramban's arrival, many relocated to Jerusalem.

I remember hearing about Torah scrolls that had been removed to the city of Shechem for safekeeping prior to the Mongol invasion. Now these cherished scrolls were brought back to be read during the first Rosh Hashanah services in the new Ramban Synagogue. For four years until his death in 1270 CE, Nachmanides faithfully visited the Kotel to pray, to meditate, and to mourn the destruction of the Temple.

Such was his influence that the synagogue that he founded in the Old City continues to exist almost 750 years later. Not only that, but also

---

87   That flourishing Jewish community, which had seen its heyday in the 12th century, ended in 1492 when the Catholic kings expelled all the Jews.

his prestige and reputation succeeded in reestablishing Jewish communal life in Jerusalem for 700 years following his death.[88]

1517 CE — Turks Capture Jerusalem

The Turkish Ottoman Empire under Selim I captured Jerusalem from the Mamluks, who had held it since 1250 CE. Unlike many of its previous occupiers, the Islamic Ottomans were relatively tolerant of Jewish religious practice and did not disturb any of its religious sites. The Ottomans had welcomed thousands of Jewish refugees who had been expelled from Spain by Ferdinand II of Aragon and Isabella of Castile in 1492. They had a positive impression of the Jews.

For 400 years under the Ottomans,[89] Jerusalem benefited from a period of relative quiet and (minimal) food sufficiency. Under the beneficent rule of Suleiman the Magnificent, the city prospered, enjoying ethnic and economic tranquility. No one dared challenge the military superiority of this Turkish Empire. In 1532 the city's aqueducts were restored. Once again, a steady supply of water was made available to the inhabitants. Fearful that the Mamluks would attempt to recapture Jerusalem, Sultan Suleiman the Magnificent began in 1537 to rebuild the impressive defensive walls that surround the city. Its completion in 1541 provided a measure of security and peace of mind to its inhabitants. These are the same fortress-walls that still surround the Old City of today.

The Ottoman Empire (now known as the Turkish Empire) was an empire that lasted from 1299 CE to November 1, 1922. At one time, during the 16th–17th century it controlled Southeastern Europe, Western Asia and North Africa — straddling three continents.

For 600 years this Islamic Empire was the powerhouse between the Eastern and Western Worlds, supplanting the Eastern Roman (Byzantine) Empire.

---

88   Communal life in the Old City was interrupted again for nineteen years following Jordan's conquest in 1948.

89   The Ottoman Empire held its own against rivals from Europe and Asia for roughly 400 years. From: www.jewishvirtuallibrary.org/.../Jerusalem1.htm...
Also: "They remained for eight jubilees (8 x 50 = 400 years), that is to say they were in Jerusalem for 400 years. Exactly 400 years later, in 1917, the Ottoman Turks ... www.alamongordo.com/tag/predictions-jerusalem/

1589 CE — Turks Shut Down the Ramban Synagogue

What an abrupt and unexpected change of heart. Four-hundred years of relative coexistence and religious tolerance came to a sudden and jarring end. The beneficent rule of Suleiman the Magnificent simply evaporated. Shocked and traumatized, the distraught Jewish community was totally unprepared for what was to come. Their faith in G-d was unshakeable. They improvised and somehow managed to get by.

The rumors I heard were disquieting. If true, I feared for the emerging Jewish community in Jerusalem. Gossip had it that the Ottoman Sultan, previously so friendly to the Jews, ordered the closing of the Ramban synagogue. The decree, once confirmed, marked the closing of the only synagogue in Jerusalem. Its congregants, mostly descendants of immigrants from the Spanish expulsion a century ago, were now forced to pray privately in their own homes. It was not until the beginning of the 17th century that a replacement synagogue, the Yochanan ben Zakkai Synagogue, was constructed to serve the needs of the small Jewish community.

October 14, 1700 — Ashkenazim from Europe

I was roused that morning from a rather restless night by the sound of hundreds of shuffling feet. Heavy eyed, I looked around me and saw hundreds and hundreds of new faces. I immediately recognized them as newcomers. They were not dressed in the Sephardic fashion, but appeared to be Ashkenazim from Europe. Not quite awake, I observed this group with particular interest. Within minutes, every available spot in front of the Kotel was occupied, and a second and third row was forming. These Jews were preparing for their first morning prayers in the Holy Land. The first faint light was not yet discernible in the eastern sky. I saw small groups looking around in the dark for water with which to wash their hands prior to prayer. There were no water faucets or even well-water hand pumps at the Kotel in those days. Others brought flasks of water with them and were performing the *Netilat Yadayim* (ritual hand washing).

By morning, the light of sunrise had begun to spread across the eastern sky. As local Jews arrived, I watched the goings-on, wondering whether these Jews would recite the *Shema* and pray the *Amida* so early or would they wait until the *"Mi'sheyakir"* hour had arrived. That is the time when the morning light has begun to make itself felt to the point where one is able to recognize a rare acquaintance from a distance of four cubits, or the time when one is able to distinguish between blue and white. At that hour, recitation of the *Shema* is permitted, though it is still too early for the recitation of *Shemoneh Esrai (Amida)*. Most of the locals, both Ashkenazim and Sephardim, wait until *Hanetz Hachamah*. Halachically, this is the time when the first part of the sun rises above the horizon. From then onward, prayer is permissible. Yet, there are some very pious Jews who come to the Kotel to pray *Hanetz*. They recite the *Shema* just before sunrise and then pray *Amida* with the sunrise.

Obviously, I was elated at the arrival of so many pious newcomers. Overnight, the narrow plaza in front of the Kotel was transformed from a sleepy, almost languid site to one that is vigorously dynamic. The last time I witnessed such spirited activity was more than a century before. To say that I was thrilled is an understatement.

Who were these newcomers? It appears that a group of 1,000–1,500[90] Polish, Moravian, and German Jews, led by the great Judah HeHasid, arrived in Jerusalem. The Jewish population of Jerusalem at the time consisted of approximately 200 Ashkenazi and 1,000 Sephardi Jews. Almost all were extremely poor, barely subsisting on charities from the Jewish Diaspora. The unexpected arrival of such a large group created a predicament for the resident community. Not only did they lack the funds to help them, but the local Jews mistrusted some of the new arrivals, thinking they might be *Sabbateans*.[91] Conditions worsened for the newcomers when their leader died shortly after their arrival in Jerusalem. Appeals for help from abroad failed. Furthermore, as they had travelled from Europe, they incurred debts that were compounded when, in exchange for permission to enter, the Ottomans insisted on financial guarantees in the name of the entire Jewish community in Jerusalem.

---

90 Sources differ as to the exact number. "The Churva", by Dovid Rossoff, suggests that the figure is in excess of 500. Others maintain that it was 1000 or even 1500.

91 Followers of Sabbatai Zevi , the false messiah who eventually converted to Islam.

Aliyah to the Holy Land

WOMEN AND MEN AT THE KOTEL (CIRCA 1912)

[Photo courtesy Eric Matson, Government Press Office- American Colony Photo Collection] [Code: D 826-075]

Photo shows mostly women with an occasional man. Some come to pray for a parent or for a child, others at the approach of childbirth, still others for a recovery from illness. Many thoughts percolate in their hearts, wafting into their inner core, yearning for deliverance. Composing their own words — for few, if any, had siddurim (prayer books) — they hear and sense the echo of their words in their own entreaties. This longing for a closer bond with G-d continues to glow within them and inspires their spontaneous entreaties.

Over the course of the next few weeks and months, I learned more about this single-minded Jewish group. Influenced by their leader's zeal and commitment, the small group of thirty-one families started out in 1697, traveling from one Jewish locality to another throughout their native Poland, exhorting penitence and a lifestyle typified by abstinence from various sorts of worldly pleasures. The goal was *aliyah* to the Holy Land where they would reach their religious and spiritual zenith. As they traveled throughout Moravia, Germany, and Italy, they gained many more followers — some say as many as 1,500. Sadly, 30 percent of the pilgrims died en route from the hardships and illnesses of the journey.

Despite all the difficulties, they persevered and established themselves in the city.

The Ottoman authorities demanded huge bribes for permission to build a synagogue. The group wanted to rebuild the synagogue that was located in the courtyard next to the Ramban Synagogue.[92] The Turks were very willing to lend the money at high rates of interest in order to help finance the cost of construction. Failure to repay resulted in the imprisonment of the borrower. Money had to be solicited to redeem the debtor. Over time, the spiral of debt made it impossible to repay.

Furious, in 1721 CE, the Ottomans set fire to the synagogue building and its contents and expelled both the old Ashkenazi community and the newcomers, with a warning not to return until the cumulative loans were repaid.

For the following eighty-nine years, it was hard to locate a single Ashkenazi Jew in Jerusalem unless he was dressed like a Sephardi in order to hide his Ashkenazi identity. Most of the Ashkenazi Jews relocated to other holy cities: Hebron, Tiberias, and Safed.

I remember the day when the destroyed synagogue, called *Churvat Yehudah He-Hasid*,[93] was finally rebuilt in 1864. It became the chief Ashkenazi synagogue in Jerusalem until it, too, was destroyed by the Arab Legion in 1948.

---

92   At the end of the 16th century, ownership of the Ramban synagogue passed into Muslim hands. For 400 years, it was used as a raisin mill, a charcoal warehouse, and finally a cheese factory. Over 100 years ago, the building returned to Jewish hands and the sound of the Torah once again emanated from the Ramban Shul in the streets of the Jewish Quarter.

93   Rebuilding He-Hasid's Ruin: 1857–64: "With new funds arriving, work could progress. In 1862 the domed ceiling was completed and Rabbi Yeshaya Bardaki, head of the Ashkenazic community, was honored with placing the final stone of the dome. Two years later, in 1864, the new synagogue was dedicated. Present was Baron Alphonse de Rothschild, who eight years earlier had been given the honor of laying the first stone." Rossoff, Dovid (1998). *Where Heaven Touches Earth*, Guardian Press, as quoted by http://en.wikipedia.org/wiki/Hurva_SynagoguerefRossoff1998.

1808–1812 CE — My Fantastic Memory

I told you about my fantastic memory. I can recall the face of everyone who has visited my fellow stones or me for at least a year following their visit. I can summon up not only the image but also the mannerisms of the individual and his style of *davening* (praying). No, there is no hidden camera inside of me. I assure you that I am solid stone. So many new faces came to the Kotel beginning with the year 1808. They were not residents of Jerusalem; I know this because most of their appearances at the Kotel were limited to a week or less. It seemed that a group of some 500 Jews known as *Perushim* made *aliyah* to Palestine from Lithuania. These followers of the Vilna Gaon would have liked to settle in Jerusalem but refrained from doing so out of fear that the Ottoman government would insist that these newcomers repay the old debts incurred by the Ashkenazi community a century ago. Descendants of the original creditors still held the old promissory notes.

MAN ABSORBED IN DEEP STUDY
People come to pray, to recite Tehillim (Psalms), as well as to learn.

1835 CE — The Four Sephardi Synagogues

I have witnessed many unexpected changes in Jerusalem's fortunes. Most were disheartening, some crushing. But every so often, a buoyant change would lift my spirits. One such experience was the decision by Mohammed Ali, the viceroy of Egypt who ruled Jerusalem at the time, to permit the restoration of the four Sephardi Synagogues of the Old City. Since their initial construction, successive Muslim rulers banned any restoration or renovation. Now they could be fixed and returned to their proper splendor!

1864 CE — Disciples of the Vilna Gaon

Disciples of the Vilna Gaon officially consecrated a new synagogue at the same site of the original burnt-out Churva synagogue. Many of them are the children of those who came in the years 1808–1812. The Churva synagogue would remain in continuous use until the Jordanians reduced the building to rubble during the 1948 Arab-Israeli war.

1869 CE

When Chabad Rabbi Hillel Moshe Gelbstein settled in Jerusalem, he patiently succeeded in having benches and tables (previously forbidden) brought to the Wall for daily prayer sessions (minyanim) and for study groups. This was of great help to Jews — especially the elderly — who wanted to study and pray at our holiest site. These prayer and Torah study sessions continued for several years until Arab resentment put a stop to it.

1877–1895 CE — Failed Attempts to Purchase Kotel Plaza

Having houses, animals, outhouses, and dirty streets occupying one's holiest place is simply not appropriate. No surprise that Jews were understandably very anxious to purchase (from the Arabs) property in front of the Western Wall. In 1877, they almost succeeded when the *Mufti* of Jerusalem accepted their offer. A difference of opinion within the Jewish community aborted the deal. This was followed by a bigger plan in 1887 when Baron Rothschild envisaged a strategy to purchase and demolish the Moroccan (Arab) Quarter as "a merit and honor to the Jewish People." The projected purchase was approved by both the Ottoman Governor of Jerusalem and by the *Mufti* of Jerusalem. Unfortunately the deal was called off after the authorities insisted that the Jews may demolish the quarter but may not build anything on the land. They would only permit planting of trees to give the place a face-lift. Furthermore (and this was the monkey wrench in the deal) the Jews would not have full control over the area. Thus, Arabs would be free to use the plaza as they chose; including the driving of mules and other animals, whose consequence would be disruption of Jewish worship and desecration of the holy site.

Further efforts to purchase the land in front of the Kotel proved disastrous for Hebrew linguist and publisher Rabbi Chaim Herschensohn who, in 1895, invested all his assets in a failed effort to purchase the land in front of the Kotel. This was followed by another futile attempt by the Palestine Land Development just prior to the outbreak of World War I. A few months before the start of World War I, the Turkish authorities, succumbing to Arab pressure, issued an official decree forbidding Jews from bringing benches and lighting candles at the Wall. The relations between the Jews and the Turks, fragile but tolerant, was rapidly deteriorating. It took the self-assured intercession by Chacham Bashi to persuade the Turks to overturn the ban.

1828–1908 CE — The Crumbling of the Ottoman Empire

During this period, the Ottoman Empire lost much territory. The centralized government was enfeebled, exhibiting signs of administrative instability. Confronted by challenges on all fronts, it sought alliances with an assortment of European countries: France, the Netherlands, the United Kingdom, and Russia.

Because of its alliances, many Muslims and Circassians immigrated to the Ottoman Empire. By the end of the 19th century, both Austria and Russia wanted to expand their spheres of influence, if not sovereign rule, over territory previously controlled by the Ottoman Empire. Were it not for the United Kingdom, which feared Russian dominance in the Eastern Mediterranean, Austria and Russia would have gobbled up the weakened empire.

CHAPTER VIII

End of the Ottoman Empire

The dissolution of the Ottoman Empire began in 1908 and ended shortly after the First World War. On the Middle Eastern front, the Arab revolt (which began in 1916) helped to turn the tide against the Ottomans. Most of the Arabian Peninsula was turned over to the British forces in 1919.

We, the stones at the Kotel, did not know what to make of the First World War. Jewish soldiers were to be found on both sides the war. Some 85,000 Jewish soldiers served in World War I for the German Empire. Over 12,000 lost their lives. Many of those soldiers who came out alive were highly decorated.[94]

The First World War pitted the British army against the Turks. At least 50,000 Jews enlisted. Five Jewish soldiers won the Victoria Cross. Jews formed their own unit, the Zion Mule Corps, fighting at Gallipoli and the Dardanelles in 1915. Later, in 1918, three Jewish units were in the Jewish Legion under General Allenby in Palestine. These regiments were disbanded after the First World War. Many Eastern European Jews were in the Pioneer Corps, working as laborers on the trenches.

Not too many people know about the young Jewish men from around Zichron Yaakov who engaged in active espionage for Great Britain while the

---

94   Still, Hitler repaid this loyalty to Germany in 1933 when he declared the Jewish soldiers "unfit to serve" and forced them out of the German military. Tragically, many of them and their families were later killed in concentration camps. We all know what followed. The 1938 pogrom known as the *Kristallnacht* (Night of Broken Glass) was the prelude to the bestiality that characterized man's inhumanity to man.

country was still under Ottoman rule.[95] Several thousand Jewish residents of Palestine, some of them trained and appointed as officers, were forced to fight on behalf of the Turkish army.[96]

The League of Nations and the British Mandate

We really did not know what to expect following the defeat of the Ottoman Empire, which had controlled Palestine since the early 16th century. News reached us that the League of Nations might entrust the British to administer Palestine. If Britain were to replace the defunct Ottoman Empire, what was to be the fate of the Jews? It was not until June, 1922 that we learned about the League of Nations decision to formalize British rule in Palestine. The boundaries of two new states were laid down within the territory of the Mandate: Palestine and Transjordan. The initial news appeared to be quite promising. The preamble of the Mandate declared:

> Whereas the Principal Allied Powers have also agreed that the Mandatory should be responsible for putting into effect the declaration originally made on November 2nd, 1917, by the Government of His Britannic Majesty, and adopted by the said Powers, in favor of the establishment in Palestine of a national home for the Jewish people, it being clearly understood that nothing should be done which might prejudice the civil and religious rights of existing non-Jewish communities in Palestine, or the rights and political status enjoyed by Jews in any other country.

With the onset of the First World War, the Zionists aspired to gain assistance from one of the Great Powers for increased Jewish immigration and

---

95   Called the Gideonites, who served as the basis for NILI (the initials of *netzach Yisrael lo yeshaker*, I Sam. 15:29) under the leadership of the agronomist Aaron Aaronson.

96   Examples are Moshe Sharett, Dov Hoz (who later deserted to the British army), Alexander Aaronson, and Elimelekh Zelikovich (Avner); the latter eventually became a senior commander in the Haganah.

ultimate sovereignty of Palestine. Arab nationalists argued for an independent Arab state covering all of the Ottoman lands in the Middle East.

The Jews, then comprising only 12 percent of the population of Palestine, needed someone who could leverage their hopes and aspirations. That someone was Chaim Weizmann, a perceptive senior scientist who was widely respected for his contributions to Britain's wartime success. He was an articulate man of integrity, experienced in European diplomacy. Weizmann understood domestic British politics as well as the European strategic viewpoint: that British Middle East policy pivoted on control of the Suez Canal and its strategic role in India and Egypt.

As British war prospects weakened throughout 1917, the focus shifted towards the Zionist aspiration for strategic reasons. Jewish Palestine was viewed as a budding helper, able to protect British interests in the region. Fears were also voiced in the Foreign Office that if Britain did not come out in favor of a Jewish entity in Palestine, the Germans would preempt them. Lastly, a number of influential Christians, especially Lloyd George and Arthur James Balfour, attached religious importance to the wished-for return of the Jews to their ancestral homeland. That was the background for the British commitment to the Zionist cause with the issuance of the Balfour Declaration of November, 1917.

December 1917 — A Promise Not Kept

When the British forces, under Edmund Allenby, conquered Jerusalem from the Turks, Allenby promised "that every sacred building, monument, holy spot, shrine, traditional site, endowment, pious bequest, or customary place of prayer of whatsoever form of the three religions will be maintained and protected according to the existing customs and beliefs of those to whose faith they are sacred."

1918 — Weizmann and the Balfour Declaration

Our initial optimism was that with the defeat of the Turks, the prospect of more equitable treatment was at hand. Our expectations soared with the Balfour Declaration, which gave us new hope for a Jewish homeland in Palestine.

Let me paint a background picture for you. The goal of the Jewish nationalist movement was the creation and support of a Jewish national state in Palestine. It originated in eastern and central Europe in the latter part of the 19th century. You are all familiar with Theodore Herzl and his steadfast determination to establish a home for the Jews in Palestine. The biblical promise of a land for the Jews and a return to the Temple in Jerusalem were preserved in Jewish consciousness for almost 2,000 years. As recently as the 1800s, less than 25,000 Jews lived in Palestine, most of them in Jerusalem.

It was Chaim Weizmann whose protracted and capable negotiations succeeded in eliciting the Balfour Declaration in support of the Zionist cause. The letter from the Foreign Secretary, addressed to Lord Rothschild, affirmed the British government's "sympathy with Jewish Zionist aspirations," viewed with favor "the establishment in Palestine of a National Home for the Jewish People," and announced its aim to help bring about this goal.

1919 — Failed attempts to purchase the Kotel area[97]

Zionist leader Chaim Weizmann, eager to enable Jews to pray at the Kotel undisturbed, offered a very substantial sum to purchase the area at the foot of the Wall and resettle the Arab occupants.[98] While the British Military Governor of Jerusalem was enthusiastic about the idea, hoping to improve the educational lot of the mostly illiterate Arabs, he encountered fierce Muslim opposition to the proposal. Twenty years later, the same British Governor wrote:

> The acceptance of the proposals, had it been practicable, would have obviated years of wretched humiliations, including the befouling of the Wall and pavement and the unmannerly braying of the tragic-comic Arab band during Jewish prayer, and culminating in the horrible outrages of 1929.

---

97   See also above 1869 and 1877–1895

98   Somewhere between £75,000 and £100,000

MECHITZAH SEPARATING MEN & WOMEN

Mechitzah is the dividing wall separating the men's prayer area from the women's prayer area. The reason given is to avoid kalut rosh (frivolity) resulting from proximity to members of the opposite sex. The prophet cautioned that men and women should stay away from each other while engaged in prayer or other religious occasions. Separate seating, a feature of all Orthodox synagogues, does not connote lack of respect for women or inequality. On the contrary, it reinforces the Jewish sense of modesty. Mixed pews can detract from a sense of reverence and kavanah that are necessary to intensify one's communication with one's Maker

1920

Arab attacks on peaceful Jewish settlements killed seven Jews. The British military emasculated the Balfour Declaration's promises to help in the establishment of a Jewish national home in Palestine. The League of Nations Mandate for Palestine was awarded to the British.

1921

The British-installed mufti of Jerusalem incited Arabs to riot. In Jaffa, forty-three Jews were killed. Instead of punishing the Arabs, the British rewarded them by temporarily suspending Jewish immigration.

Under the British Mandate (1922–1948)

With the British conquest of Jerusalem on December 9, 1917, all of Palestine came under its military rule. Jerusalem was made the capital of the British-held League of Nations Palestine Mandate.

Still, the fate of the region, resulting from Arab pressure and conflicting British objectives, was far from settled. In the ensuing years the British did everything possible to impede, obstruct, and encumber Jewish immigration and the realization of the 2,000-year-old dream of a Jewish homeland.

1922

The League of Nations Mandate for Palestine was emasculated once again by the British, who removed all of Palestine east of the Jordan (78 percent of Palestine) from the territory of the League of Nations Mandate for Palestine and transferred power to Emir Abdullah, who established the Emirate (later Kingdom) of Transjordan.

The British officially banned the placing of benches near the Wall. Many recalled that the ban imposed by the Ottomans in 1915 was overturned after the intervention of the Chacham Bashi, the then Sephardi religious leader. This time around, all appeals failed.

BLOWING A YEMENITE SHOFAR
The Yemenite shofar is different from the traditional Jewish shofar. The distinguishing sign is its appearance. It is more spiraled and bigger in size. Its outer surface from the mouthpiece to the middle portion is highly polished. The rest has a natural appearance and texture. Unlike the typical shofar, the Yemenite shofar is made from the horn of a Greater kudu (a woodland antelope found throughout eastern and southern Africa).

1926

The year marked another unsuccessful effort made by the Palestine Zionist Executive to buy the whole area adjacent to the Wall in order to create an open space with seats for aged worshippers to sit on.

1928 — Mechitzah Triggers Major Altercation

John Chancellor, British High Commissioner of Palestine, reportedly asserted that the Western Wall should come under Jewish control and wondered "why no great Jewish philanthropist had not bought it yet." (Surely he was aware of the repeated attempts to purchase the land in front of the Kotel, all of which were rejected.)

A major altercation erupted between the Arabs, Jews, and Mandate authorities when a *mechitzah* (a screen used to separate men and women at prayer) was placed at the Wall in 1928. This confrontation was triggered by the Arabs, despite General Allenby's pledge to permit the Jews to worship unmolested. The ban was extended once again, forbidding the placement of chairs or benches anywhere in the alleyway near the Wall. In practice, a compromise was reached where such screens were moved into place when large numbers of worshippers came to pray. Under Arab pressure, the District Commissioner stationed a British officer to enforce the ban. As heartless as it seems, his task was to make sure that elderly Jews were prevented from using chairs.

On September 28, 1928, on Yom Kippur — the holiest day of the year — British police vehemently dismantled a makeshift *mechitzah*. The police, using parts of the wooden frame as clubs, hit women who tried to thwart the removal of the screen. In a scene hard to imagine, the police then uncaringly pulled out the chairs from under elderly worshippers. The desecration of the site on such a holy day triggered international objection over the British action. Defending his action, the British commissioner admitted that he acted under a complaint from the Supreme Muslim Council. He blamed the Jews for violating the Ottoman status quo. Nevertheless, he expressed regret over the events that followed.

CHAPTER IX

The Jewish Connection to the Temple Mount

I have tried my best to explain the Jewish connection to the Temple Mount and Western Wall. That deep-seated link and bond goes back more than 3,000 years. Jewish tradition and history are intertwined with this tiny piece of real estate.

Creation began here from the stone (Foundation Stone) at the top of Mount Moriah. Adam, the first human being, was created on Mount Moriah. It was on top of this Foundation Stone that Abraham bound his son Isaac, readying him for the ultimate sacrifice to G-d. Jacob's ladder was linked to Mount Moriah. King Solomon constructed the First Temple here almost 3,000 years ago on this site. The Temple's Holy of Holies (built around the Foundation Stone) contained the original Ark of the Covenant, until the Babylonians destroyed the Temple in 586 BCE. Seventy years later, the Second Temple was built on the same site. Later, in the first century BCE, the platform surrounding the Temple was greatly expanded by King Herod. The Temple was the hub of Jewish spiritual and communal life until the destruction of the Second Temple by the Romans in 70 CE.

The Kotel, that huge section of the western supporting wall of the Temple Mount, has survived intact. The area in front of the Wall and the Wall itself have evolved as the most sacred place in Jewish religious and national consciousness because of its connection with the Holy of Holies in the Temple, from which the *Shechinah*, the Divine Presence, never departed.

The Controversy Over the Western Wall During the Mandate Period

The legitimacy of the Jewish claim to the Holy Land extends back 4,000 years when HaShem instructed Abraham to leave his homeland of Ur Kasdim and go *"to the land that I will show you"* (Genesis 12:1). The nation of Israel existed 2,000 years before the advent of Islam in the 7th century CE. Jews have continued to live in the Holy Land almost from time immemorial. I cannot understand the basis for Palestinian claims to sovereignty of Jerusalem, let alone the biblical Land of Israel. Such assertions are fraudulent. There is no basis for the Arab entitlement either in biblical history, in archaeological findings, or in view of the history of the past 2,000 years.

I find their contention that Jerusalem be the capital of a Palestinian state outrageous! Can any unbiased historian, biblical researcher, or archaeologist deny that Jerusalem has been the Jewish capital since the time of King David? Why, if the Arab claim had any legitimacy, didn't Jordan establish it as the Palestinian capital during the nineteen years it occupied Jerusalem? Why isn't Jerusalem mentioned even once in the Koran? It is mentioned "many hundreds of times" in the Hebrew Bible.[99] It is clear that Mohammed never visited Jerusalem — for if he did, surely I would have taken note of his "night journey." The whole of Jerusalem is legally and justly the capital of the Jewish State of Israel.

Do not listen to the history-deniers. I can personally attest to the fact that the Jewish presence in Jerusalem preceded the Muslim arrival in

---

99   Ohr Somayach, basing its opinion on *Jerusalem, Eye of the Universe* by Rabbi Aryeh Kaplan (http://ohr.edu/ask_db/ask_main.php/291/Q1/), states that "... it is true that the word 'Jerusalem' does not appear there. Most simply, this is because it was not yet called Jerusalem. Under Jebusite rule and earlier, Jerusalem was divided into two cities, the western part called Jeru (*Yere*) and the eastern part called Salem (*Shalem*). Both of these names *do* appear in the Five Books: 'And Malki-Tzedek, King of Shalem' (Genesis 14:18). 'And Abraham called that place...Yere' (Genesis 21:14). Around the time of Joshua's conquest, the Amorites consolidated the two halves of the city, and they combined the two names: Jeru-salem. From this point on in history, our Bible refers to Jerusalem countless times."
Furthermore, the Chumash refers nineteen times to *"the place that G-d will choose"* as the center for Jewish life and religion (e.g., Deuteronomy 12:11, 14, etc.). The Prophets' Samuel and Gad finally reveal to King David that this chosen place is Jerusalem and the Temple Mount. Jerusalem played a prominent part in Jewish history and writings more than two thousand years before Islam's rise and the writing of the Koran, which makes no mention of Jerusalem.

636 CE by more than 1,500 years. Despite attempts to rewrite history, there was a *Beit haMikdash* where the Dome of the Rock stands today. I have not budged from this spot in over 2,000 years. During those very many years, I have witnessed so many tears, so many painful memories in my city of Jerusalem. No wonder some call my Wall "the Wailing Wall." Jerusalem is a city of tears, but it is more, much more, for here we will witness the coming of the *Mashiach* and the rebuilding of the Third Temple. The streets of Jerusalem will be filled with song and laughter.

The Muslim Inflammatory Claims

All this talk about a Jewish homeland in Palestine struck fear in the heart of the Arab mufti of Jerusalem. Attempts in the 19th century by a number of Zionist groups to gain control of the Wall and its surroundings failed. Baron Rothschild offered the Arab owners of the property very substantial sums to "buy back" the area, but the Arabs were adamant in refusing. Quite the opposite, the Arab religious establishment, encouraged by the Turks (and later the British), went out of their way to prevent Jewish observance and to break up any Jewish presence at the Wall. The Arabs created a labyrinth of alleyways, making access to the Wall difficult. The embryonic rise of Arab nationalism and religious fervor created a feeling of despair on me and my fellow stones.

The Muslim claim to Jerusalem came about after the death of Mohammed in 632 CE.[100] Many have pointed out that the Arabic name of Jerusalem *Al-Quds* (The Holy One) is derived from *Beit-el-Muqadas* (i.e., *Beit haMikdash*), the Hebrew name for the Temple Mount. Jerusalem is not mentioned once in the Koran.[101]

The mufti of Jerusalem began to inflame the Muslim community against the Zionists, saying publicly that they planned to seize control of the Wall. In order to irritate the Jews, the Mufti created another opening at the southern end of the alley that runs along the base of the Wall, thus altering the rarely used alleyway from a dead end into a thoroughfare for people, donkeys and other animals. In addition, the Muslims intentionally held noisy and often shrill rituals in the immediate area in an attempt to disrupt any Jewish worship at the Kotel. As the Jewish people's dreams for a land of their own began to percolate, it was the Kotel that embodied their national aspirations. From the end of the 19th century throughout the period of the British mandate, the Arabs constantly interrupted Jewish prayer at the Kotel, not only by prohibiting *shofar* blowing but also by banning benches or even a small table from which the Torah scroll could be read. As if that were not enough, they repeatedly protested to the British about the Jews placing such items as a *shtender* (small lectern, podium) or a small table for prayer books from which the Torah scroll could be read.

---

100 Islam's claim that Mohammed set foot in Jerusalem is without basis, since he died six years before Jerusalem surrendered to the Muslims; still, they claim he came here on his night journey.

101 Though there are allusions to the *Al-Aqsa* Mosque in Jerusalem (the Farthest Mosque, where many Muslims believe is where Prophet Mohammed prayed prior to his ascent to Heaven in the year 620). Mohammed's journey to the Farthest Mosque is mentioned in the Koran.

CHAPTER X

Arab Violence — 1929 Riots

I could not believe my ears. The scene that erupted was stressful and grave. As hundreds of enraged Arabs exited the *Al-Aqsa* Mosque, they screamed in frenzy that the Jews had come to the Western Wall to curse Mohammed and that Jews have attacked and are planning additional attacks against mosques. The rabidly anti-Semitic mufti of Jerusalem, Haj Amin el-Husseini, again incited the Arabs. How well I remember the riots of 1929. Screams became louder and louder as an inflamed Muslim mob converged on the Jews praying at the Kotel, running amok, rampaging and smashing ritual objects. This disturbance was mild compared to the extensive rioting that followed throughout Palestine. Nor was this just an isolated sermon from one mosque. This agitation was a well-planned provocation throughout Palestine. Hysterical mobs raced throughout the land, becoming one of the worst pogroms by Arabs against Jews in Palestine.

Of course, the accusations against us were sheer fabrication. This campaign of false rumor and propaganda was well-orchestrated. One hundred and thirty-three Jews were murdered by Arab mobs. The British suppressed the assaults. Ever ready to blame the Jews for the murderous violence against them by the Arabs, the British recommended reducing Jewish immigration. Arab hostility to Jewish prayer at the Kotel was intense. It was fueled by deceptive information. Like fire out of control, these distorted accusations of Jews endangering Islamic mosques were systematically spread from mosque to mosque, further stirring up the Arab populace.

Woe is me! Was I reliving Job (10:15) who cried out in anguish to G-d 3,200 years ago: "If I be wicked, woe unto me; and if I be righteous, yet will I not lift up my head. I am full of confusion; therefore see Thou mine affliction."

The riots led to massacres of Jews in Hebron and other cities. To add insult to injury, the British commission of inquiry ultimately decided that the Muslims had unqualified ownership of the Wall and adjoining property. As a concession to the Jews, the commission gave the Jews some degree of access to the Western Wall for limited worship.

Still, severe restrictions were imposed on the Jews. They could only come to the Kotel in small groups, and were barred from the Kotel on Fridays and on Muslim festivals. Furthermore, they were forbidden from bringing *Sifrei Torah* to the Kotel *or* to place any chairs in front of the Wall. Topping off these unfair constraints was the humiliating dictate that the *Shofar* was never to be blown at the Kotel, not even on Rosh Hashanah or Yom Kippur, lest it offend the Arab population. Any attempt to fulfill the commandment of blowing the *Shofar* was met by intervention of the British police, who would arrest the "perpetrators." So much for the "specific guarantees regarding freedom of movement and access to the Holy Sites contained in the Treaty of Berlin (1878) [which] had been preserved under the terms of the Palestine Mandate," and which had been confirmed by the Covenant of the League of Nations.

The Decade Following the 1929 Arab Riots

"I am full of confusion," as Job (10:15) said. What was happening?

After 2,000 years of anguish and travail, why was Jewish blood being spilled again?

The decade following the 1929 Arab riots was a turbulent one for all. Despite openly favoring the Arabs, the British sought to quell sporadic rioting and spontaneous strikes by the Arab community. Widespread outrage in the Arab community at various supposed "provocations" sparked the 1935–1936 insurrections, during which thousands of Jewish farms and orchards were destroyed. Jewish civilians were attacked and killed, causing some Jewish communities to evacuate.[102] The British Peel Commission

---

102 Beisan and Acre

recommended a partition between a small Jewish state and an Arab state. The Arab rejection of the proposal led to violent uprisings that lasted until 1939. British forces, reinforced by 6,000 armed Jewish auxiliary police, overpowered the Arab militants, but lost control of Nablus and Hebron. The violent, unprovoked Arab attacks on the Jews of the pre-state *Yishuv* led to the establishment of Jewish underground military groups, first and foremost the *Haganah*. With the realization on the part of world leaders that reconciliation between Arabs and Jews was unlikely, the concept of partition gained ground.

1939 — White Paper Restricts Immigration of Jews to Palestine

Word came to me that the British called for a conference to be attended by the Zionist and Palestinian Arab leadership, as well as that of neighboring Arab states. The Arabs refused to sit in the same room with the Zionists and no solutions were reached. As expected, the British sided with the Arabs and issued a White Paper that severely restricted immigration of Jews to Palestine, continuing in its betrayal of its commitments under the League of Nations Mandate.

1947 — Partitioning Proposed

I felt the unease amongst those coming to pray at the Kotel. Word had it that the United Nations proposed partitioning the British Mandate (the remaining 22 percent of Palestine)[103] into separate Arab and Jewish states. The plan was accepted by the Zionist movement but rejected by all Arab parties. Jewish communities in many Arab countries across the Middle East were attacked; hundreds were murdered. Arab militias and terrorist groups infiltrated Palestine and attacked Jews.

---

103   78% having already been given to Transjordan

CHAPTER XI

INDEPENDENCE

1948 — A Decisive Year

On the eve of the projected partition (May 14, 1948), I could hear the fierce fighting that broke out in the city between Jews and Arabs. With the Mandate nearing its end in 1948, Arabs and Jews jostled to secure their positions. Israel was fighting for its life. The United Nations sought to partition Palestine into Arab and Jewish states, with Jerusalem and its environs (including Bethlehem) as an internationally administered enclave.

I remember Israel's War of Independence very well. The war began when the British abandoned their Mandate of Palestine in the middle of May, 1948. The Arabs rejected the United Nations partition plan. The tremors turned to shock waves as five Arab countries invaded the territory of the former British mandate. The powerful armies of Egypt, Iraq, Jordan, Lebanon, and Syria attacked the infant State of Israel.

Greatly outnumbered and ill-equipped, every single citizen knew deep in his heart what he was fighting for. This was more than just a fight for his homeland. His personal survival and that of his family and friends was at stake. During that war, Jordanians captured the Old City of Jerusalem. It is not easy for me to recall the depressing sensation. My fellow stones and I felt a sense of numbness. All around us, the air was filled with a mixture of commotion and calm all at the same time. The suffering was palpable. If stones could cry, we would shed enough tears to flood the area around us.

What was being done to HaShem's city? Jerusalem means the city of peace! How could the suffering around us be reconciled with the concept of peace?

The war ended with a 1949 armistice agreement. Little did we know that 1948 marked the beginning of an Arab-initiated conflict that would continue for many decades to come.

May 28, 1948, was a particularly black day for me and my fellow stones. The Jewish Quarter of the Old City of Jerusalem fell to the Arab Legion. The Jews of the Old City surrendered. The Arabs were now in control of our sacred city. Once again, numerous ancient sites holy to the Jewish religion were under the domination of foreigners.

1949 — Baruch HaShem, We Survived

Baruch HaShem, we survived. Remember that in 1948, the Jewish population of Israel totaled 650,000. After Hitler decimated the Jewish population of Europe, killing six million, only twelve million Jews survived in the whole world. This means that only 5.4 percent of world Jewry lived in the Jewish state.

How 650,000 Jews (many of whom were survivors of concentration camps) were able to withstand the assault of so many Arab countries is a miracle. Outnumbered and outgunned, HaShem led us to victory. Still, it was a bittersweet victory for the Jewish People, because its heart and soul — the Kotel in the Old City of Jerusalem — was beyond its reach.

Except for Iraq, all the other Arab aggressors who attacked Israel signed armistice agreements with Israel. However, all of them refused to recognize Israel or negotiate a solution to the Palestinian-Arab refugee problem created by the war. The belligerent Arab assault gave rise to 700,000 Palestinian-Arab refugees, most of whom were placed in refugee camps by neighboring Arab states who refused to accept them.[104] Discount the

---

104 "The Arab refugees who had migrated to various Arab nations were not similarly well-received. They were regarded not as Arab brothers but as unwelcome migrants who were not to be trusted. Squalid refugee camps were set up as showpieces to induce the West's sympathy and kept that way. The UN, through UNRWA (UN Relief and Works Agency), provided assistance to the camps when the host country could not or would not. These

myth that there were four or five million Palestinian refugees. Most of these are the descendants of those who fled. There are only 50,000 of the original refugees who remain alive today. The Arab countries refused to permit the resettlement of these refugees. They were helpless pawns in the hands of extreme Arab governments. The United Nations General Assembly passed Resolution 194, calling for the return of Palestinian-Arab refugees within the context of an Arab/Israeli peace. All Arab states opposed the resolution and opposed peace with Israel.

Nineteen Years of Jordanian Rule

During the nineteen years when the Old City of Jerusalem was under Jordanian rule, Jews were forbidden from entering the Old City and other holy sites located elsewhere in East Jerusalem. This was a clear violation of the UN mandate to permit Jews and Christians to visit their holy sites. Not only did the Jordanians refuse access to Israelis but they also began a systematic destruction of the Jewish Quarter, including many ancient synagogues.

I could hear what was going on. Later, good Christians and Arabs friendly to the Jews spoke of the devastation that took place after the fall of the Jewish Quarter during and after the 1948 Arab-Israeli War. Synagogues were burnt, desecrated, and turned into horse stables. Tombstones were stolen from cemeteries to be used as paving stones. What I could not accept was the wanton desecration and systematic looting of Jewish sites. The frenzy that accompanied the vandalism is unspeakable. Almost sixty ancient synagogues (some of them 700 years old), libraries, *yeshivot*, and religious institutions were ravaged. A dozen were utterly and intentionally destroyed. The few buildings that remained intact were disfigured and used as barns for donkeys and horses. The Jordanians were determined to eradicate any vestige of Jewish presence. My immediate

---

camps became a training ground for terrorist youth to be targeted at Israel. The host country, like Syria, would provide training, weapons and explosives, but refused to absorb the Arab refugees as equal citizens. Keeping them in misery made them valuable and irreplaceable as angry front-line terrorists, attacking Israel as proxies for the Arab armies who lost to the Jews on the field of battle in declared wars. Citizenship or legal residency in host countries is denied in Lebanon where the absorption of Palestinians would upset a delicate confessional balance."
From: http://www.science.co.il/Arab-Israeli-conflict/Refugees.asp

area became a slum. The stench from the accumulated mountains of garbage and human waste was intolerable, even for an inert stone such as me. The international community and the United Nations were deaf to the worldwide appeals to stop the destruction and the defilement of Judaism's foremost site, the Western Wall.

We felt sad and dejected. Despite 2,000 years of turmoil, I never felt such a menacing anxiety. It is hard to describe this state of inner turmoil. You humans, at times, suffer from this nervous behavior. I have watched you pacing back and forth. This was more, much more, than a mood-state in which one is ready or prepared to attempt to cope with upcoming negative events. I felt utterly helpless. It was a horrible feeling of dread of imminent death. It was an intimidating fear like I have never felt before. It was a staggering mixture of alarm, worry, and apprehension.

I have never been diagnosed with any kind of anxiety disorder. Stones do not exhibit phobias, obsessive-compulsive behavior, or post-traumatic stress disorders. But for the first time in my long existence, I have felt physical effects. I could feel my heart palpitating, I could feel the fatigue, nausea, chest pain, and tension headache. Were you to check my blood pressure, heart rate and perspiration, you would find all the signs of a panic attack. Yes, what you saw was a stone sweating and trembling. Try as I might, I could not pull myself out from this situation.

The shocking sacrilege and defilement by the Jordanians was appalling. For thousands of years, even under Muslim rule, Jews were permitted (to a limited extent) to pray at the Western Wall. Abruptly, a 2,000-year ritual was banned and the world said nothing! Jews were barred from the Western Wall, the Mount of Olives, and additional places sacred to Jews. One of the most outrageous and offensive stories I heard about was the removal by Jordanian Arabs of 40,000 tombstones from the ancient cemetery on the Mount of Olives.[105] These tombstones were used as paving stones for roads and as construction material in Jordanian Army camps, including use as latrines.[106] Neither the United Nations, nor the

---

105 *City of Stone,* Meron Benvenisti

106 http://www.nytimes.com/2009/05/10/world/middleeast/10jerusalem.html?_r=1&pagewanted=2&em
"Israel 1948-1967: Holy Sites Desecrated". palestinefacts.org. http://www.palestinefacts.org/pf_1948to1967_holysites.php. Retrieved 2007-06-27.
Alon, Amos (1995). *Jerusalem: Battlegrounds of Memory.* New York: Kodansha Int'l. pp. 75.

international community at large, made any effort to stop this ghoulish activity. That such macabre desecration was perpetrated by a civilized country following World War II is unpardonable. That it was condoned by the civilized world is unconscionable. It was not until the Old City was recaptured by Israel in 1967 that the full extent of Arab-Jordanian crimes against humanity was fully revealed. This cemetery, where more than 150,000 Jews have been buried from biblical times until today, had been ravaged. Hundreds of graves were found uncovered with human bones scattered. Portions of the cemetery were converted into parking lots, a gasoline station, and a paved road that cut through the cemetery, destroying hundreds of Jewish graves, some from the First Temple period. Jordan's King Hussein gave permission for the Intercontinental Hotel to be built on top of the mountain.

Sadar Khalil, appointed by the Jordanian government as the official caretaker of the cemetery, built his home on the grounds using the stones robbed from graves. In 1967, the press published extensive photos documenting that Jewish gravestones were found in Jordanian Army camps, such as El Azariya, as well as in Palestinian walkways, steps, bathrooms, and pavements.[107]

The Arab refugees who had migrated to various Arab nations were not similarly well received. They were regarded not as Arab brothers but as unwelcome migrants who were not to be trusted. Squalid refugee camps were set up as showpieces to induce the West's sympathy and kept that way. The UN through UNRWA (UN Relief Agency) provided assistance to the camps when the host country could not or would not.

These camps became a training ground for terrorist youth to be targeted at Israel. The host country, like Syria, would provide training, weapons and explosives, but refused to absorb the Arab refugees as equal citizens. Keeping them in misery made them valuable and irreplaceable as angry front line terrorists attacking Israel as proxies for the Arab armies who lost to the Jews on the field of battle in declared wars. Citizenship or legal residency in host countries is denied in Lebanon where the absorption of Palestinians would upset a delicate confessional balance[108].

"After 1967, it was discovered that tombstones had been removed from the ancient cemetery to pave the latrines of a nearby Jordanian army barrack."

107   From: http://www.science.co.il/Arab-Israeli-conflict/Refugees.asp

108   From: http://www.science.co.il/Arab-Israeli-conflict/Refugees.asp nt

The world was silent to the Jordanian display of blasphemy and disrespect, in total violation of all the norms of civilized behavior. Despite an unambiguous commitment by Jordan under the Israeli-Jordanian Armistice Agreement of 1949,[109] Jordan refused to grant Jews access to the cemetery and to permit continued burial of Jews on the Mount. Now the Palestinians insist that this most important Jewish cemetery in the world be transferred to their control. Based on that horrific experience of 1948–1967, they have the audacity to demand that Israel should accede to this outrageous demand. The Mount of Olives, which over the course of 3,000 years has been the resting place of the legendary dead of the nation, represents a religious and national memorial. It contains the tombs of Zechariah and Avshalom, of Rabbi Chaim ibn Attar, author of *Ohr Hachaim Hakadosh*, of eminent rabbis from the 15th to the 20th centuries, including Rabbi Avraham Yitzchak Kook, the first Ashkenazi Chief Rabbi of Israel, his son Zvi Yehuda Kook, and Israeli Prime Minister Menachem Begin. During the course of many centuries, the Mount of Olives Cemetery served as a site for Jewish assembly and Jewish prayer, even prior to the construction of the Holy Temple.

1956 — Suez Canal Closed to Israeli Shipping

I heard hushed voices. Something was different today as different groups congregated all over Israel. War news came quickly and was amplified many times as worshippers came to petition HaShem for the safety and security of Israel and its inhabitants. It seems that Egypt blockaded the Gulf of Aqaba and closed the Suez Canal to Israeli shipping. Nassar, Egypt's president, called for the destruction of Israel. Israel, England, and France went to war to force Egypt to open the Canal. Israel captured Sinai after a lightning campaign; the US threatened to impose sanctions on Israel if it failed to withdraw from Sinai, which it did.

---

109 Jordan guaranteed Israeli Jews free access to the Western Wall under Article VIII of the armistice agreement. "In fact, during the nineteen years of Jordanian rule in East Jerusalem, no Israelis were allowed to visit this site which was most holy to them." Martin Gilbert, *Jerusalem in the Twentieth Century* New York: John Wiley & Sons, 1996, p. 241.

1957 — HaGomel

Some of the soldiers came to the Kotel to thank HaShem and to *bench HaGomel*.[110] They mentioned that Israel began to withdraw from all of Sinai. The United Nations Emergency Force (UNEF) was stationed there to supervise the peace as the Sinai was demilitarized. We could breathe easier knowing that the US guaranteed Israel's freedom of passage in the Straits of Tiran and thus guaranteed Israel's southern port, Eilat, against future Egyptian blockades.

---

110   Recite the prayer of thanksgiving

CHAPTER XII

THE YEAR OF A MIRACLE

1960–1961 Adolf Eichmann Captured

Hundreds, perhaps thousands, of people milled around Jerusalem on a warm day in May 1960 applauding one another. I myself could not believe the electrifying news: Israeli Security Service agents seized Adolf Eichmann in Argentina and took him to Jerusalem to stand trial in an Israeli court.

(Otto) Adolf Eichmann was the notoriously infamous Nazi *SS-Obersturmbannführer* and one of the major organizers of the Holocaust. After World War II, this evil war criminal fled from Austria and made his way to Argentina where he lived under the name Ricardo Klement. He was now in an Israeli prison!

The Eichmann trial stirred up worldwide attention. Nazi atrocities had long ceased to be front news. Many European countries glossed over the horrifying facts. Some nations dodged the issue of culpability to avoid confronting their role during the Nazi occupation. Survivors, too, buried the gruesome *Shoah* experience, some refusing to tell their shocking tales. Testimonies of Holocaust survivors were crucial. The tribunal gave encouragement to many Holocaust survivors who now felt able to reveal the indescribable suffering that enveloped their lives during that traumatic chapter in history.

Jews throughout the world, and especially in Israel, experienced an emotional release. With this evil oppressor behind bars, I shared with many worshippers who came to the Kotel a feeling of spiritual release and purification. His capture and imprisonment brought about an intense emotional experience.

Israeli Attorney General Gideon Hausner signed a bill of indictment against Eichmann on fifteen counts, including crimes against the Jewish people and crimes against humanity.

For those and other charges, Eichmann was found guilty and sentenced to death. On June 1, 1962, Eichmann was executed by hanging. His body was cremated and the ashes were spread at sea, beyond Israel's territorial waters. The execution of Adolf Eichmann remains the only time that Israel has enacted a death sentence.

All the elements of psychotherapeutic catharsis were at play: the capture, the story of how Eichmann was smuggled out of Argentina, his imprisonment, trial, conviction, sentencing, execution, and the disposition of his ashes in the sea. These elements enabled Jews, especially survivors, to experience the deep emotions associated with those grisly events of the *Shoah* that had been repressed or ignored, and had never been adequately addressed.

1967 — The Six-Day Phenomenon

Excuse me!

I heard Israeli jets overhead. Ever since 1948, I stopped to bless those pilots on their way to a mission or just on training flights.

I cannot begin to tell you how tense the situation was in the early summer of 1967. Since the time of King David, except for the nineteen years between 1948 and 1967, there has always been a Jewish presence in the ancient city of Jerusalem, the capital of Israel.

For those nineteen painful years, Jews were barred from access to the Kotel or its environs. I cannot remember any other time since the Roman occupation where the Western Wall was totally inaccessible to Jews. While the newer, western part of the city was in Israeli hands, the ancient Old City was under Jordanian control. Only a small area of eastern Jerusalem on Mount Scopus was held by Israel from 1948–1967.

That state of affairs ended in June, 1967 with the spectacular and significant liberation of East Jerusalem from the merciless clutches of the Jordanians. Jerusalem was reunited. The city's liberation — a decisive event in the history of Israel — marked a seminal milestone in the 4,000-year history of the Jewish people.

First, let me convey to you how my fellow stones and I felt. Jerusalem, the heart and soul of Israel, whose prophetic history has been betrayed throughout the ages, was being threatened again. For almost 2,000 years, spanning centuries of Jewish exile and dispersion from its Holy Land, I have witnessed countless wars being fought over the stones of Jerusalem. Oh, how much blood has been spilled! How many tears have been shed on our holiest spot on Earth? Even before I was born, Jerusalem, this City of David, has been the scene of countless battles. Historians tell me that Jerusalem has fallen under the control of twenty-six different rulers, during which time it has been reduced to rubble on at least five different occasions. With each destruction, the victor sought to expunge the city's ancient Jewish history. It did not matter whether the conquerors were pagan, Christian, or Muslim. The fact that the Jews were Jews was sufficient reason to desecrate Judaism's holiest places and oppress those faithful to HaShem. I ask you: where else in the whole world have so many battles and brutal atrocities been repeatedly waged as in Jerusalem? But try as they may, its conquerors failed to destroy the Jewish people. The Kotel, the one symbol that has inexplicably remained standing despite the destruction of the Temple, embodies the permanency of the Jewish people.

The period leading up to the Six-Day War was stressful. Nasser, Egypt's president, proclaimed his objective to obliterate Israel and drive the Jews into the Mediterranean Sea. Could the IDF (Israel's army), outnumbered and outgunned on all fronts and in all services, withstand such a genocidal assault? Israel's total strength of 264,000 soldiers (including reserves) had to face 525,000 Arab soldiers. Israel's 800 tanks faced 2,424 Arab tanks. Israel's 350 aircraft had to combat 939 Arab aircraft. Here, in the summer of 1967, Israel faced a seven-nation military alliance fanatically and enthusiastically committed to her annihilation.

The large number of casualties expected prompted the Jerusalem *Chevra Kadisha* (burial society) to prepare 10,000 body bags. Israel braced itself for the worst. Disaster plans included turning Jerusalem's parks into cemeteries. The animals in Jerusalem's zoo were tranquilized to preclude the possibility that they might be let loose, resulting in pandemonium.

Artifacts from the Israel Museum, including the Dead Sea Scrolls, were hurriedly boxed for underground storage. There they would safely rest, along with Knesset archives, in secure facilities.

Euphoria from Heaven

Those six days in June, 1967 felt like an eternity. Would nineteen years of revolting behavior on the part of the Jordanians come to an end? My emotional state, fragile to begin with because of the fall of my city in 1948, remained in a tense state of suspension. Gunfire burst forth all around me. I could feel the reverberations with each volley of gunfire. For the life of me, I could not fathom who was winning. Just then, I saw dozens of well-trained Jordanian legionnaires setting a trap for the Israeli fighters. The sight almost succeeded in crushing my spirits.

If stones could pray, I prayed. If stones could cry, I cried. If stones could bleed, I bled.

I dreaded the possibility that the fledgling Israeli army would be repelled. I felt myself going to pieces. Panic struck. I wanted to run away to avoid witnessing Israel's defeat. But how? I could not escape my surroundings. I have been wedged into this place for 2,000 years. I was sinking deeper and deeper into depression. I had no hands with which to cover my eyes, no possibility of turning my back to the unfolding events. I had not seen a genuine Jew in nineteen years! Suddenly, I saw battle-fatigued Israeli paratroopers led by Motta Gur. They broke through to the Old City through the Lion's Gate. Euphoria from Heaven! The shock waves (good ones, this time) created an electrifying excitement. The Western Wall and Temple Mount were liberated and the Jews would once again be able to come to the Western Wall to pray.

PRAYERS DURING SUCCOT

Throngs gather at the Kotel during Succot (Booths, Tabernacles) following the Days of Awe. The Jew is commanded to dwell in the Succah for seven days. In addition it is a mitzvah for every Jew to take hold of the arbah minim (the Four Species).

The Area in Front of the Kotel

For almost 800 years following the conquest of Jerusalem by Saladin's son, the prayer area in front of the Kotel was a constricted passageway measuring twelve feet wide and extending ninety-two feet in length. Over the centuries, Muslims built their homes close to the Wall, shrinking access to it. On one side of this narrow alleyway was the Kotel and on the other side were Muslim houses. Public access to the Wall was through the Moroccan Quarter, a maze of narrow pathways. In May, 1840, Ibrahim Pasha issued a decree forbidding the Jews from paving the passageway in front of the Kotel. The decree further warned the Jews against "raising their voices and displaying their books there." He did not, however, bar them from visiting the Kotel. It was not until the Six-Day War that the area was cleared out to create a large plaza enabling sizable groups of worshippers to visit and pray there.

Moshe Dayan's Gift to the Arabs — a Staggering Blunder

Our people have experienced enough failures and enough injustices. Repeatedly, we have come away empty-handed. Too often, our aspirations and expectations came to nothing. Finally, after the struggle for independence in 1948 and the miraculous recovery of our ancient and Holy City in 1967, we were entitled to celebrate our victory. We had triumphed. We subdued the Jordanian occupiers of our Holy City and regained the trophy that is the Kotel.

Nevertheless, having vanquished our enemy, we displayed an undeserved sensitivity to their feelings. As a gesture of goodwill, Moshe Dayan, then minister of defense, permitted the Jordanian Wakf to administer their religious sites in the Old City. Instead of appreciating our magnanimity in the face of their ignominious defeat, the Muslims have rewarded us with four decades of hate-filled killings and mutilations.

In retrospect, my fellow stones and I view that gesture as a staggering blunder. Ever sensitive to the feelings of Muslims and Christians, the State of Israel embraced a generous and high-minded approach to newly-liberated Jerusalem. What a contrast to 1948 when the Jordanians barred Jews from the Kotel! Muslims were permitted to retain administrative control over their holy places.

In a puzzling and controversial decision, Israeli authorities forbade Jews from praying on the Temple Mount. Furthermore, non-Muslims are barred from visiting the Temple Mount on Muslim holidays and their visits are severely restricted on other days.[111]

1973 — Yom Kippur War

I scanned the sea of people on this Yom Kippur day. There was a certain stillness and peacefulness on this holiest day of the year. The upper plaza, too, was crowded. Every inch of the Kotel area was crammed full with men and boys, women and girls. For twenty-five hours, from just before sunset on the ninth of Tishrei until after nightfall on the tenth, Jews are commanded to afflict their bodies. They abstain from food and drink, do not wash or anoint their bodies, do not wear leather footwear and abstain from marital relations.

Suddenly, I heard hushed tones of agitation. It seemed that Egyptian and Syrian forces, backed up by forces from other Arab nations, launched a surprise attack against Israel on Yom Kippur. The terrifying news spread like wildfire, but there was no panic. Hundreds of young men jumped up and ran out of the Kotel area carrying their *tallitot*[112] and *machzorim*[113] as they headed towards their IDF units. With the help of HaShem, after initially suffering big losses, Israel recaptured lost ground and then pushed into Egypt and Syria. Israel turned the tide with a US resupply of weaponry but agreed to a cease-fire before reaching either Cairo or Damascus.

After the war, the Muslims conspired to reduce oil production, driving up oil prices and setting off a global economic crisis.

1975 — Jackson-Vanik Amendment

We at the Kotel were delighted to hear some good news for a change. The Jackson-Vanik Amendment enacted by the US Congress tied American trade benefits to the Soviet Union to freedom of emigration for Jews.

---

111 To further placate Muslim feelings since 2006, the State of Israel has looked the other way while Palestinians illegally excavate below the Temple Mount. By law, the Antiquities Authority may stop such excavations but again, appeasement seems to be the order of the day.

112 Plural of *tallit* (prayer shawl)

113 Plural of *machzor* (Holiday prayer book)

This milestone lifted the spirits of millions of Jews, especially those who have been clamoring to emigrate from the Soviet Union. More Jews will be able to visit the Wall!

1979 — Peace Treaty with Egypt

It was with mixed emotions that I heard about the peace treaty signed between Israel and Egypt. Sure, I was happy for peace. I was sad that the treaty called for Israel to return the entire Sinai to Egypt. I was further crestfallen to learn that Israel would have to dismantle its communities there and uproot 5,000 Jews. Israel was victorious; why was it forced by America to hand over its military airbases and Israeli-developed oil fields in return for Egyptian recognition and diplomatic and trade relations? After all, it was Israel who won in self-defense against an unprovoked attack! The treaty ended the war but the Egyptian populace continues to treat the treaty with vocal disgust.

1993 — Israel Resuscitates the PLO

I am not a politician. I am a mere immobile stone witnessing what is happening all around me. But I cannot help a feeling of betrayal. I was shocked to learn that the new peace accords permitted the arch-terrorist Yasser Arafat to return to the West Bank.

How could Israel's leaders resuscitate the PLO, an ailing organization? The Oslo Accords provided for the creation of a Palestinian interim self-government, the Palestinian Authority, which would have responsibility for the administration of the territory under its control. The Accords also called for the withdrawal of the Israel Defense Forces (IDF) from parts of the Gaza Strip and West Bank. It did not promise Palestinian statehood. I am sure that the Accords were a mistake. The Palestinians agreed to recognize Israel, renounce terrorism, outlaw terrorist groups, confiscate illegal weaponry, and end incitement against Israel and Jews. The PA promised to reject violence — a promise violated hundreds and hundreds of times at the expense of thousands of Israelis who were murdered and wounded. What happened to their commitment to acknowledge the State of Israel or stop terrorism? They have reneged on everything.

1994 — Chabad-Lubavitcher Rebbe Dies

It was a sad year for me and for Jews all over the world. Rabbi Menachem Mendel Schneerson died on June 12, 1994. For reasons known only to him, the Rebbe never set foot in our Holy Land. How I longed for him to visit us at the Kotel. Known as the Chabad-Lubavitcher Rebbe, he was instrumental in creating one of the world's largest and best-known Chasidic movements, probably heading the largest Jewish religious organization in the world today. Chabad maintains a network of over 3,600 institutions in over 1,000 cities, spanning 70 countries. Chabad institutions provide outreach to unaffiliated Jews, as well as religious, cultural and educational activities at Chabad-run community centers, synagogues, schools, and camps.

November 4, 1995 — Rabin Assassinated

I was shocked and stunned to learn of the assassination of Prime Minister Yitzchak Rabin. The shooting took place on the 12th of Mar-Cheshvan, 5756 (Hebrew calendar), at the end of a rally in support of the Oslo Accords. The killer was an Israeli Zionist named Yigal Amir, who strenuously opposed Rabin's peace initiative and particularly the signing of the Oslo Accords. For a Jew to kill another Jew is simply unthinkable.

That it occurred in the Hebrew month Cheshvan, (classically referred to as Mar-Cheshvan) started me thinking. The prefix *Mar* means "bitter." Three other depressing events in our history occurred in the "bitter" month of Mar-Cheshvan: (1) The flood in the time of Noah; (2) the death of our matriarch Rachel, Jacob's beloved wife; and (3) Methuselah's death.

1995 — Israel Acquiesces Once Again

How can I, a mere stone, knock some sense into the Israeli political leadership? Israel's acquiescent conduct once again stunned me. In the past two years, the PA had not delivered on any of its promises. Despite this staggering failure, Israel's leadership again signed a follow-up agreement in which the PA undertook, once again, to end incitement and hostile propaganda against Israel and to prepare its public for peace, including to do so through its educational system. In return, Israel undertook to transfer further territories to PA control, including major Palestinian population centers. Unfortunately, it seemed clear to me that once again we would keep our commitments and they wouldn't keep theirs.

1997 — Holy City of Hebron Given to Arabs

Déjà vu. Here we go again. Why another worthless agreement? This time Israel undertook to relinquish control over most of Hebron, and did so. The PA again undertook to arrest terrorists, fight terrorism and educate the Palestinian public for peace, but did not. Yet the world continues to blame Israel and demand further concessions.

1998 — Israel Withdraws From Judea and Samaria

I was shaken and upset. Those coming to the Kotel were expressing their outrage. Hasn't our government humiliated itself in its dealings with the Palestinians? Worshippers were using such words (of course in Hebrew) as disgrace, degradation, and scandalous. The Palestinians refused to carry out any of their commitments. We all know that these paper agreements are meaningless. I must have been missing something. Israel and the PA signed the Wye River Memorandum, under which Israel undertook to withdraw from further territory in two phases; the PA undertook, yet again, to take all necessary measures to fight terrorism, to confiscate illegal weaponry and to end incitement to hatred and murder against Israel. Israel fulfilled its commitment by withdrawing from 13 percent of the West Bank in the first phase but refused to go further when the PA did not carry out its commitments. Where are the teeth to these agreements? So many unnecessary widows and orphans have been coming to shed tears at the Wall...

Since the commencement of the Oslo peace process in 1993, Israel has made extensive, sometimes irreversible compromises. But the PA, quite the opposite, has not only failed to honor any of its commitments but has absolutely refused even to repeal the ten articles of its Constitution that call for Israel's destruction and terrorism against Israel.

I have finally figured out how the blueprint for peace works. Drafted by the US and Western Powers, the pattern is for Israel to withdraw from territory or hand over resources and entitlement. Unpublicized threats hang over Israel's head, forcing it to comply. The PA, on the other hand, undertakes to dismantle terrorist groups and prepare its public for peace — but never does.

2000–2001 Oslo Accords Signed — Disaster Waiting to Happen

HELP! I was beside myself! Everything seemed to be out of control.

The signing of the Oslo Accords in 1993 was the beginning of a hare-brained slippery slope. Israel gave and the Palestinians took. In the Camp David negotiations and subsequent negotiations leading to the Clinton Parameters, Israel agreed to Palestinian statehood in all of Gaza, over 90 percent of the West Bank, the uprooting of many Jewish communities in the West Bank, the ceding of the strategically vital Jordan Valley and the division of Jerusalem. The PA did not agree to this plan, made no counter-proposal and launched a terrorist war against Israel that claimed over 1,000 Israeli lives in the succeeding five years.

2003 — Israel Pressured to Give Up More of its Biblical Homeland

What chutzpah! Have you read the terms of the proposed "Roadmap"? It has been read to me by one of the worshippers after morning prayers. It is replete with one-sided stipulations. The Plan, another in a series of peace plans, was destined to fail. Its disaster-prone terms will not bring peace. It failed to call for new terrorism-free Palestinian leadership but did call for Israeli withdrawals from the areas it had re-entered since October 2000. It demanded Israeli withdrawal ahead of, not in response to, Palestinian action to end terrorism and accept Israel's right to exist. It insisted that Israel freeze Jewish construction in the West Bank — something that had never been a feature of any of the signed Oslo agreements. Perhaps under pressure and/or threats from the US, Israel accepted the plan subject to (soon to be forgotten) fourteen reservations.

2006 — UN Imposes Cease-Fire to Israel's Detriment

I shed many tears in the past 2,000 years, especially after the *Shoah* when six million of our family of Jews were slaughtered by the Nazis. I shed tears again when I heard about the Hamas kidnapping of IDF Corporal Gilad Shalit from his IDF army post. Tears shed are not a sign of weakness. They are a sign of a *lev tahor* (a pure heart).

The violence continued. A suicide bombing near the old Central Bus Station in Tel Aviv killed eleven. Israel responded with military operation. The Second Lebanon War erupted after Hezbollah attacked an Israeli military patrol on Israel's side of the border, killing eight soldiers and kidnapping two others. The UN Security Council unanimously adopted cease-fire Resolution 1701, ending the Lebanon war.

2007 — Terrorist Hamas Gulps Down Gaza

I had a feeling that I should remain asleep and not wake up that morning. I had a premonition that the news would not be good. I didn't want to wake up. I was having a much better time asleep. But it was almost sunrise and the *vatikin* crowd had prepared themselves for the morning prayer services. I woke up into a nightmare. It seemed, as I later learned, that after heavy infighting in Gaza City, Hamas fighters completely took control in Gaza as the West scrambled for a response to the arrival of Islamist power on Israel's doorstep. The US hosted the Annapolis (Maryland) Peace Conference, hoping to revive Israeli-Palestinian peace talks.

2008 — Yeshiva Students Massacred

I was overcome by the feeling that something terribly wrong was happening. The dreadful news came almost immediately. A Palestinian gunman attacked a Jerusalem *yeshiva*, killing eight young students. We were not ashamed to weep. It is our right to grieve. It had been said that "tears are only water, and flowers, trees, and fruit cannot grow without water. But there must be sunlight also. A wounded heart will heal in time, and when it does, the memory and love of our lost ones is sealed inside to comfort us."[114] May the memory of those eight *kedoshim* be for a blessing.

---

114 Brian Jacques, *Taggerung*

2010 — 1,027 Murderous Arab Terrorists Exchanged for One Kidnapped Israeli Soldier

You ask, "What happened in the year 2010 and later?" In a word, more of the same. If I thought it would help, I would throw myself down and gnash my teeth and curse those who have terrorized us. But that is not our way. We do what we need to do and pray to HaShem for salvation.

As we immerse ourselves in some of the sad happenings of 2010, we try to separate its numerous elements, understanding its delicate gradations. In our *Shemoneh Esrei*, we ask HaShem to grant us "perception, understanding, and intellect" through which sadness could be divided into its infinite spectrum. Although I did not have a radio, the news somehow reached me. Israel exchanged 1,027 Palestinian and Israeli-Arab prisoners for Israeli Army soldier Gilad Shalit, who had been held in captivity for five years. Shalit came here, to the Wall. Everyone, myself included, cried.

CHAPTER XIII

Search for History and Heritage

I encourage you to visit Jerusalem. Let me personally welcome you to the Kotel, the holiest of Jewish sites. No, I am not paid to promote tourism to Israel. I honestly feel that a visit to the Western Wall is an "absolute must," regardless of your religion. The sight of so many people praying at this mystical Wall will have a lasting effect on you. Over the many centuries, millions of Jews have come to the Western Wall. For many, it was a search for their history and heritage. Especially moving to me is to see the young ones who come with open, questioning hearts. Since 1967, many come from assimilated backgrounds. They come from the four corners of the world. Some approach hesitatingly, picking up a free *kippah,* looking left and right to see what others are doing. In due course, they make their way toward me and my fellow stones. Bit by bit, they become conscious of the holiness of this spot. Undoubtedly, for many it has been one of the most inspiring experiences in their lives. Think of my fellow stones and me as a link between the Jewish future and the holy treasures of the past. I feel fortunate to be here to help instill Jewish pride and, hopefully, to kindle the flame of knowledge for returnees to Jewish tradition. That very first visit to the Kotel can do more to guarantee Jewish survival then all the conferences and discussions can ever succeed in doing. The very first visit to the Kotel is the best first step to a worldwide Jewish renaissance.

I Envy You

In some ways I envy you. Not that I am complaining. I would not want to be anywhere else in the world but where I am now. Still, hearing the sounds of guitars and singing filling the air during evening hours is tempting. After more than 2,000 years marked by sadness and dreariness, it is heartening to experience a festive atmosphere in the Old City. Increasingly since 1967, its mood, tone, and character has been shaped by students from all over the world learning in various *yeshivot* (academies of Torah learning) in and around the Old City. What a pleasure it is to see the happy faces of these students and of the many tourists who come to the Kotel. The ambience is in such stark contrast to the pre-1948 days, and especially to the centuries of repression as wave after wave of foreign powers captured Jerusalem and subjugated its people.

The Guy with the Camera

See that fellow over there? Not that one. Look to his right. See the person with the expensive camera? You can just feel his excitement as he painstakingly photographs men and boys praying at the Kotel. He has remained at that spot for quite a while now, unhurriedly turning and snapping photo after photo with sheer delight. I have watched him for almost an hour. The expression on his face is electrifying. He may be a professional photographer or an amateur. I have seen many photographers coming to the Kotel with cameras, both simple and sophisticated, who click away, focusing on a variety of targets. It appears that he is trying to convey a vision and an emotion. Perhaps he is an artist trying to express what he sees and feels as he captures others communing with G-d. Now don't get me wrong. I recall some 150 years ago when a European photographer set up a wooden sliding-box camera in the alleyway in front of the Kotel. He came with an assistant and what appeared to be a portable chemical laboratory.

Much has happened since then, from the Kodak Brownie box roll-film cameras in the early 1900's, to the 35-mm cameras, to the automatic diaphragm and instant black-and-white film Polaroid cameras, until most recently, the digital still cameras. Right after the Second World War, 8MM home-movie cameras made their appearance, to be followed by camcorders and the like. You are fortunate that photography has captured for future generations memorable scenes of the Kotel from the late 1800's until the present.

CHAPTER XIV

Customs, Segulot[115] and Sanctity of the Wall

Over the years, I have witnessed many different customs and practices, some of which have persisted, while others have faded away or have been discouraged by rabbinic authorities.

One of the most interesting is called *kriyah*.

Kriyah

For many centuries, Jews who came to the Kotel tore their garments (known as tearing *kriyah*) upon seeing the Kotel (the site of the destroyed Temple) for the first time, or if one had not seen it for more than thirty days. This is an ancient ritual of mourning over the destruction of the *Beit haMikdash*. Ashkenazi practice was to tear the garments (generally a shirt) from the collar down towards the heart. The tear should be approximately three inches, done while standing and, if possible, with one's hands (though sometimes a knife or scissors are used to start the tearing). Weeping bitterly, they would recite the associated prayer: "Our Holy Temple, which was our glory, in which our forefathers praised You, was burned and all of our delights were destroyed."[116] I have heard the different prayers recited after the *kriyah*. Some follow the *Mishnah Brurah* and recite Psalm 50 (*Mizmor l'Asaf*). Others say *Baruch Dayan ha'Emet*, which

---

115 Plural of *segulah*, something that has an intrinsic value but no logical, rational reason for it. See also Exodus 18:1, 20:23

116 *"Beit Kodsheinu v'Tifarteinu asher hillelucha bo avoteinu haya l'sreiphat eish, v'chol machmadeinu haya l'chorva."* Translation of the Hebrew from Epstein, Donneal. *Halachos for the Traveler*, Feldheim 2000, Pg. 70.

is customarily said at the funeral service or in the shivah house of a mourner. Others continue with a passage from Nehemiah (9:33). In those days, visitors really felt the pain of loss when they tore *kriyah*.

Their tears were shed over the destruction and over the wretched plight of their fellow Jews. They were tears of sorrow and grief which were destined to be tears of courage and hope. The initial flow of tears began 2,000 years ago and has sadly swelled to an intense flood, gushing and surging with every additional tragedy. I have witnessed its course with its cyclical rise and fall that mirror the pulse of our people. For those who came to the Kotel in years gone by, *kriyah* was a sad, mournful encounter with the Jewish nation's tragic past.

HAND WASHING
Hands should have been washed prior to beginning of any prayers. However, (1) wash your hands again with water direct from faucet (i.e., netilat yadayim cup not required) if you urinated, scratched your head, touched your shoes, combed your hair, touched soil, or inserted your bare finger into your nose or ear or (2) wash with a single pour on each hand from a netilat yadayim cup if you touched a part of your body that is normally covered or handled any insect (dead or alive) with your bare hands.

How times have changed! Some still observe this halachah,[117] although for many it is a perfunctory rite. According to a number of *poskim* there is no longer an obligation to tear *kriyah* since the Jewish People are now in control of the Temple Mount.

Yet, even for those who accept the obligation to do *kriyah*, some have found loopholes to avoid doing it. Here comes Mr. Goldberg. He visits Israel once or twice a year. I overheard him explaining to a friend that he escapes this obligation by arriving on a Friday afternoon before sunset when *kriyah* doesn't apply. The friend responded that he skirts the issue by wearing clothes borrowed from someone else (which may not be torn, since they do not belong to the wearer). I'm not sure how I feel about all this.

Other Customs Include:

1. **Walking backwards:** When leaving the Kotel, the custom is to walk backward away from the Wall for part of the time. It is considered a sign of disrespect to turn your back on the Wall. When backing away from the Wall, look over your shoulder to avoid bumping into others!

2. **Ablution:** Ritual hand washing is to be commended. You'll find several "washing stations" around the plaza. At each station there are two-handled washing cups called "*Netilat Yadayim*" cups, which people use to ritually wash their hands before praying at the Wall.

3. **Tzedakah:** Charity collectors at the Kotel have posed a serious problem. On the one hand, it is a Jew's obligation to give *tzedakah* before praying. Professional beggars are aware of this and flock to the Kotel. Some sit quietly and hope you won't pass them by; others disrupt worshippers as they empty their hearts. I am embarrassed by the behavior of those who shatter the worshipper's *kavanah* (concentration). In the words of one visitor: "It is often very difficult to concentrate on the whole *Tefillah* at the best of times, and for me at least, it can ruin all chances when a hand shaking a few

---

117 *Shulchan Aruch, Orach Chaim* 561

coins is pushed in front of my face with the sole intention (usually successfully) of capturing my attention and thereby interrupting my *davening*."

True, G-d may be more likely to heed our prayers if we, too, listen to the pleas of others. Indeed some charity collectors are begging for poor brides and destitute families. The Rabbi of the Kotel has the responsibility of striking the right balance or risk continued frustration of those who want to pray with *kavanah*.

4. **Cleaning of the Stones:** The officiating Rabbi of the Kotel prohibits any cleaning of the stones. This issue arose after a troubled tourist spray-painted the stones. It took a number of months for the offensive graffiti to fade away.[118]

5. **Respect:** Rabbinic authorities have declared that the area immediately in front of the Kotel is to be treated with the same respect accorded to a synagogue.

6. **Segulot:** A well-known Kabbalistic tradition among Jews is to pray for forty consecutive days at the Kotel for any one petition. Formulated by Rabbi Yisroel Yaakov Fisher, it is based on Moses' repent before G-d on behalf of the Jews who committed the sin of the Golden Calf. G-d accepted Moses' apology and acquiesced to his prayer following the forty days that Moses remained in Heaven praying for forgiveness. Jewish tradition presumes that prayers recited for forty consecutive days have great power, especially if recited at the Kotel, the closest site to the Holy of Holies, from where prayers from all over the world ascend to Heaven.

I have heard many extraordinary stories, well-authenticated, of people whose prayers were miraculously answered and whose lives spectacularly transformed after finishing forty days of prayer at the Western Wall. I can also attest to the fact that the task of coming to the Wall, day-in and day-out, for forty consecutive days is quite a demanding one. Absolute commitment is required, regardless of the weather. Weekday and Shabbat,

---

118 Shragai, Nadav (October 5, 2006). "Western Wall rabbi forbids proposed burning of prayer notes." *Haaretz*. http://www.haaretz.com/hasen/spages/770030.html. Retrieved 12-16-2007.

holiday or fast day, blistering heat, rain, cold, wind, or storm — you may not skip a day!

Nor is it sufficient just to show up at the Kotel and perfunctorily recite some prayer. You have to pray with *kavanah* — total concentration on communing with HaShem. I have observed Jews standing at the Kotel with such a strong focus on prayers and on their relationship with G-d that the gates of heaven literally opened to receive their petitions. With each passing day, these committed Jews experience the amplified power of prayer in this holy place.

There are many mystical reasons why praying for forty consecutive days evokes a favorable response from HaShem. The symbolism in the number forty is evident from the many references in *Tanach*.[119]

---

119 The rain that brought about the Flood in the times of Noah lasted forty days (Gen. 7:4, 12, 17) "Forty days passed between the emergence of the mountain-tops and the opening of the Ark's windows"
(Gen. 8:6).

- Spies explored Canaan for forty days. (Num. 13:25);
- Israel wandered in the wilderness for forty years. This period of years represents the time it takes for a new generation to arise.
- Jews (and the Greeks) maintained that the fortieth year was the height or pinnacle of man's life; and from this fact forty years came to represent a generation.
- Moses' life can be divided into three forty-year increments. The first forty years he lived in the courts of Pharaoh. The second forty-year period of Moses' life was spent in Midian as a shepherd. The third forty-year period Moses returned to Egypt to pressure Pharaoh to let his people go and led them through the wilderness on their way to the Promised Land.
- Jacob's embalming took forty days (Gen. 49:3).
- Moses fasted forty days and forty nights before receiving the Torah. (Ex. 24:18).
- Elijah wandered without food for the same period (I Kings 19:8);
- Ezekiel lay on his side for forty days because the Kingdom of Judah had continued to sin for forty years after the Ten Tribes were exiled.
- Goliath confronted the army of Israel for forty days (I Sam. 17:16).
- Nineveh was granted forty days for repentance (Jonah 3:4).
- A mother's purification following the birth of a boy is forty days (Lev. 12:2, 4); following the birth of a girl is twice that number of days (Ibid. v.5).
- Several Israelite leaders and kings are said to have ruled for forty years, that is, a generation. (Examples: Eli, Saul, David, Solomon.)
- A *mikvah* consists of forty *se'ah* (approximately 200 gallons) of water;
- Forty lashes is one of the punishments meted out by the Sanhedrin, though in actual practice only thirty-nine lashes were administered.
- Isaac and Esau both married when forty years old (Gen. 25:20; 26:34).
- Caleb was forty years old when sent as a spy (Josh. 14:7)
- Several of the judges ruled for forty years (Judges 3:11, 5:31, 8:28; I Sam. 4:18)
- Several kings reigned for forty years: David, Solomon, and Joash (II Sam. 5:4; I

Past Customs, no longer practiced are:

1. Removing one's shoes: The 17th century custom[120] of removing one's shoes when visiting the Kotel has been judged unnecessary, unlike the sanctified zone of the Temple Mount.

2. Kneel and prostrate: Prior to the Middle Ages, some rabbis urged the pious to approach the Kotel garbed in white garments, kneel and prostrate reverentially and recite, "This is nothing other than the House of G-d and here is the gate of heaven." Prostrating, that is, putting the body in a prone position, is no longer normative Jewish practice except during the Days of Awe.

3. Cool water for the worshippers: In years gone by, before the advent of water fountains, some women would offer cool water for the worshippers.

4. Fragrant herbs: Another quaint and somewhat ancient custom was for some women to sit at the entrance to the Kotel every

---

Kings 2:11, 11:42; I Chron. 26:31, 29:27; II Chron. 9:30, 24:1)

- Israel was oppressed by the Philistines for forty years (Judges 13:1).
- Jacob sent Esau forty cows (Gen. 32:16). Benhadad sent "forty camels' burden" as a gift for Elisha (II Kings 8:9).
- The governors before Nehemiah obtained forty shekels of silver under duress from the people (Neh. 5:15).
- Abdon had forty sons (Judges 12:14); Solomon, forty stalls of horses (I Kings 5:6).
- Barak's army consisted of forty thousand men (Judges 5:8);
- In the Tabernacle, forty sockets of silver supported the twenty boards (Ex. 26:19 et seq.; 36:24, 26).
- In Solomon's Temple, each of the ten lavers of brass contained forty baths; and in the Temple described by Ezekiel the "hekhal" and the sidecourts measured forty cubits in length (Ezek. 41:2, 46:22).
- The *Mishna* states that the fortieth year is the age of reason ("*ben arba'im labinah*," Avot 5:26).
- Rabbi Yochanan ben Zakkai (*Rosh Hashanah* 31b), and Rabbi Akiva (Avot D'Rebbe Natan 4) set out upon their rabbinical careers when they were forty years old.
- Forty days without rain is the condition for ordering a public fast (*Ta'anit* 19a).
- Forty less one is also given as the number is of the "principal labors" that are forbidden on the Sabbath (*Shab.* 69a, 73a).
- The planet Venus forms a pentagram in the night sky every eight years, returning to its original point every forty years with a fortyday regression (some scholars believe that this ancient information was the basis for forty becoming sacred).

120 Aner, Ze'ev; Ben Dov, Meir; Naor, Mordechai (1983). "IV: Sanctity, Law and Customs". *The Western Wall*. Israel: Ministry of Defense Publishing House. pp. 83–97.

Shabbat, offering fragrant herbs and spices to enable worshippers to complete the requisite 100 blessings.

5. Washing down the cobblestone: Prior to 1948, when the alleyway in front of the Kotel was quite narrow, pious women would cast lots for the honor of brushing away any debris in front of the Kotel and then washing down the cobblestone of the alleyway.

   I am amazed at how much ink has been spilled and words exchanged about seemingly trivial matters pertaining to me and my fellow stones. However, our history and tradition is replete with debates, l'Shem Shamayim (for the sake of Heaven). Therefore, I will just touch on a few such issues that have been deliberated by rabbinic authorities:

6. In years gone by, Jewish codifiers argued that it was not permitted to place one's fingers inside the cracks of the Wall because the crevice itself constitutes part of the Temple Mount itself and therefore retains its holiness.

7. Some cautioned against having any benefit from the Wall. Thus, they assert that leaning against it or using it for shade debases its holiness. Included in this admonition was the placing of prayer books or candles in the larger crevices.

8. There was a time centuries ago when pilgrims "would place nails in the cracks and paint their Hebrew names on the Wall. These practices stopped after rabbinic consensus determined that they were a desecration of holiness."[121]

9. Another objectionable practice in the past was for tourists (and even those planning to travel abroad) to remove a chip from the Kotel or some of the sand from between its cracks as a segulah. In 1898, this was deemed a desecration.

10. Rabbi Ovadia Yosef, of blessed memory, in Yalkut Yosef, prohibits the removal of even small chips of stone or dust from the Wall. He does, however, permit removal of vegetation that grows in the Wall for use in an amulet, since these are devoid of any sanctity.

---

121 Ben Dov, Meir; Naor, Mordechai; Aner, Ze'ev (1983). "Sanctity, Law and Customs". The Western Wall. Israel: Ministry of Defense Publishing House. pp..83–97.

CHAPTER XV

SITES CLOSE TO THE WALL

Aish HaTorah Institutions

Look at that building across the plaza overlooking the Kotel. That's the Aish HaTorah institution, which recently dedicated their new building. Aish HaTorah is known for its programs that bring unaffiliated Jews closer to traditional Judaism.

Jewish Quarter

I can see the edge of the Jewish Quarter from where I sit. To get to the Jewish Quarter from the Kotel, you will have to climb about 120 stairs. I would love to visit the Jewish Quarter, but there is a small matter of logistics. Obviously, my girth and weight are part of the problem! Yet, I will bet that if you bring over a bunch of Technion engineers, they will be able to plan and implement what is sure to be a complex task. Meanwhile, you will have to settle for a description of the Old City based on what I have heard from others.

The Old City consists of four quarters. The Jewish Quarter is the smallest. The Muslim Quarter is the largest. Prior to the Arab riots of 1920–1936, Jews owned or rented at least 30% of what is now the Muslim Quarter. Jews lived there for generations. How well I remember the Arab rioters, incited by the Mufti of Jerusalem. They fanatically assaulted and slaughtered Jews, causing most to flee from the Old City. By the year 1939, any trace of Jewish blood had been removed as an impurity. The cleansing of the Jews from the Muslim Quarter foreshadowed the Nazi concept of *Judenrein* (literally "free of Jews").

In 1948, the embryonic State of Israel suffered the loss of Jerusalem's Jewish Quarter to the Jordanians. Incidentally, the other two quarters are the Christian Quarter and the Armenian Quarter.

Chabad Synagogue

As I write these words, I recall how painstakingly the Jewish Quarter was renovated and rebuilt as families and institutions began to reestablish themselves there. Climb those 120 steps and see the rebuilt Jewish Quarter for yourselves. More than 400 families now live there. Visit the Chabad Shul, the only synagogue not destroyed by the Jordanians, who converted it to a textile factory. The synagogue, built in the 1860s, is designated as the Tzemach Tzedek Synagogue, named in memory of the third Lubavitcher Rebbe. In the early 1900s, the building was expanded and today is a flourishing focal point for Torah learning, especially the teachings of *Chassidut*.

The Churva Shul

Walk around the corner from the *Tzemach Tzedek* to visit two celebrated synagogues, the Churva and the Ramban. The Churva was renowned as the biggest and most striking synagogue of the Old City's Ashkenazi Jewish community. Like every other site in the Jewish Quarter, it was blown up by the Jordanians. It was partly rebuilt after the Six-Day War, resulting in the lone arch that became one of the symbols of the Old City. The arch, as high as it is, is only two-thirds of the height of the original structure. It was not until the year 2000 that the Israeli government approved plans to rebuild the synagogue in its previous design.

Now, the Churva Shul has been entirely rebuilt and is open to public prayers. (Muslims built the lone mosque of the Jewish Quarter, located next to the Churva and Ramban, for the sole purpose of establishing a place of worship that would be higher than the Churva. The mosque is unused today.)

The Ramban Synagogue

Just beside the rebuilt Churva lies the Ramban synagogue, which is the long, dark synagogue described in the writings of the Ramban when he journeyed to Jerusalem in 1267 and successfully revitalized the Jewish community. Nachmanides (Rabbi Moshe ben Nachman), also known as the Ramban, was a frequent worshipper at the Kotel. His *shul* is the oldest functioning synagogue in the Old City of Jerusalem. Unlike some other synagogues built more than a half-millennium ago, the Ramban Shul does not have any Gothic or Islamic structural elements.

Many have asked me why the synagogue is located ten feet below street level. That was done to comply with Muslim laws. Non-Muslim houses of prayer could not be taller than mosques. Jews living in Muslim lands were treated as second-class inhabitants (*dhimmi*), deprived of most legal rights. It was a humiliating and degrading category but Jews bore the yoke of servility with patience and endurance. Throughout the centuries, Jews living in Muslim lands realized that it was G-d's will. So long as they were free to follow the Torah way of life, they were prepared to accept life's difficulties.

Four Sephardic Synagogues

As you proceed south to the Jewish Quarter parking lot, you will discover the four Sephardic synagogues. These interesting and exquisite buildings were also desecrated and partially destroyed by the Jordanians. After 1967, the synagogues were restored and are in constant use. The four are: (1) Yochanan ben Zakkai Synagogue; (2) Istanbuli Synagogue; (3) Eliahu Ha'Navi Synagogue; and (4) Emtsai Synagogue. For many years, and certainly prior to 1939, the Jewish population of the Old City was predominantly Sephardi. Each of these four synagogues followed its own customs, thus enabling each of the main streams of Sephardi Jews to follow its traditional prayer rites.

Other Sites in the Jewish Quarter

On one of the east-west pathways of the Jewish Quarter, you will find the Old Yishuv Court Museum, where you can see more of the history and way of life in the Jewish Quarter before 1948. I have been told that there is a fascinating historical site in the lower floor of this museum. There you will find the little "Ari" Shul, where the illustrious Kabbalist, Reb Yitzhak Luria, *ztz"l* was born. Variously called the Ari, Ari-Hakadosh, or Arizal, he is considered the father of contemporary Kabbalah. Although born in Jerusalem in 1534, he received his Jewish education in Egypt, and finally settled in Safed in 1569.

These are some of our neighbors. Of course, there are others, including the Wohl Museum, and the *Tiferet Yisrael* (or "Nissan Bek") synagogue, with its domed roof, also destroyed by the Jordanians in the 1948 Arab-Israeli War.

Take note, as you come down the stairs, of the "Burnt House" ruins that housed the *Kohanim* in the time of the *Beit haMikdash*. There are many more archaeological attractions and sights in and around the Old City. Remember that prior to 1900, Jerusalem was only the Old City. It was not until 1860 that the Jews, who constituted the largest community in the Old City, expanded their settlement to outside the Old City walls.

Ever since 1967, archaeologists have uncovered layer upon layer of history in the Old City. Come back sometime in the future and I will tell you more about its history, much of which still lies undiscovered. Of course, you can wait until archaeologists continue their dedicated probes beneath the surface or rely on my infallible memory to round out your knowledge about our history.

Wilson's Arch — Men's Prayer Area

As you stand facing the Wall, look to the left. That covered underground prayer area just north of the outdoor plaza dates back to the Herodian period (70 BCE).[122] As you look inside you will see Wilson's Arch, named after a 19th century explorer of Jerusalem. This arch is one of a succession of arches that continued westward, from the Temple Mount, across the Central Valley, to the western hill of Jerusalem. Archaeologists have discovered additional arches in recent times. Enter and you will find bookcases with prayer books and songs. Worshippers come to this covered part of the Wall to seek shelter from rain or sun. During the course of the day, services are continuous.

---

122 Some archaeologists dispute the date of the arch. Some maintain that it dates back to the Umayyad Period (651–750 CE).

The Old City Walls and its Entrance Gates

The Old City of Jerusalem is completely enclosed by an immense wall built by Sultan Suleiman in 1541 CE. The Old City walls, which average forty feet in height and more than seven feet in width, contain along its two-and-a-half mile perimeter forty-three observation towers and eleven gates, seven of which are currently open.[123] I cannot see the walls from where I was placed, but you surely saw it as you entered through one of its many gates. Many times during the past 450 years, I have overheard many visitors describe this commanding structure. Tourists and visitors have spoken and photographed this matchless architectural treasure. Undoubtedly, you have toured Jerusalem and visited its many archaeological and historical sites. Truthfully, have you encountered anything that could rival the walls surrounding the Old City? I have been told that the Old City has been walled since it was first established 5,000 years ago. The first city wall to surround Jerusalem was built in the year 1800 BCE, a full 800 years before King David conquered Jerusalem. From that time, more than 3,300 years ago, the Old City walls and its gates were knocked down and rebuilt as successive foreign armies battled for control of Jerusalem. In 1535, the Turkish Sultan Suleiman the Magnificent restored damaged sections of the wall by building on top of remains from prior periods.

Did you know that there is a path on top of the wall? After the Six-Day War, the Israeli government began restoring damaged sections of the city's wall. In addition to the removal of fortifications installed by the Jordanians, landscape gardens were planted and paths were paved along the ruins uncovered at the foot of the wall. But perhaps most interesting is the walkway that Israeli authorities built on top of the walls surrounding the Old City. The promenade, with its protective railings, is quite safe and has become very popular for visiting tourists and Israelis alike. Oh, how I wish I could climb on top of the ramparts and walk along that path! Visitors to

---

123 The seven open gates are: Jaffa Gate, Lions Gate, Herod's Gate, Damascus Gate, New Gate, Zion Gate, and Dung Gate. The closed gates are: Triple-Arched Gate, Double-Arched Gate, Single Gate, and Golden Gate. The Triple-Arched Gate and the Double-Arched Gate are also known as the Hulda Gates, and are the pair of now-sealed entrance-gates in the Southern Wall at the eastern and western corners, respectively. The Single Gate, which led to the underground area of the Temple Mount known as Solomon's Stables, can also be found on the Southern wall. These three now-sealed gates were constructed prior to the Ottoman period.

the Kotel have told me about the stunning panorama of the city beyond the walls. I am more interested in seeing how people live inside the Old City.

Those who have sauntered along the pathway describe their feelings as they looked down at the inner pulse of the Old City. Some say that you can very nearly put forth your hand and pat the minarets and church belfries (not that you would want to!). Although the path along the walls may be accessed from the Jaffa, Damascus, Lion's and Zion Gates, experienced visitors suggest that you locate the access staircase for the Ramparts Walk at the Jaffa Gate. Inside and to the north of the Jaffa Gate, you'll find steps leading to the walkway along the ramparts.

At one time, there were a total of eleven entrance gateways in Jerusalem's Old City walls. The oldest of the gates is the Golden Gate (now sealed). Tradition has it that the *Shechinah* (Divine Presence) used to enter through the Golden Gate and will do so in the future when the *Mashiach* will come.[124] Tradition also has it that a new gate will replace the present one, which has been sealed by the Muslims. There was a time many years ago when Jews used to pray at this gate for mercy. That is where it got the Hebrew name, *Sha'ar ha'Rachamim*, the Gate of Mercy. Today there are only six entrance gates leading to the Temple Mount. Until 1887, each gate was closed before sunset and opened at sunrise.

Some archaeologists claim that the Golden Gate was built 1,250 years ago by Byzantine artisans hired by the Umayyad Caliphate. Located in the middle of the eastern side of the Temple Mount, the gate was used for ritual purposes in biblical times. In order to thwart the entrance of the *Mashiach* to Jerusalem, the Ottoman Sultan Suleiman I sealed off the Golden Gate in 1541. In a further (and surely futile) attempt to prevent the *Mashiach's* entrance to the Old City of Jerusalem, the Muslims built a cemetery in front of the gate in the mistaken belief that Elijah, the forerunner to the *Mashiach*, being a *Kohen*, would never step on the cemetery grounds and hence would not be able to enter through the gate. They were ignorant of Jewish law, though; I am told that a *Kohen* is permitted to enter a non-Jewish cemetery. To this day, the Golden Gate remains sealed, along with the Hulda Gates.

---

124   Ezekiel 44:1–3

SWEARING IN CEREMONY

An IDF Swearing-In Ceremony (Tekes Hashba'ah) for recruits takes place regularly at the Western Wall Plaza. Soldiers are given a gun and a Tanach — a sophisticated weapon and a distinctively Jewish "weapon." Soldiers in the religious Nachal Chareidi unit do not swear. Instead they declare, "Ani Matzhir." Soldiers salute next to guns and Tanachs.

CHAPTER XVI

SPECIAL EVENTS

My fellow stones and I are here all year round, 24 hours a day, 7 days a week. We host many national and private ceremonies, including Memorial Day ceremonies, military ceremonies, national prayer gatherings and private Bar Mitzvah celebrations.

You are very important to us and we welcome the opportunity of welcoming you! You are in for a double treat if you come on one of the joyous holidays. The Days of Awe — Rosh Hashanah and Yom Kippur — are exceptionally inspiring. You are in for an experience of your life if you come as thousands fast and mourn on the 17th of Tammuz, on Tisha b'Av or one of the other public fast days. There are other events that I find stirring and stimulating as well and I will share them with you.

Before we proceed, please mark your calendar to come on April 8, 2037, for the *Birkat haChama*, ("Blessing of the Sun").[125] Sorry you just missed the last one on April 8, 2009. This event occurs only once every twenty-eight years.

Let me tell you something. I assure you that any prayers you say from the heart at the Kotel will be heard by G-d. Know that you are now closer to the Source of all blessings than anywhere else is in the world. If your prayers are from the heart and sincere, no matter what language they are

---

125 *Birkat haChama* will occur next on April 8, 2037 (23rd of Nissan, 5797); April 8, 2065 (2nd of Nissan, 5825); April 8, 2093 (12th of Nissan, 5853)...

in, they will surely be heard and answered. Take it from me. I have been around for more than 2,000 years. When you stand in front of me or any of my fellow stones, take the opportunity to speak to G-d directly. Open your heart and communicate your innermost thoughts to Him. Leave the rest to Him. Have faith that the Temple will be rebuilt, that the *Mashiach* will come soon and all the sadness will be replaced with gladness and joy.

HAGBAH — ASHKENAZI RITE
In the Ashkenazi tradition, after the Torah reading is finished, two men are called for Hagbah, the lifting of the Torah, and Gelilah, the rolling and wrapping of the Torah. The Hagbah raises the Torah off the Shulchan (reading table), and turns right and left so everyone can see the open Sefer Torah. He then sits down and the one called for Gelilah winds the Torah closed, ties or closes the gartel (sash) to hold the Torah shut, and then places the cloth mantel (covering) on the Sefer Torah.

Kabbalat Shabbat

I particularly like Friday evenings. I can hear voices singing, as one group after another descends from the Jewish Quarter in the Old City.

Presently other voices join in as Jews of all stripes welcome the Sabbath Queen. Called *"Kabbalat Shabbat,"* this mystical ritual is sung before *Ma'ariv* on Friday nights. Promoted by Kabbalists in the 16th century, its theme is that Shabbat is the "Bride of Israel" who descends upon the Jewish people as the *Shechinah* (Divine Presence). The tradition of the *Shechinah* as Queen and Bride continues to this day as Jews worldwide usher in the Shabbat. *Kabbalat Shabbat* has two meanings: "welcoming" the Shabbat and "accepting" the Shabbat.

Of course, I remember Friday evening prayer services prior to the 16th century. Somehow, they lacked the more relaxed pace and richer musical style that was introduced by the Kabbalists. Especially after 1967, with the exponential increase in Jerusalem's *yeshiva* populations, one is bathed in the grandeur and elegance of these ceremonies that bring so much majesty into our midst.

Bar Mitzvah at the Kotel

I am amazed at how popular the ritual of celebrating a boy's Bar Mitzvah at the Kotel has become. I'm not against things modern. This ritual of celebrating a boy's thirteenth birthday (according to the Hebrew date) and his entry into the community of Judaism has taken place for centuries in synagogues throughout the world. In years past, and even today, especially in the Diaspora, the boy reads from the Torah in his local synagogue. The preferred day is usually Shabbat morning, but at times, it takes place on Monday or Thursday mornings or on Rosh Chodesh — which avoids having non-observant family members or relatives violate Shabbat by driving to the Kotel.

I have had the singular pleasure of watching as thirteen-year-old boys attained their religious adulthood. There is something wholesome about them. Some are tall, some are short. Some are Ashkenazim, others Sephardi, Yemenites or Ethiopian Jews. Some come from religiously observant families, but most come from traditional or secular backgrounds. While in some parts of the world the Bar Mitzvah is associated with gala parties totally devoid of any religious component, here in Israel the male adolescence ceremony is bound by religious ritual. The young man can now be counted in a minyan (prayer quorum) and is now obligated to observe the *mitzvot* (commandments). According to Jewish law, he is now fully responsible for his actions. The newly

BAR MITZVAH BOY PRAYING AT THE KOTEL

A Jewish boy who reaches the age of thirteen celebrates the milestone of "becoming a man" by being called to the Torah for an aliyah. In many Orthodox synagogues, the young man himself will read directly from the Torah with the proper cantillations (musical notes), having been tutored to do so. There is no obligation for him to read from the Torah, but it is a sign of accomplishment if he does so.

"minted" Bar Mitzvah boy will be praying with *tefillin* (probably) for the first time and will be called to the Torah for his *aliyah*.[126]

Spiritual Elevation

There is something so refreshing about a thirteen-year-old putting on *tefillin* for the first time.

When we do *mitzvot* for the first time, we get a spiritual elevation — a "high" of sorts.

With this newness comes an excitement, an enthusiasm, an awakening to the glory of the experience. Do you recall when you first put on *tefillin* or when you visited the Kotel for the first time? There was a special feeling of love and warmth that radiated from those experiences.

---

126 Interestingly, prior to 1400 CE, there were no formal Bar Mitzvah ceremonies. Indeed, the major codifiers of the Oral Law, such as Isaac Alfasi (11th cent.) and Maimonides (12th cent.) do not mention it.

However, after a while, the newness and excitement unfortunately fades and the *mitzvot* become routine. They are performed by rote with no enthusiasm, with no excitement, with no life — like a body without a soul.

King David understood human psychology. In the 27th psalm, he says, "One thing I ask from HaShem, this is my only request: To dwell in the House of HaShem all the days of my life; to behold the sweetness of HaShem and to be like a visitor in His sanctuary."

Rabbi Dov Ber Weisman comments on this seeming contradiction:[127]

> If David wanted to live in HaShem's house all the time, that is permanently, then why at the end does he ask to be only a visitor? The psalm reminds us that our life force and happiness should be as "dwellers in the House of HaShem" but that is not enough. At the end of the *pasuk*, King David prays that we should, at the same time, be "visitors in HaShem's sanctuary," striving to still maintain the emotional and intellectual freshness of a visitor — of learning Torah, of doing *mitzvot*, of *davening* at the Kotel for the first time. Our goal is to maintain that enthusiasm, joy, and life blood on the same high level, to perform *mitzvot* both in body and spirit.

My fellow stones and I pray that this newness, this freshness and sparkle that each Bar Mitzvah boy experiences when he puts on *tefillin* for the first time will always be there.

These boys are a link in the "Chain of Generations" and symbolize a new age group that reaffirms our confidence in the future and in the guiding Hands of HaShem. I cannot help but feel that *Am Yisrael* is entrusting to these Jewish youth the destiny of our people and of our land. Together,

---

127   Rabbi Dov Ber Weisman, born and bred in Dallas, Texas, is a true cowboy at heart. Currently, he is one of the most popular lecturers in Atlanta, Georgia, where he gives weekly classes on the Torah portion, holidays, and other Jewish topics.

banded as one, they represent a unique essence whose very existence embodies a longing "for all that is sacred in our humanity and all that is human in our sanctity."[128]

Western Wall Tunnels

Ever since the opening of the Western Wall Tunnels to the public, I have noticed entire families celebrating the auspicious occasion of the Bar Mitzvah by taking a memorable tour of the tunnels. I would love to accompany them but cannot set myself free. (Immobility has its advantages and disadvantages!)

The tunnels are the continuation of the Western Wall, uncovered after being obscured for over 600 years by houses in the Muslim Quarter. I have been told that this is a "must-see" tour. It is literally a voyage through time that recreates the history of the Wall through archeological remnants and interactive models of the Second Temple.

What an exceptional way to top off an unforgettable Bar Mitzvah experience! The intensity of a Bar Mitzvah at the Kotel, the special ambience within the Western Wall Tunnels, linking our cultural heritage and connection to Jerusalem — all in the presence of family and friends — combine to create a memorable experience.

Chabad introduced a new twist to the ceremony. Once again, in June, 2009, they celebrated a mass Bar Mitzvah at the Kotel for 107 Israeli boys from needy families. The celebration included the participation of Israel's chief rabbis and the Chief Rabbi of the Western Wall. Each of the boys received a new set of *tefillin*.

On the Way to the Wedding

During the week before a wedding, the Ashkenazi custom[129] is for the bride and groom not to see (or speak to) each other. Despite this custom, some (mostly Sephardic) Israeli brides and grooms come to the upper Kotel plaza to be photographed prior to their wedding. At other times, only the happy bride in her gown and veil, with her entourage of family and friends, stop for photographs and blessings prior to

---

128 To paraphrase Richard M. Joel, President of Yeshiva University

129 Some traditional Sephardi couples also follow this practice.

proceeding further to the nearby wedding. Wedding ceremonies are not supposed to be conducted at the Kotel.

SIMCHAT TORAH AT THE KOTEL — 1974
[Photo courtesy Yaacov Saar; Government Press Office][Code: D146-026]
This joyous Jewish holiday marks the conclusion of the annual cycle of public Torah readings, and the beginning of a new cycle. Simchat Torah is a part of the Torah-mandated holiday of Shemini Azeret (Eighth Day of Assembly), which comes right after the festival of Succot. In this photo, you see young men rejoicing and dancing around the elevated Torah. All the Torah Scrolls are carried around in a series of seven hakafot (circuits). The dancing and singing with the Torah scrolls usually lasts for several hours.

Yom Yerushalayim at the Kotel

Would you believe it? Tonight we are celebrating the anniversary of the liberation of the Old City and its reunification with Jerusalem under Israeli control. Listen to the exhilarating voices coming from every bend and turn of the Old City, singing the unforgettable songs of the Six-Day War. The intensity of the sound from the mosque on top of the Temple Mount has always been disruptive to the Kotel worshippers. Today the *muezzin's* high-pitched call to prayer seems to be louder than ever. But no amount of amplification of the Islamic wail could overwhelm the *ruach* (religious spirit) that permeates the air. I feel it, and I am sure all 100,000 who come to the Kotel feel the spirit. For nineteen years we were denied access to our holiest site. On this night, on June 7, 1967, on the 28th day of the month of Iyar in the year 5727, on the Hebrew calendar, Israeli forces recaptured the Old City of Jerusalem.

Am Yisrael Chai

Today, as the sounds of prayer and thanksgiving ascend from these ancient walls and soar heavenward, we can be proud of the life force that so clearly exemplifies *Am Yisrael Chai*. Look at the strength of character of these Israelis. Set your eyes on the blue-and-white-clad teenagers as they dance in front of the Kotel and throughout the streets of Jerusalem. Could our grandparents and great-grandparents ever have imagined such a sight? Youngsters, with their elders, converge on the Kotel, joined by thousands of *kibbutzniks*, laborers, professionals, and politicians of all stripes coming together to this historic site. Army bands, street performers, and musicians, winding their way through the Jewish Quarter or the Dung Gate, contribute to the ambience, all displaying a strength of character, courage, and determination that so characterizes modern Israel. How I wish that I could capture the essence, the mood of the day — not so much for future generations, but for the past. But then how would I transmit it to those who have come before us?

Wait! I hear the sounds of a street parade with the IDF band performing to thousands of spectators lining the streets. I can just picture the enthusiastic crowds jostling for position with thousands of Israeli flags fluttering in the breeze. Many roads have been closed and numerous bus routes were put on hold for the duration of the parade. The only way to get to the Old City is by walking. Jerusalem's streets are jammed with a huge, buoyant crowd as it works its way toward the Kotel.

My favorite event is *Beit Orot's* all-night party. That *Hesder Yeshiva* on the Mount of Olives really knows how to throw a party! It is the place to be for the National Religious *yeshiva* crowd. The singing and dancing is almost non-stop until the exhausted bands stop playing around 4:30 A.M. At that point, the mass of enthusiastic youngsters set out with their flags in hand to retrace the path taken by the paratroopers of 1967. As they have done in past years, they walk down the same road from the Mount of Olives, turning left at the Kidron Valley precisely as the paratroopers did many years ago. They continue along the Jericho Road as far as Lion's Gate, finally climbing the hill to enter the Old City. The timing is perfect. They arrive at the Kotel in time for the *Vatikin* early-morning prayers. What an expression of faith! They recite the *Shema* in unison just before sunrise and then pray the silent *Amida*[130] with the rising sun.

Chanukah Candle Lighting at the Kotel

The tradition of kindling Chanukah lights each night of the eight-day long festival is exciting. The miracle of Chanukah happened at the Temple. It is most appropriate, then, that the ceremonies recalling the miracles take place at the Kotel, since it is closest to where the Holy Temple stood. The oil-lights are lit at three different locations at the Western Wall. The uplifting events start at the back of the plaza where the *yeshiva* boys light their candles, followed by singing and dancing. Then there is the official lighting of both the big flames on the balcony and on the huge *Chanukiyah* at the Kotel itself. Each day, three important people are honored with lighting the menorahs at the Kotel. These include the chief rabbis, government leaders, and prominent rabbis. The celebrations continue with dancing and music at the Kotel plaza.

Birkat HaChamah

I must tell you about a special event that I have been privileged to witness every twenty-eight years. The last time it occurred was on the day before the holiday of Passover, the 14th of Nissan (April 8th, 2009). Thousands came to the Western Wall plaza to join in the rare recitation of *Birkat haChama* ("Blessing of the Sun"). *Birkat haChama* commemorates the return of the sun to the point it was in at the time of Creation. In the early hours of the morning, well before dawn, they began arriving from all over Israel and began to walk toward the Kotel. From conversations that I overheard, the hotels were filled to capacity with Jews from all over the world who came for this special occasion. They came by foot, car, bus,

---

130   The Shemoneh Esrei – silent recitation of the eighteen blessings.

and taxi. The throngs coming to the Kotel for this occasion fulfilled the mitzvah of *"b'rov Am."*[131] During the days of the *Beit haMikdash, Hakhel* was also done *"b'rov Am."*

What can be more momentous than giving testimony to G-d's ultimate authority over the cosmos? Surely *Birkat haChama*, especially when recited so close to the site of the *Beit haMikdash*, ratifies this truth. Jews all over the world gathered to recite this very same blessing, all facing Jerusalem. Those at the Kotel are actually facing east, looking at the western side of the Temple Mount. You could feel the anticipation and excitement as everyone waited for the sun to rise. Then, all at once, the hushed silence was broken as young and old recited the blessing for the occasion: "He who performs the acts of Creation." Early-morning prayer services began at 5:50 a.m., and were followed by the actual *Birkat haChama* at 6:30 a.m.

What a rare and special gathering! Those not familiar with the ritual expressed extraordinary curiosity days and weeks before the event. Newspapers and radios commented on this remarkable happening. There were many notables present, including the chief rabbis and other great rabbinic and religious figures. Many reminisced about the last time the ceremony took place in 1981, and prior to that in 1953. All were hoping that they would still be around to recite *Birkat haChama* on its next occasion in the year 2037.

The day was special for another reason. *Birkat haChama* fell out that year on the day before Passover, a rarity that occurred only ten times in the history of the Jewish people. Thus, following the services, a *siyum* was held, marking the completion of a tractate of Talmud. Refreshments were served to all. This permitted the firstborns to "override" the obligatory fast that always takes place the day before Passover. The crowd of thousands quickly dispersed to enable all to prepare for the upcoming holiday.

I overheard someone saying that for the first time in at least 2,000 years, a group was planning to go up to the top of Masada to recite the *Birkat haChama*. I don't mind competition, and the blessing can certainly be said anywhere, but isn't Masada an enigmatic location? Perhaps I am too old-fashioned to follow the trends.

---

131 *B'rov am hadrat melech* ("in large numbers there is glorification of the king") is a Jewish tenet urging that *mitzvot* be carried out together with as large an assembly as possible, thus according HaShem greater honor.

The Shalosh Regalim (Three Pilgrimage Festivals)

My fellow stones and I remember quite well how thousands of pilgrims came to the *Beit haMikdash* during the time of the Second Temple, some 2,000 years ago. For us Kotel stones, the *Shalosh Regalim* (Three Pilgrimage Festivals) were always happy times. Thousands of Jews from northern Israel and from Judea would make their way to the Torah-mandated festivities.[132]

PRIESTLY BLESSINGS
The Kohanim raise their outstretched hands elevating them so that they are level with their shoulders. The right hand should be a bit higher than the left hand. The back of the Kohen's hands face upwards. Normally, a petitioner would have his palms facing up (and the back of his hands facing down) in symbolic anticipation of the bounty to be placed in his hands. In this case, however, the blessings from G-d are passed to the congregation by the Kohanim, hence their palms are down and the backs of their hands up to symbolize the "placing" of the blessings upon them. During the recitation, the Kohanim cover their hands and faces with their tallitot (prayer shawls).

---

132 For men, optional for women

Once here, they would participate in the ritual worship conducted by the *kohanim* (priests). They would come to offer sacrifices to HaShem. They were diligent in their observance of the Festival of Matzot (Passover), of the reaping festival (Shavuot) and of the harvest festival (Succot). Adult Jewish males meticulously observed three Torah commandments during these festivals: (1) going to Jerusalem; (2) bringing *Chagiga* (individual sacrifices) as well as those brought on behalf of the nation; and (3) rejoicing on the festival.

The sacrifices on behalf of the entire nation are different for each festival. Passover, the festival of the Spring, commemorates the Exodus from Egypt and the agricultural significance of the new barley crop (the *Omer*).

Shavuot, the harvest festival, is my favorite. It marks the end of the barley harvest and the start of the wheat harvest, and commemorates the giving of the Torah at Mount Sinai.

The last in the cycle is the festival Succot, which marks the harvest gathering of the crops, as well as recalling the forty years that the Israelites wandered in the desert.

Sadly, after the destruction of the Temple, Jews were deprived of the opportunity presented by the Three Festivals. As you know, the sages substituted prayers for Temple sacrifices. As a result, we recite Musaf (additional) services on each of the festivals that incorporate references to the festivals.

An especially propitious time to visit the Kotel is during the holidays of Passover and Succot, when the *Birkat Kohanim* (priestly blessings) are recited, an event that attracts thousands of people. A word of caution: If you are planning to come during the morning prayer services to receive these blessings be prepared for the huge crowds.

Shavuot

I love the holiday of Shavuot, alternately referred to as "the feast of harvest" or the "Festival of First Fruits,"[133] one of the three *Regalim* (pilgrim festivals).[134] Shavuot always falls out on the fiftieth day of the counting the *Omer*. This festival commemorates our acceptance of the Torah (both oral and written) at Mount Sinai. On this day, in Temple times, Jews would bring the first fruits of the harvest to the Temple.

---

133 Exod. 23:16

134 There is even a designation of Isru Chag, "The day after the festival."

Simchat Torah / Shemini Atzeret

A beautiful custom has evolved in Jerusalem on Simchat Torah. Different groups, often whole families and friends, walk through the streets toward the Kotel. The one carrying the Torah, all the while singing and dancing, leads them. What a sight! Thousands of people, of all ages, proceeding to the Kotel, where the singing and dancing intensifies as the *hakafot* begin.[135] In the Diaspora, the holiday of Simchat Torah comes first, followed by Shemini Atzeret, which is observed the following day. In Israel, the two holidays coincide.

Kol Nidrei at the Kotel

There is something extraordinary about Kol Nidrei services at the Kotel. Unless you are an octogenarian (or older!), you may be unaware of the heroic efforts to blow the shofar at the Western Wall during the days of the British Mandate (in the late 1920s). The British, capitulating to Arab demands and Arab violence at the Kotel, banned shofar blowing at the Wall.

In one well-known episode in 1929, the British immediately arrested a rabbi for blowing the shofar at the close of Yom Kippur. Despite the fact that he had fasted for the prior twenty-five hours, he was jailed without food until midnight. He was released only after then-Chief Rabbi Avraham Yitzchak Kook advised the police commander that he himself would not eat until the rabbi was released. (The entire story appears later on in this book.)

As far back as the 12th and 13th centuries, I have seen Ashkenazi Jews coming to the Kotel, clothed in a white *kittel*, (a robe which serves as a burial shroud for male Jews),[136] many with a white kippa, and all wearing non-leather shoes or slippers. Adult males were draped in the traditional *tallit*, many covering their heads with it. Wearing a *kittel* on Yom Kippur is symbolically linked to its use as a burial shroud and to the verse "our sins shall be made as white as snow" (Isaiah 1:18).

---

135 The ceremony on Simchat Torah and on other occasions in which congregants carry Torah scrolls around the synagogue.

136 Sephardic Jews do not follow this custom.

I look at the sea of people in front of me. There is a hush, now audible, as they look around searching for fellow worshippers who follow their particular *nusach* and *minhag* (prayer rite and custom). As they greet each other, many customarily ask *mechila* (asking for forgiveness) from others whom they may have offended during the course of the past year, whether knowingly or not. Still others try to find an available plastic chair. They have come here with a passionate desire to cleanse their personal slates, to wipe away the clutter of their daily lives for twenty-five hours and to focus totally on who they are and what they have become. As they lift up their prayer books this evening, they entreat HaShem to absolve, forgive, annul, and declare void all their vows. *Kavanah*, concentration in prayer, is somehow easier here in front of the Kotel than in synagogues elsewhere.

Different Groups

There are so many different groups here, each group following its own traditions. Years back the majority were Sephardic Jews, the Ashkenazim a minority. After 1967, the numbers appear to be balanced. Here and there, subdued conversation continues. But by and large, a quiet serenity has overtaken the Kotel plaza. Portable Torah Arks had been previously positioned on *bamot*, the raised platforms [in this case, on wheels].

Let's converge on one such Ashkenazi group. The Ark is opened and two men have been given the honor of removing from it two Torah scrolls. Then, each holding a scroll, they stand on either side of the *chazzan*. The evocative formula is chanted, beginning with the words: "*B'Yeshiva shel malah, b'Yeshiva shel mattah*" — "In the tribunal of Heaven and the tribunal of Earth, by permission of G-d, blessed be He, and by the permission of its holy congregation, we hold that the lawful pray with the transgressors."

The Kol Nidrei prayer, which is recited at the Kotel and in synagogues throughout the world, has had a very chaotic history. Until a few centuries ago, it was not as widely accepted as it is today. "Introduced into the liturgy, despite the opposition of rabbinic authorities, repeatedly attacked in the course of time by many halachists, and in the nineteenth century expunged from the prayer book by many communities of Western Europe, it has often been employed by Christians to support their assertion that the oath of a Jew cannot be trusted."[137]

The prayer itself dates back to the Geonic period.[138] Over the many centuries, the haunting tunes of Kol Nidrei echoed here at the Wall. However, it was not always so. Many discontinued the recitation after Amram Gaon,[139] about the middle of the 9th century CE, dismissed the Kol Nidrei prayer as

BOOSTING JEWISH BATTLE MORALE
Periodically, the IDF Rabbinate conducts sessions at the Kotel Plaza designed to uplift soldiers' spirits. In 2009, the Chief Rabbinate distributed 10,000 MP3 players with prayers to boost the morale of soldiers fighting in Gaza and with recorded sermons to combat soldiers — both religious and secular, Jewish and gentile — who were then serving in Gaza. Maimonides, the Jewish philosopher and legalist, urged soldiers to "trust in God and know that war is being waged for the sanctification of His name...and not to fear." The IDF rabbis emphasize that the war Israel is fighting is justified because its aim is "to save the Jewish people from its enemies," a halachik definition mentioned by Maimonides.

---

137 Jewish Encyclopedia [http://www.jewishencyclopedia.com/articles/9443-kol-nidreanchor9]

138 The Geonic period extended from about 690 CE until the 11th century.

139 Amram Ben Sheshna was the Gaon of Sura, whose famous *siddur* (order of prayers and blessings for the entire year as laid down by the Tannaim and Amoraim) contains the text of the prayers for the entire year, as well as the laws and customs pertaining to the different prayers.

a *minhag shetut* ("foolish custom"). Thereafter, for almost 1,000 years, some worshippers at the Kotel and elsewhere declined to recite this prayer.

The ancients frequently vowed to HaShem (to bring offerings, give charity, or to perform other good deeds). The Torah[140] is clear that it is better not to vow than to make vows and take the chance of forgetting, delaying, or violating them.[141] To extricate themselves from a possible sin, they sought some mechanism for dispensation from such vows. Thus the sages evolved the rite of absolution from a vow (*hatarat nedarim*) performed by a tribunal of three laymen. The now-famous Kol Nidrei plea evolved to clear the conscience of those seeking reconciliation with HaShem. The dispensation formula chanted by the *chazzan* in the name of the assembled congregation on the eve of Yom Kippur declared that the petitioners solemnly retract, in His presence, all vows and oaths that they had taken during the period intervening between the previous Day of Atonement and the present one,[142] and made them null and void from the beginning, entreating on their behalf a pardon and forgiveness from the Heavenly Father.[143]

Karaites and Christians pounced on the ease with which Jewish vows could be annulled to discredit the validity of any oath, declaration, or undertaking made between a Jew and others. They ignored our explanations that the dispensation from vows in the Kol Nidrei refers only to those that an individual voluntarily assumes for him alone and in which no other persons or their interests are involved. In other words, the formula is restricted to those vows that concern only the relation of man to his conscience or to his Heavenly Judge. The intent of the Kol Nidrei is to shield the individual from heavenly punishment. Overlooked was the fact that these vows were between man and G-d and did not annul any vow, promise, or oath that affected

---

140 Deuter. 23:23

141 Ramban

142 An important alteration in the wording of the Kol Nidrei was made by Rashi's son-in-law, Meir ben Samuel, who changed the original phrase "from the last Day of Atonement until this one," to "from this Day of Atonement until the next." Thus the dispensation of the Kol Nidrei was not as formerly *a posteriori* and concerned with unfulfilled obligations of the past year, but *a priori* and having reference to vows that one might not be able to fulfill or might forget to observe during the ensuing year.

143 Jewish Encyclopedia [http://www.jewishencyclopedia.com/articles/9443-kol-nidreanchor9]

another person, a court of justice, or a community. The attacks forced the Geonim to curtail the ability to annul vows. Indeed the Kol Nidrei was rejected by both of the Babylonian academies and regarded as a dubious mechanism for the dispensation of vows.

Now you can understand why some ancient worshippers at the Kotel on Yom Kippur eve did not recite Kol Nidrei and some did. Those Jews who followed the rituals of Amram Gaon in his *siddur* did not recite Kol Nidrei. Jews following the Catalonian or the Algerian ritual did not recite it, nor did Provençal and Spanish Jews. Those from other lands did recite it.

CHAPTER XVII

Fast Days

There is something different about the demeanor of worshippers on a fast day. It is apparent in their deportment. There is something in the stance and in the mannerism of the Kotel regulars.

The *Shulchan Aruch*[144] obliges the Jew to fast on the following occasions: (1) Tisha b'Av; (2) 17th of Tammuz; (3) 3rd of Tishrei; and (4) 10th of Tevet. The Fast of Esther, generally observed on the 13th of Adar, is not one of the four public fasts ordained by the Prophets. Consequently, we are more lenient in its observance; pregnant women, nursing mothers, and those who are weak are not required to observe it.

Some might think that the most important aspect of the public fast is abstinence from food or drink. In truth, these four public fast days merely lay the groundwork for repentance. The objective is atonement, thereby cleansing the soul and enabling the worshipper to intensify his level of holiness. The nature of the commemoration dictates the degree of strictness (or leniency) applicable to the communal mourning. By the way, Yom Kippur does not fall into this category of communal fasts. True, it is a day of fasting, but it is essentially a Festival.

17th of Tammuz (Sheva Assar b'Tammuz)

In my mind, the onset of the month of Av is associated with two millennia of misfortune, tribulation and disaster. The Crusader bloodbaths,

---

144   (Code of Jewish Law) 549:1

in which whole communities were slaughtered, and brutal pogroms throughout the ages, reinforced this linkage between the month of Av and adversity.

When the 17th of Tammuz rolls around, I recall the five tragedies that happened to the Jewish nation. It marks the start of a three-week period of national mourning over the destruction of Jerusalem, which ends with Tisha b'Av. Those mourning rites deepen from the first day of the month of Av, and intensify on Tisha b'Av to the point where they are akin to the mourning customs for the death of a close relative.[145]

Five catastrophes befell the Jews on this day:

1. Moses threw down the Tablets at the sight of people dancing around the Golden Calf. This was G-d's handiwork that was being smashed.[146]

2. The daily offering ended in the First *Beit haMikdash* (The Holy Temple).

3. The walls of Jerusalem were breached prior to the demolition of the Second *Beit haMikdash*, which I unfortunately experienced along with the following two calamities.

4. Apostomos burned the Torah in the *Beit haMikdash*.[147]

5. Apostomos set up an idol in the *Beit haMikdash*.

The three-week period of national mourning between the two fast days (Fast of Tammuz and Tisha b'Av) is known as *Bein haMetzarim* ("Between the Straits").

Tisha b'Av (9th of Av)

Pious Jews gradually ease into the mood of Tisha b'Av by refraining from any pleasurable activities (recreation, trips, walks, etc.) from midday on. Many come to the Kotel to recite Minchah early in the afternoon then hurry home to eat the *Seuda haMafsekes* (the cessation meal). *Tachanun*, prayer of supplication, normally recited during Minchah, is omitted. Customarily, they refrain from eating fish or meat and drinking wine, and from eating more than one cooked dish.

---

145   *Ta'anit* 30a

146   Exod. 32:19

147   *Ta'anit* 6:6 [he was probably a Roman officer]

Incidentally, Jews are proscribed from eating meat and drinking wine during the nine days preceding Tisha b'Av. The last item eaten is a hard-boiled egg with ashes scattered on it as a sign of mourning. This meal of cessation is eaten while seated on a low stool (or the floor). While normally it is meritorious to eat with at least two other men, so that the Grace after Meals may be said with a *zimun*,[148] on this last meal it is preferable that one eat alone and recite the Grace alone in a subdued tone.

Do not be confused by those bottles of water people are carrying. One may still eat and drink until sunset. Notice that people do not greet each other on Tisha b'Av, nor do they shake hands. If greeted by someone unacquainted with these mourning restrictions, it is permitted to respond in a subdued tone and manner. Most worshippers at the Kotel internalize the Talmudic statement that "each generation in which the Temple is not rebuilt should regard itself as responsible for its destruction." Eicha (the Book of Lamentations) is read aloud by the *chazzan*, with everyone else reading along in a subdued tone. The last sentence, *Hashiveinu*, is read aloud first by the congregation and then repeated aloud by the *chazzan*. Following Eicha, special dirges called *Kinot* are read in a hushed voice by both the *chazzan* and the congregation.

Tisha b'Av at the Kotel in Days Gone By

There were no chairs or benches in those days. The men came with tears in their eyes, kissed and caressed the stones and then sat on the ground mournfully lamenting the destroyed *Beit haMikdash* — the focal point of ancient Judaism that embodied G-d's Presence in the world. This was especially so on Tisha b'Av, the Jewish day of fasting, to commemorate the destruction of our Holy Temple.

Dressed in tattered clothing, those Jews who were permitted to enter Jerusalem would pour out their tears over its stones and implore G-d to redeem His Chosen People. During the evening services, with heads bowed and tears streaming from their eyes, they would read from the scroll of Eicha. There was no electric lighting in those days. Their light came from oil lamps, candles, and in later years from kerosene

---

148 A *zimun* is an invitation to three or more males eating together, to thank G-d together by reciting "grace" after a bread meal.

lamps. At the completion of the services, those who did not go home slept on the ground.

The following morning, different groups chanted *Kinot*, bewailing the loss of both Temples and subsequent tragedies. Sephardic Jews would read the Book of Job on the morning of Tisha b'Av. I recall the moving scenes — so emotional and sad. The intensity of the prayers was directly related to the extent of the most recent persecution by local authorities. How sad and heartbreaking that so many of the rituals go unobserved by so many of our people.

Tisha b'Av marks the destruction of the First and Second Temples in Jerusalem — events that took place on the same date but 656 years apart.[149] Some say that this tragedy was foretold in the Torah when the ten spies returned with a dispiriting report to dissuade the Israelites from possessing the Promised Land. This day also marks the collapse of the second rebellion against Rome, when the city of Beitar was destroyed and the Romans massacred over 100,000 Jews in 132 CE.[150] On this day, too, the Romans razed the site of the Temple, utterly demolishing every structure. The Roman Emperor Hadrian built a pagan temple on the site of the *Beit haMikdash*.

In addition to the above calamities that befell the Jewish people, under Hadrian in 135 CE Jerusalem became a pagan city from which Jews were barred.[151] You will recall my telling you about the First Crusade, which was declared on this day in the year 1095 CE.[152] Roughly two hundred years later, in the year 1290, King Edward I expelled all Jews from England on this day. On this same ninth of Av, in the year 1492, all Jews were expelled from Spain. On this day in 1555, Pope Paul IV moved all the Jews in Rome into the first ghetto. The First World War began on this day in 1914 when Britain and Russia declared war on Germany. The Nazis, may their name be erased, on Tisha b'Av, 1942, began to transport Jews from Warsaw's ghetto to the murder facility at Treblinka. By Yom Kippur, 1942, over 250,000 Jews had been sent from Warsaw to Treblinka to be murdered there. On this day in 1994, a deadly bombing of the AMIA (the

---

149   The First Temple was destroyed by the Romans in 586 BCE and the Second Temple was destroyed in 70 CE.

150   http://en.wikipedia.org/wiki/Tisha_b'Av

151   called Aelia Capitolina

152   www.history.com/this-day-in.../pope-urban-ii-orders-first-crusade

Jewish community center in Buenos Aires, Argentina) killed eighty-six people and wounded some 300 others.

And the tragedies continue. In more recent times, on the day after Tisha b'Av in 2005, Israel began the expulsion of Gush Katif residents in the Gaza Strip. The expulsion was pushed off by a day, so as not to coincide with Tisha b'Av. The Second Lebanon War took place in the three weeks leading up to Tisha b'Av in 2006. Coincidence? Albert Einstein once said, "Coincidence is G-d's way of remaining anonymous."

How to come to terms with the stark reality of our history punctuated with such agonizing periods of destruction? Many come to the Kotel to draw inspiration from Zechariah's prophecy (8:18–19) that one day these fast days will be turned into days of joyous festivals:[153]

"The word of HaShem , Master of Legions, came to me, saying: The fasts of the fourth [month], the fast of the fifth, the fast of the seventh and the festival of the tenth will be to the house of Judah for joy and for gladness and four happy festivals. [Only] love truth and peace!"

Zechariah begins this (eighth) chapter with the words of comfort. At the end of the exile, G-d will direct his zeal to the defense of Jerusalem and vengeance against its enemies:

"The word of HaShem, Master of Legions, came [to me], saying:

'Thus said HaShem, Master of Legions: I have become zealous with great zeal on behalf of Zion; I have become zealous with great wrath on its behalf' " (Ibid. 8:1)

Then it continues to outline the blessings that G-d will pour on Jerusalem, culminating in verse 14 and 15:

"For thus said HaShem, Master of Legions: Just as I had planned to bring misfortune upon you when your forefathers angered Me — said HaShem, Master of Legions — and I did not relent [from doing so], so have I turned back these days and planned to benefit Jerusalem and the house of Judah. Do not fear!"

Incidentally, after the conclusion of Tisha b'Av, I have often heard Egyptian Jews wishing one another *"B'karov Tzion b'nechmat lirot tizke"* (You should merit witnessing the restoration of Zion in the near future.)

What a beautiful custom!

---

153   The Babylonians breached the walls of Jerusalem in the fourth month [17th Tammuz]; they destroyed the Temple in the fifth month.

CHAPTER XVIII

WOMEN PRAYING AT THE WESTERN WALL
"The Ashkenazi women stand away off and jump little jumps as they respond to every kedushah prayer they hear. The Sephardic ladies love the Wall with a special love and most of them come to it enveloped in white sheets. Those who cannot read the texts of the prayers make modest prayerful signs to the Wall. All, when they leave, kiss each stone individually and back away as though they were leaving the royal presence, stretching out their fingers towards it with eyes raised on high." [Mordechai ben Hillel haKohen (1889)]

Women at the Kotel

I can hear the quiet sobbing of many of the women on their side of the partition, imploring HaShem that it should be a good year for all Jews. I, and my fellow stones, wholeheartedly welcome women to the Kotel, just like men. Traditionally, just as there is a *mechitzah* (divider between men and women) in Orthodox synagogues, so there has been, since 1967, a *mechitzah* at our Wall.

It is true that in the past centuries, due to restrictions imposed by foreign rulers, men and women prayed side by side at the Kotel. Indeed you may view a newsreel film from 1911 that authenticates that statement.[154] Photos dating back more than 160 years also show men and women praying together. Nevertheless, we have a tradition, authenticated in *halachah* (Jewish religious law), for the preservation of modesty and humility that deems public and loud women's prayer inappropriate in the presence of men. In Orthodox Judaism, mixed services (men and women praying together) are totally inappropriate, nor are men allowed to hear women sing, a prohibition called *Kol Isha*. This prohibition applies at all times and forbids a man to pray or study Torah in the presence of a woman who is singing aloud. This is not a sign of discrimination, intolerance, or unfairness. Rather it is recognition that inappropriate thoughts triggered by a woman's singing can become overwhelming, making proper *kavanah* (intense concentration of prayer) difficult to attain.

Now, I recognize that there are many sincere contemporary Jews who reject that position. But one can hardly discard a belief held by the great majority of our people for over two millennia. Your forefathers, perhaps even your grandparents or great-grandparents, not only lived by, but esteemed these very resolute laws.

That women and men are to pray in separate areas may seem old-fashioned to you, but these norms continue to be our treasured tradition as they are for hundreds of thousands of Jews in the present-day world. The vast majority of Jews who come to the Kotel on a regular basis to pray are offended when their prayers are distracted by women's voices raised in loud song. Again, I repeat, women and girls are free to come to pray as individuals at a separate section at the extreme right of the Western

---

154 The film is courtesy of the Spielberg archive: http://www.youtube.com/watch?v=T0zpbDGjHAE

Wall. This area is reserved for women, who are not allowed into the men's section, in keeping with Orthodox Jewish tradition.

I have noticed that since 1988, a group of women decided that they should be allowed to pray as a group at the Kotel. For millennia, women prayed at the Wall as individuals. Furthermore, these women, since called Women of the Wall (WOW), demanded the right to read from a Torah scroll and to wear *tallitot*. Once a month on Rosh Chodesh, WOW members gather to form a minyan and pray at the Kotel. Their repeated appeals to the courts were generally unsuccessful. Nevertheless, an accommodation has been reached whereby they pray at a nearby archaeological area in order to read the Torah.

Some claim that the Western Wall was never considered an "Orthodox synagogue" until the late 1960s when the plaza was cleared and a *mechitzah* was erected. I state clearly that the Kotel is open to all, Jews and non-Jews alike. Nobody checks to see whether you are Orthodox, Conservative or Reform. However we do ask you to be respectful of the traditions that have governed attendance at the Wall for twenty centuries.

Notwithstanding the above, it pains me to witness the behavior of some men and boys against Women of the Wall. Our Torah way is not to spit on the women, throw chairs, or scream defamatory epithets. Such disparaging conduct brings shame on to the Jewish People at this holiest site in Judaism.

CHAPTER XIX

My Special "Customers"

I am always happy to greet newcomers to the Kotel. Many non-Jewish visitors are profoundly moved by the heartfelt piety of Jews praying in their own unique way at the Western Wall. Over the past 2,000 years, Jews have come from the outermost corners of the world to recite their prayers at this site. Many non-Jews have come: ordinary people and famous people, sovereign rulers, emperors, kings and queens, prime ministers and other heads of state. I have greeted soldiers and civilians, professionals, merchants and working-class people. I especially like to meet the youth. There is something very appealing about them as they — especially those from foreign lands — anxiously and guardedly come up to the Kotel. True, there are those who approach self-assuredly, but these are rarely first-time visitors.

Non-Jewish Visitors

The Kotel is not a sacred site for Jews only. All who come, Jew and non-Jew, are received with the same sense of dignity. The *Beit haMikdash* was a place of prayer for all. When King Solomon built the First Temple, he expressly petitioned G-d to answer the prayers of non-Jews at the Temple as well.[155] The prophet Isaiah called the Temples "a house of prayer for all nations." The Prophet Zechariah (14:16) says:

---

155   1 Kings 8:41–43

"And it shall come to pass, that every one that is left of all the nations that came against Jerusalem shall go up from year to year to worship the King, the G-d of Hosts, and to keep the Feast of Tabernacles (Succot)."

While far from being a *navi* (prophet), I can assure you that there will be a time when the nations of the world will come to visit our Third *Beit haMikdash*.[156]

European Heads of State

Towards the end of the 19th century, prominent Europeans and heads of state visited the Western Wall as part of their pilgrimages to the Holy Land. One such royal couple that I greeted was Germany's Kaiser Wilhelm II and his Queen Augusta-Victoria, who came to Jerusalem in October, 1898.

March 21–26, 2000 — Pope John Paul II

Initially, I had mixed emotions about welcoming the Pope. Somehow, I felt that Pope John Paul II was different from his predecessors. I must admit, he won me over with his historic apology for sins committed by Christians against Jews and referred to the Jews as the Catholics' "elder brothers." Pope John Paul II was the first Pope to pray at the Wall. During his visit to the Kotel, he inserted a letter in a crack that read:

"G-d of our fathers, You chose Abraham and his descendants to bring your Name to the nations: we are deeply saddened by the behavior of those who in the course of history have caused these children of yours to suffer, and asking your forgiveness we wish to commit ourselves to genuine brotherhood with the people of the Covenant."

Signed: John Paul II

May 12, 2009 — Pope Benedict XVI

I did not feel any warmth for the second papal visit to the Kotel. I cannot help but compare the previous Pope John Paul II with Benedict XVI. The Polish-born John Paul's trademark (at least in my mind) was

---

156 The issue of the restoration of sacrificial worship is beyond the scope of this book. All I can say is that we pray and hope for the *Mashiach* to come and play a major role in a future Jewish eschatology.

nurturing Catholic-Jewish relations. Recent moves and statements by Pope Benedict have left me wondering.

Most recently, he moved to bring Holocaust-era Pope Pius XII a bit closer to sainthood. Holocaust researchers have long accused Pius of having failed to act as Nazis murdered innocent Jews during the Holocaust. Benedict's visit to Rome's synagogues notwithstanding, his endorsement of Pope Pius XII progress toward sainthood attracted extensive criticism from Jewish organizations. The Vatican's claims that the wartime Pope acted secretly to relieve Jewish suffering cannot be independently substantiated until the Vatican agrees to fully open its secret archives... which it refuses to do.

It is certainly not up to me to decide whom to honor with sainthood. Nonetheless, I agree with those who view it as a hostile act. World Jewish Congress President Ronald Lauder said, "As long as the archives of Pope Pius about the crucial period 1939 to 1945 remain closed, and until a consensus on his actions — or inaction — concerning the persecution of millions of Jews in the Holocaust is established, a beatification is inopportune and premature."

Nor was this the first episode that angered me about Benedict. I recall his decision in 2008 to reinstate a Good Friday Latin prayer that appeared to call for the conversion of the Jews. True, the uproar prompted the Vatican to change some of the prayer's wording, but that only happened because we complained.

Another troubling act was the Pope's lifting of a 1988 excommunication order against Richard Williamson, a Holocaust-denying bishop who chose to live outside Vatican laws and conventions. Nor can I forget the Encyclical of his namesake, Pope Benedict XIV, who promulgated on June 14, 1751, a spewing venomous diatribe against the Jews.[157]

---

157 "Because the Jews control businesses selling liquor and even wine, they are therefore allowed to supervise the collection of public revenues. They have also gained control of inns, bankrupt estates, villages and public land by means of which they have subjugated poor Christian farmers. The Jews are cruel taskmasters, not only working the farmers harshly and forcing them to carry excessive loads, but also whipping them for punishment. So it has come about that those poor farmers are the subjects of the Jews, submissive to their will and power. Furthermore, although the power to punish lies with the Christian official, he must comply with the commands of the Jews and inflict the punishments they desire. If he doesn't, he would lose his post. Therefore the tyrannical orders of the Jews have to be carried out."[http://www.jewishvirtuallibrary.org/jsource/anti-semitism/Pope_Benedict_on_Jews.html]

To his credit, Benedict visited synagogues in his native Germany and in the United States and visited the Kotel on his trip to Israel. While I would never open a note inserted into the Kotel, it is interesting to read the contents of the note, made public by the Vatican. It read:

"G-d of all the ages, on my visit to Jerusalem, the 'City of Peace,' spiritual home to Jews, Christians, and Muslims alike, I bring before you the joys, the hopes, and the aspirations, the trials, the suffering, and the pain of all your people throughout the world."

The Pope ended his prayer with a quote from the Book of Lamentations, "The Lor-d is good to those who wait for him, to the soul that seeks him."

At a brief ceremony prior to the Pope's personal prayer at the Wall, the Chief Rabbi of the Kotel read in Hebrew from the first book of Kings, and the Pope read psalm 122 in Latin, which read in part: "Pray for the peace of Jerusalem; those who love you will be serene. May there be peace within your Wall, serenity within your palaces. For the sake of my brethren and companions, I shall speak of peace in your midst. For the sake of the House of HaShem, our G-d, I will request good for you." The Talmud teaches us to give people the benefit of the doubt. That is a good dictum, motivated by the highest ideals of Judaism. Nevertheless, I cannot lose sight of the reality that surrounds us or of the historic role that Christianity played in the sufferings of the Jews. As much as I want to judge others favorably, I must look ahead to see what negative impact such actions might have on *Klal Yisrael*. With this background, you can understand why I was unenthusiastic about Pope Benedict's visit.

Other Notables who Visited after 1948

I recall the visits of three United States presidents (Bill Clinton, George W. Bush, and Barack Obama), as well as Russian President Vladimir Putin and Edouard Shevardnadze (President of Georgia). While I did not see the First Lady Laura Bush, who was in the women's section, I learned that she also placed a note in the crevice of the Kotel.

I could fill many books with the names of important visitors to the Kotel.

The Makoya Sect

An event that is both unusual and surprising takes place several times a year when groups of Japanese Christians, members of the Makoya sect, visit the Kotel. These Japanese men and women make a pilgrimage to Israel every year to pray for the peace of Jerusalem and for Israel. They passionately identify with Israel and regard the establishment of the State of Israel and the unification of Jerusalem as a fulfillment of biblical prophecies. The Makoyas avoid proselytizing, respect religious pluralism, tolerance, and coexistence. They journey to Jerusalem, and especially to the Kotel, for religious reasons. At the Kotel, they recite prayers and lamentations after which they assemble in the upper plaza, where they form a choir to sing Zionist songs in Hebrew. The Makoya (which means Tabernacle) have maintained close ties with Kibbutz Hefziba for more than thirty years, where more than 600 Japanese students have studied Hebrew. Additionally there is a Makoya Jerusalem Center, where 60–70 students study Hebrew, Bible, and Judaism. Interestingly, though they are Christians, they do not use the cross as their symbol. Instead, they have adopted the seven-armed biblical menorah as their religious emblem, and display it on their badge or pendant. They view the cross as a symbol of "anguish," whereas the menorah symbolizes "hope," which accords with their religious outlook on life.

KOTEL HAKATAN — THE SMALL KOTEL

Shockingly, in 2006 a man was arrested for blowing Shofar at Western Wall. "Shades of the 1920s: A Jewish man was hauled off to the Old City police station in the middle of prayer for sounding the Shofar during Rosh Hashanah services at the area known as the Kotel HaKatan. The incident occurred around 7:30 in the morning, at the northern-most section of the accessible Western Wall — a little-known area called the Kotel HaKatan, the small Wall. It is considered to have extra sanctity, as it stands opposite the presumed spot of the Holy of Holies of the Beit haMikdash". [Hillel Fendel (Israelnationalnews.com)]

CHAPTER XX

Outlawing Sacred Rituals at the Kotel

Man Arrested for Blowing Shofar at Western Wall[158]... In 2006!

by Hillel Fendel (Israelnationalnews.com)

Shades of the 1920s: A Jewish man was hauled off to the Old City police station in the middle of prayer for sounding the shofar during Rosh Hashanah services at the area known as the *Kotel haKatan*. The incident occurred around 7:30 in the morning at the northern-most section of the accessible Western Wall — a little-known area called the *Kotel haKatan*, the small Wall. It is considered to have extra sanctity, as it stands opposite the presumed spot of the Holy of Holies of the *Beit haMikdash*.

Yesterday morning (Sunday), a group of some ten men and two women gathered at the site, as they have done for several years on Rosh Hashanah, for early-morning prayers. The holiday prayers feature the blowing of the *shofar* (ram's horn) at several different times. Towards the end of the first shofar sounding, a Border Guard police officer came in, made an unclear motion with his hand as if to ask what was going on, and then left. He said nothing. Shortly afterwards, Eliyahu K., the twenty-year-old prayer leader, blew the shofar a second time, in the midst of his silent prayer (in accordance with Sephardic custom). Police officers came in once again and began trying to pull him away. However,

---

158 Note: The *Kotel haKatan* (small Kotel) is not normally referred to as the Western Wall, though technically it is.

Eliyahu was in the midst of reciting the *Amida* — a long passage during which one must stand in one place without moving — and he therefore did not move.

The police officers informed their supervisors by radio that he was praying and refused to move, and reinforcements were soon sent — no fewer than twenty police officers, according to several witnesses. They then started dragging him out, and when they stopped for a moment, he got up and resumed his prayers. They then began to drag him away again, and shortly afterwards again stopped for a moment — and he resumed his prayers. At this point, the police officers allowed him to complete his prayers.

In the meanwhile, the other members of the prayer group came out and tried to prevent the police officers from taking Eliyahu away. At this point, the police officers started swinging their clubs violently; no one was hospitalized, but "it was a big brawl," in the words of one witness, with many people being dragged around and beaten while wearing their prayer shawls and Sabbath suits.

Meanwhile, Eliyahu was taken to the small police station at the Western Wall plaza, and several of his friends followed him there. They wanted to go up the steps into the police station, and demanded that at least the shofar be returned, but the police again came down with their clubs. They finally took Eliyahu by foot, accompanied by his fiancée, all the way around the Old City, past Mt. Zion and through Jaffa Gate, to the Kishle police station inside Jaffa Gate. At this point, there was no longer any violence, and Eliyahu was released around 11:30 after being charged with attacking a police officer, disturbing a police officer in the line of duty, and disturbing the public order.

One witness related, "It's not only that they stopped him from blowing the shofar, but rather the fact that the police beat us up very harshly. I was on my way to the Wall for prayers when I saw 5–7 police officers going with Eliyahu and protecting him very closely. I walked after them, and then a few of his friends came, and then the violence started. We asked the policemen to return the shofar, and they started kicking us and punching us."

The worshippers said that an Arab woman who said the sound of the ram's horn disturbed her children had apparently called the police. A Jewish resident of the Old City told Arutz-7: "How ironic. The loud Arab weddings and nightly prayers by the *muezzin*[159] [over a powerful loud-speaker] at 4:30 a.m. disturb our sleep every night." Similar complaints are heard from Jews living near Arab villages in Judea and Samaria.

A member of the Jerusalem Police spokesman's office, contacted by Arutz-7 for a statement on the matter and asked whether this signified a new policy towards shofar-blowing at the Wall, said, "When we have an answer for you, I will get back to you."

The head of the local council of the Jewish Quarter of the Old City, Shmuel Yitzchaki, could not be reached for comment by the time of this report.

The rabbi of the Western Wall, Rabbi Shmuel Rabinovitch, told Arutz Sheva, "This is a very grave incident, and I have asked the local police commander, Yossi Priente, to check into it — both the violence and the prevention of the shofar blowing. It reminds us of the days of the British Mandate when Jews [had to make] super-human efforts to blow the shofar at the Western Wall."

He was referring to the late 1920s, when the British, in an attempt to appease the Arabs, and following violence at the Wall, forbade shofar-blowing at the Wall. In one famous incident in 1929, a man named Moshe Segal blew the shofar at the conclusion of Yom Kippur and was immediately arrested by the British. Though he had fasted for the previous twenty-five hours, the British detained him without food until midnight, when he was released. It was later reported that the release came about when then-Chief Rabbi Avraham Yitzchak Kook informed the commander that he himself would not eat until Segal was released.

Moshe Segal again sounded the shofar nearly forty years later. This milestone occurred shortly after the Six-Day War during the first Yom Kippur service at the Wall under Israeli sovereignty.

---

159 The Muslim official of a mosque who summons the faithful to prayer from a minaret five times a day.

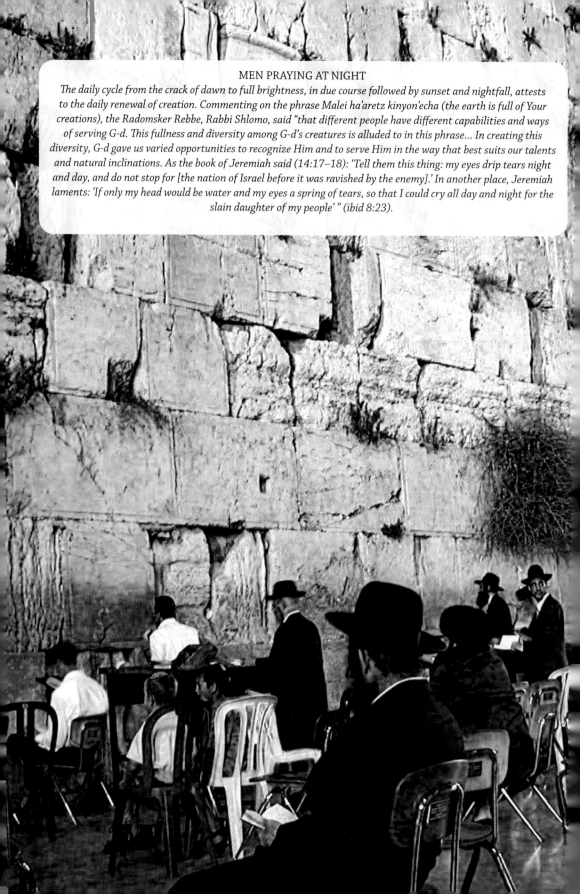

MEN PRAYING AT NIGHT

The daily cycle from the crack of dawn to full brightness, in due course followed by sunset and nightfall, attests to the daily renewal of creation. Commenting on the phrase Malei ha'aretz kinyon'echa (the earth is full of Your creations), the Radomsker Rebbe, Rabbi Shlomo, said "that different people have different capabilities and ways of serving G-d. This fullness and diversity among G-d's creatures is alluded to in this phrase... In creating this diversity, G-d gave us varied opportunities to recognize Him and to serve Him in the way that best suits our talents and natural inclinations. As the book of Jeremiah said (14:17–18): 'Tell them this thing: my eyes drip tears night and day, and do not stop for [the nation of Israel before it was ravished by the enemy].' In another place, Jeremiah laments: 'If only my head would be water and my eyes a spring of tears, so that I could cry all day and night for the slain daughter of my people'" (ibid 8:23).

CHAPTER XXI

VISITING THE WESTERN WALL — SECURITY AND ETIQUETTE

Security

If you're planning to visit the Kotel, prepare for a serious security check upon entering. Security is high, even once inside, but that is understandable, given the highly sensitive nature of the location. Please follow any orders given by the security officials at the entrance to the Plaza. Men and women are requested to use separate checkpoints. I apologize for any inconvenience, but due to terrorist threats, you will be asked to present any bags, attaché cases and the like for inspection. Some might have to undergo quick body frisks. This security protocol is for your protection and for the protection of the millions of people who come each year to visit the Western Wall.

The need for tight security has created some problems. I recall one unpleasant incident in particular. In May, 2000, on *Yom Tov Sheini* of Pesach (Diaspora Jews are obligated to observe the first two days of Pesach and Succot), religious visitors from abroad were unable to enter Kotel area. They refused to pass through the electric gates, trying to avoid desecrating the Yom Tov. The overseas visitors politely asked the security guard to permit them to enter via the adjacent vehicle gate to search them by hand rather than obligate them to pass through the electric scanning gateway, explaining the religious restriction. The guard reportedly replied,

"It's not America here. Either pass through it or return to the city." This was not the first time that the issue arose. A resident of the Jewish Quarter of the Old City of Jerusalem claimed that a prominent rabbi from the Jewish Quarter sought to bypass the electrical gate on his way to the Kotel on the last day of Pesach, but was refused. Indeed, I was told that the official rabbi of the Jewish Quarter, HaRav Avigdor Nebenzahl, had not prayed at the Kotel on Shabbat for a two-month period prior to this incident because he refused to pass through the electric gate.

SOLDIERS, YOUTH AND ELDERLY MAN AT THE KOTEL
Note the two figures at the right. One is helping the other to correctly position the head tefillin so that it lies exactly above the middle of the forehead and so that its bottom-most edge rests at the point where the hairline begins above the forehead. Resting a portion of the head tefillin on the forehead contravenes a Torah directive.

The last time Rav Nebenzahl tried to enter through other means, the guards refused to let him pass and he was forced to pray alone near the barrier. Only after the Rabbi of the Wall, Rav Shmuel Rabinowitz, sent an urgent letter to the police commander of the Wall was he able to pass. Instructions were then issued to all the guards and police to permit those wishing to bypass the electric scanning gateway to enter from the side (non-electric checkpoint) gate on Shabbat and Jewish holidays.

Sanctity

After you have passed through the security checkpoint, you will see a wide-open plaza in front of an immense tall wall of stone. Depending on when you visit, you may find dozens or hundreds of worshippers at all hours of the day or night. You might see young and old, bearded and clean-shaven men with bowed heads, perhaps leaning against the ancient stones burnished from centuries of gentle fingers affectionately touching the stones as they utter their hopes and aspirations to their Creator. On the other hand, you might observe someone weeping over a personal tragedy. Touching or stroking the face of the stone as the range of deeply felt emotions gushes out of the human heart has a therapeutic effect on the supplicant.

Of course, not all those at the Kotel come to plead for help. Many come to thank HaShem or to celebrate a happy occasion.

Please respect the sanctity of the Western Wall. It is a place of worship. Frivolous behavior is out of place. The area in front of the Wall is separated in two — one side for women and one for men. Please shut off cell phones to avoid disturbing other people's prayers. You should be modestly attired so as not to offend the sensitivities of the men and women who are praying at the Wall. Men should wear either a hat or *kippah (yarmulke)* as a show of respect [head coverings are available at the entrance]. Avoid short-shorts, tank tops, and scanty dress. Do not be surprised if you see female attendants loaning out shawls to help cover visitors whose clothing is not quite right

It is improper to smoke at the Kotel. It is absolutely prohibited to smoke on the Sabbath and Festivals anywhere near the Kotel. Please do not use a camera or a cell phone on the Jewish Sabbath or Jewish holidays. Remember that the Jewish Sabbath begins Friday at sunset and continues through Saturday night. Jewish festivals and holy days begin the previous evening at sunset. Pets (except for guiding dogs) are not allowed into the Western Wall plaza.

Do not be confused by the busy and somewhat chaotic dynamic of the Kotel. Minyanim (prayer quorums) are assembled spontaneously throughout the day. Walk in at any time of the day and you will see men with black hats or crocheted *kippot (yarmulkes),* some dressed in long, black coats, others casually garbed. You'll find Chassidim, Haredim,

National Religious types as well as secular Jews circulating amongst tourists with camcorders or cameras, young hippies dressed unconventionally and non-Jews on world adventures exploring the fascination that is the Kotel.

Many like to come to the Kotel late at night, when the Wall radiates a sparkle of spirituality amidst the darkness that envelopes it. The ritual of reciting the Book of Psalms aloud begins around midnight, when the sky appears to retract as the stars and the moon take over. Jerusalem's streets feel empty and alone as its people sleep, while here at the Kotel an indescribable tranquility seems to hold sway. I am about to wrap up the day's gamut of deeply felt emotions consigned to me and my fellow stones. The heat of the day has given way to cool breezes that accompany the prayer recitations. It is almost 3 a.m. and the dedicated night visitors prepare to leave for a few hours of well-deserved sleep.

CHAPTER XXII

DESTRUCTION OF ANTIQUITIES ON THE TEMPLE MOUNT

Gevalt! (Yiddish expression of alarm)

It is December, 2001. In blatant disregard of our Jewish heritage, the Palestinians are digging a ditch from the northern side of the Temple Mount compound to the Dome of the Rock as a prelude to infrastructure work in the area. What alarms me is the indiscriminate use of a backhoe and tractor, which will — and has — caused serious damage to the artifact-rich site. I am enraged, shocked, and dismayed at the spinelessness of the Israeli government in not stopping the work being carried out by the Arabs (or Palestinians) who seek to deny the historical fact of Israel in antiquity, especially the presence of the ancient Jewish Temples. Their wanton destruction of archeological evidence is simply an effort to deny these findings to Israel and the world.

I am stunned! What could possibly justify this kind of devastation in such an archaeologically sensitive site? Who, in their right mind, would authorize such a contemptible activity? It is unforgivable.

Where is the public outcry? I'm appalled at the silence of Christians and Jews worldwide. The impotence of leading archaeologists to stop this desecration is mind-boggling! From what I hear, the police have approved the dig, but the Israel Antiquities Authority declined to respond to the *Waqf's* excavations and would not comment on whether one of its archaeologists had approved the move. The Committee for the Prevention of Destruction of Antiquities on the Temple Mount, an apolitical group comprised of archaeologists and intellectuals from the Left and the Right, criticized the use of a tractor for excavation at the Temple Mount "without real, professional and careful archaeological supervision involving meticulous documentation." Leading archaeologist Eilat Mazar said: "There is disappointment at the turning of a blind eye and the ongoing contempt for the tremendous archaeological importance of the Temple Mount." It is so sad to see these archeological treasures going to waste, which are of such significance to all of us, because of the Palestinian desire to create facts on the ground. It is clear that the government — out of fear — is hesitant to act or renew supervision at the [politically sensitive] site."

Contrast this with the violent protests from Muslims in Israel and around the world when Israel began excavations near the Temple Mount in order to rebuild the Mugrabi bridge walkway.

AERIAL VIEW: KOTEL IN RELATIONSHIP TO TEMPLE MOUNT

The Muslims built the Dome of the Rock on the site formerly occupied by the Temple. This was an affront to the Jews whose connection to the Temple Mount goes back more than 3,000 years. Jewish tradition and history are intertwined with this tiny piece of real estate. After the struggle for independence in 1948 and the miraculous recovery of our ancient and Holy City in 1967, Israel granted the Jordanians administrative control of the Mount. To this day, Jews are severely restricted from praying on the Temple Mount — our holiest site.

CHAPTER XXIII

Stories Prior to 1930

I have been privileged to host all kinds of visitors who have come to the Wall during the past centuries. Hundreds of travelers and pilgrims, Jews and non-Jews, wrote poignant and evocative descriptions of the Western Wall. Regrettably, there are hardly any references to the Kotel during the Middle Ages and are only sporadic during other periods. This is almost certainly due to the fact that Jews were not allowed to come within reach of it, let alone pray at it. The following stories, poems, and songs illustrate how the Wall has touched the hearts of Jews throughout the ages.

Fourth Century CE

"The sanctity which is attached to the Western Wall in Jewish tradition today evolved over the generations. The 4th century rabbi, Rav Aha, is reported in the *Shemot Rabbah* as having said that 'the Divine Presence never leaves the Western Wall'... Indeed some scholars believe that Rav Aha was referring to the Western Wall of the Temple itself, and when the Wall was destroyed, its sanctity was, so to speak, transferred to the Western, buttressed Wall (our Kotel), which still survived. Others maintain[160] that the reference cannot be to the actual Temple Wall, because Hadrian demolished the Temple completely and built a Temple to Jupiter in its place long before the sources were written and it would

---

160   See A.M. Lunz, Monograph *The Western Wall*, 1912

have been absurd to say about something that had been destroyed that it would never be destroyed."[161]

333 CE

An anonymous French Pilgrim who visited the Holy Land in 333 CE wrote about the Western Wall in his book, the *Bordeaux Pilgrim*. This substantiation of Jewish prayer at the Western Wall emerges repeatedly in accounts written by Christian travelers in the following centuries. "The Jews come there (the ruins of the Temple), once a year, weeping and wailing near a stone which survived the destruction of the Temple. There are two mountains of Hadrian there and not far away is a stone riddled through with holes to which the Jews come once a year. They anoint it (the stone), and wail and keen and rend their garments and so they return from there." Presumably, the 'stone riddled through with holes' refers to the Western Wall.[162]

11th Century

An 11th century chronicle, *Sefer haYuhasin (Megillat Ahimaatz)*, talks about the Western Wall.

1170

Benjamin of Tudela visited the Western Wall in 1170 and wrote: "The Temple Domini now stands on the Temple site. On that site, Omar ibn al-Khattab built a large and exceedingly beautiful Cupola. In front of that place is the Western Wall... and Jews go there to pray in front of the Wall in the courtyard... All the Jews, each and every one of them, write their names on the Wall."[163]

1210

Samuel Ben Shimshon came to Jerusalem in 1210: "We came to Jerusalem from the West and when we saw it we tore our garments, as

---

161 Reprinted with permission from: Meir Ben-Dov, Mordechai Naor and Zeev Aner (1987). *The Western Wall*, Ministry of Defense Publishing House, pg 65

162 Ibid. pg. 66

163 Ibid.

is proper, and we were filled with pity and we wept the great weeping. I and Rabbi Jonathan of Lunel entered by the gate near the Tower of David and we came to prostrate ourselves before the courtyard, and we bowed down before the gate, opposite which, from the direction of Ein Etam, which was the priests place of ablution, is a gate in the Western Wall."[164]

1333

Isaac ben Joseph ibn Chelo, a Kabbalist, wrote about the Western Wall in his book, *Shevilat Yerushalayim* (The Pathways of Jerusalem).

1488 — Its Stones Are Great and Thick.

From the 15th century onwards, descriptions of the Western Wall and its environs and the prayers there increased. Rabbi Obadiah of Bertinoro, who emigrated to Eretz Yisrael in 1488, wrote: "As to the Western Wall, which is still in existence — or at least part of it — its stones are great and thick. I have never seen such massive stones in any ancient building, not in Rome or elsewhere."[165]

1522

In 1522, when the Ottoman Turks already ruled the country, an anonymous traveler wrote: "The Western Wall, which survives, is not the whole of the Western side but only a portion of it, between 40 and 50 cubits long. For one half of its height, it is from Solomon's time as a larger ancient stones show. Below and above that section is new building."[166]

18th and 19th centuries — A Place of Devotion

Fortunately, a number of Jerusalem residents and travelers to the Holy Land recorded their observations describing past events relating to the Kotel, especially in the 18th and 19th centuries. The

---

164 Ibid.
165 Ibid. pg. 68
166 Ibid. pg. 68

Kotel and its surroundings persisted to be a place of devotion for the Jews.[167]

1786 — Non-Jew from Belgium

In 1786 a Belgian tourist Jean Zoualert wrote about the Wall: "Jews come to this place from all over the world out of the special respect they have for Solomon's Temple and the Holy of Holies in which was stored The Chair Of Glory, The Cherubs, and the Ark Of The Covenant, as well as the Manna and Aaron's Rod."[168]

1838 — Non-Jewish Geographical Researcher

In 1838, Edward Robinson, the father of modern geographical research into Eretz Yisrael, wrote of his visit to the Wall: "I went… to the place where the Jews are permitted to purchase the right of approaching the site of the Temple, and of praying and wailing over its ruins and the downfall of their nation. The spot… is approached only by a narrow, crooked Lane, which there terminates at the Wall in a very small open space. The lower part of the Wall is here composed of the same kind ancient stones, which we had before seen on the eastern side. Two old men, Jews, sat there upon the ground, reading together in a book of Hebrew prayers. On Fridays they assemble here in great numbers. It is the nearest point in which they can venture to approach their ancient Temple… Here, bowed into the dust, they may at least weep undisturbed over the fallen glory of their race; and bedew with their tears, the soil, which so many thousands of their forefathers once moistened with their blood."

1839

In 1839, Dr. Eliezer Levy, Sir Moses Montefiore's secretary, wrote: "On the third day I visited the thing most famous throughout the whole

---

167 See Löfgren, Eliel; Barde, Charles; Van Kempen, J. (December 1930). Report of the Commission appointed by His Majesty's Government in the United Kingdom of Great Britain and Northern Ireland, with the approval of the Council of the League of Nations, to determine the rights and claims of Muslims and Jews in connection with the Western or Wailing Wall at Jerusalem (UNISPAL doc A/7057-S/8427, 23 February 1968)

168 Meir Ben-Dov, Mordechai Naor and Zeev Aner. *The Western Wall*, Ministry of Defense Publishing House 1987, pg.74

Diaspora, the Western Wall, a memorial to ancient times... Jews gather in this holy place on Friday evenings to pray before G-d for the welfare of their brethren who live in foreign lands. They mentioned their benefactors by name and pray for each one separately.... We yesterday went to inspect the Western Wall of the Temple of Solomon (sic). How wonderful that it showed to have so long defied the ravages of time! The huge stones seem to cling together; to be cemented by a power mightier than decay, that they may be a memorial of Israel's past glory: and oh! May they not be regarded as a sign of future greatness, when Israel shall be redeemed, and the whole world shall, with one accord, sing praises to Israel's G-d!"[169]

1842

A non-Jewish Englishman, George Fisk, visited Eretz Yisrael in 1842 and, like many others, merges a portrayal of the then current pitiful state of affairs with fervent hopes for a better future:

"...On reaching the spot, we found a row of aged Jews sitting in the dust in front of the Wall, all of them engaged in reading or reciting certain portions of the Hebrew Scriptures ... Among them were several Jewesses, enveloped from head to foot in ample white veils. They stepped forward to various parts of the ancient Wall, kissed them with great fervency of manner, and uttered their petitions in a low whisper, at the points where the stones came in contact. Then I thought of Israel, when by the wonders of Babylon they sat down and wept; and could but lift up my heart for the hastening of the time when their King shall be again in the midst of them-no longer in humiliation, but in glory, and when all 'shall know him from the least to the greatest." [170]

Isaac Yehuda, well known in Jerusalem's Sephardic circles, recollects in his writings how men and women used to gather in a circle at the Wall to hear sermons delivered in Ladino. He relates how his great-grandmother, who arrived in Palestine in 1841, "used to go to the Western Wall every Friday afternoon, winter and summer, and stay there until candle-lighting time, reading the entire Book of Psalms and the Song of Songs...she would sit there by herself for hours."

---

169 Ibid. pg. 70

170 Ibid. pg. 74

1850 — Writing About the Kotel – Rabbi Joseph Schwarz

Rabbi Joseph Schwarz comments: "Thousands of Israelites constantly deplore there and weep for the fall of Jerusalem. It is touching to see how every Jew bends his head, moaning reverentially, at the foot of this holy Wall, and lifts up his tearful eyes to heaven, and exclaims, sobbing, "How long yet, O L-rd!" This spot is visited by travelers of all

MAN PRAYING WITH KAVANAH, HANDS ON KOTEL
Kavanah is the religious concentration associated with prayer, i.e., devotion in prayer. One who prays with kavanah is fully absorbed and focused on the prayer and on his nearness to G-d. It also connotes intent when one is engaged in performing a mitzvah or other religious rite.

nations; and no one can ever quit the place unmoved and with indifference. It is no vain fancy!

I have indeed often seen there non-Israelitish (sic) travellers melt into tears. No one can describe the feelings experienced on this sacred spot. One paints to himself in spirit the former exalted state of the Israelitish (sic) people in the highest degree, and then feels suddenly that it is sunk into the dust and robbed of its glory; but his imagination places again before him the future exaltation — he feels himself inspired, and exclaims, 'Surely this is the gate of heaven!'(Gen. 28:17) This Wall is visited by all our brothers on every feast and festival; and the large space at its foot is often so densely filled up, that all cannot perform their devotions here at the same time. It is also visited, though by less numbers, on every Friday afternoon, and by some nearly every day. No one is molested in these visits by the Mahomedans, as we have a very old firman (decree) from the Sultan of Constantinople that the approach shall not be denied to us."

1858 — Felix Bovet, a Protestant Theologian who Visited Palestine[171]

"The Christians who conquered the Land of Israel did not know how to hold it, and it was never anything more to them than a battleground and a graveyard. The Saracens, who took it from them also left, and it was then taken by the Turks and the Ottomans, who are still here. They have made a desert of it, and it is seldom possible to walk without fear. Even the Arabs, who dwell there, do so as sojourners. They set down their tents wherever there is pastureland, and seek refuge in the ruins of the towns. They did not create anything, as they were, in truth, strangers, not masters of the land. The spirit of the desert, which had brought them hither, could in the same fashion take them away and leave nothing behind. G-d, who has given Palestine to so many nations, has not permitted any one of them to establish itself, or to take root in it. No doubt it is reserved for His people, Israel."

1859

In his 1859 book, *Nach Jerusalem*, Ludwig A. Frankl commented: "I set my steps towards the ruins of the Temple, to the one Wall that has

---

171 Reprinted with permission from Prof. Ted Bolen, *The Master's College*; Bible Places.com;

survived, the wailing place of the Jews who gather there every Friday evening to pray the evening service and to bewail the Temple that was destroyed... After we passed through many streets, we came into a narrow, winding street and from there to the Wall. It is 158 feet long and 60 feet high, which height is made up of 23 stone courses of which the bottom nine are hewn stones, some of which are between 20 and 30 feet in length and 5 feet wide. Each of these slabs of stone is rounded and on their faces, which have been smoothed as though within instrument, there is a shining border about a finger's depth. Lying there, row on row, thin lines can be seen between them and so the whole Wall looks like a Wall of avenues of which the upper courses are of a later origin. From the shape of some of the hewn stones that jut out of the Wall, modern research has concluded that they are the remains of arches leading from the Temple Mount Zion. There can be no doubt that this Wall, with its courses of foundation stones under the ground, is a memorial for the Jews from Solomon's time which, as Jossipon put it, will never collapse. Anyone who has seen it can testify that it will not collapse until the very foundations of the earth will be shaken.[172]

"From a distance, we could already hear the sound of the wailing, a cry of pain, which pierced the very heart. In chorus, the appeal rang in our ears, 'How long, O Lor-d!' Jews were gathered there in their hundreds, some in the address of the Ishmaelites and others in the style of Poland, and, facing the Wall, they bowed and prostrated themselves. At a great distance from the men, stood the women all totally enveloped in white gowns-white doves, tired from their flying, resting on the ruins. When the Cantor reached those parts of the prayers to be said by the congregation, their voices rose among the choir of male voices, and spreading their arms on high, they looked in their wide white gowns for all the world, like wings spread upwards to the open gates of heaven. Afterwards, they smote their foreheads against the hewn stones of the Temple Wall. Then, when the Cantor, exhausted and wasted from his efforts, quietly and slowly weeping, turned his head to the Wall, then suddenly in a moment a deathly silence covered all."[173]

---

172 Reprinted with permission from: Meir Ben-Dov, Mordechai Naor and Zeev Aner (1987). *The Western Wall*, Ministry of Defense- Publishing House;pg. 70-71

173 Ibid. pg. 71

1860 — Mark Twain

In 1867, Jerusalem's population was 8,000 Jewish, 6,000 Muslim, and 3,800 Christian. Mark Twain recorded his 1867 visit to Jerusalem.[174]

"The population of Jerusalem is compose (sic) of Muslims, Jews, Greeks, Latins, Armenians, Syrians, Copts, Abyssinians, Greek Catholics, and a handful of Protestants... It seems to me that all the races and colors and tongues of the earth must be represented among the 14,000 souls that dwell in Jerusalem. Rags, wretchedness, poverty and dirt, those signs and symbols that indicate the presence of Muslim rule more surely than the crescent-flag itself, abound. Lepers, cripples, the blind, and the idiotic, assail you on every hand...

To see the numbers of maimed, malformed and diseased humanity that throng the holy places and obstruct the gates, one might suppose that the ancient days had come again... Jerusalem is mournful, and dreary, and lifeless. I would not desire to live here."

At that time, Jerusalem was under Ottoman rule and the Old City was a small lonely city with a Jewish majority who lived both within the Old City and the surrounding areas, including the area now deemed by many as "Palestinian East Jerusalem." As photos taken in the early 19th century at that time testify, many areas surrounding the Old City (the Mount of Olives, the City of David area, and Silwan) were largely unoccupied.

1863 — Rev. James W. Lee[175]

"On Friday afternoon, March 13, 1863, the writer visited this sacred spot. Here he found between one and two hundred Jews of both sexes and of all ages, standing or sitting, and bowing as they read, chanted and recited, moving themselves backward and forward, the tears rolling down many a face; they kissed the Walls and wrote sentences in Hebrew upon them... The lamentation which is most commonly used is from Psalm 79: 'O G-d, the heathen are come into Thy inheritance; Thy Holy Temple have they defiled.' "[176]

---

174 *Innocents Abroad*, Mark Twain visits Palestine (1867) Chapter 53

175 Ted Bolen, The Master's College; Bible Places.com; Excerpted from *Earthly Footsteps of the Man of Galilee*, pg.147

176 Ibid.

..."The old men and old women will yet sit in the streets of Yerushalay-im and the ruins of Yerushalayim will fill up with little boys and little girls playing in her streets."[177]

1864 — Norman McCleod

Norman McCleod, a distinguished Scottish clergyman wrote: "...One day I visited the Jews 'wailing place', certainly one of the most remarkable spots in the world. To see representatives of that people met here for prayer — to see them kissing those old stones — to know that this sort of devotion has probably been going on since the Temple was destroyed, and, down through those teeming centuries, which saw the decline and fall of the Roman Empire, and all the events of the history of modern Europe — to watch this continuous stream of sorrow, still sobbing against the old Wall, filled me with many thoughts. What light amidst darkness, what darkness amidst light; what undying hopes in the future, what passionate attachment to the past; what touching superstition, what, belief and unbelief! I found some slips of paper, bearing prayers written in neat Jewish characters, inserted between the stones of the old Wall."[178]

1881 — Charles Wilson[179]

Major General Charles Wilson obtained a commission in the Royal Engineers in 1855 and, while working in Palestine to improve the water supply of Jerusalem, wrote about various historic sites.

"Jews may often be seen sitting for hours at the Wailing-place bent in sorrowful meditation over the history of their race, and repeating oftentimes the words of the Seventy-ninth Psalm. On Fridays especially, Jews of both sexes, of all ages, and from all countries, assemble in large numbers to kiss the sacred stones and weep outside the precincts they may not enter."[180]

---

177 Zechariah 8:4-5
178 Ibid. pg 75–76
179 Reprinted with permission: Dr. Todd Bolen, Bibleplaces.com (*Picturesque Palestine*, Vol. 1, pg. 41)
180 Ibid.

1887 — Josias Leslie Porter[181]

An Irish explorer J.L. Porter has written about historic sites and ruins in Eretz Yisrael. A facsimile edition of the book first published in 1886 (limited edition):

It is a small paved quadrangle; on one side are the backs of low modern houses, without door or window; on the other is the lofty Wall of the *Haram,* of recent date above, but having below five courses of beveled stones in a good state of preservation. Here the Jews are permitted to approach the sacred enclosure, and wail over the fallen Temple, whose very dust is dear to them, and in whose stones they still take pleasure... Some were on their knees, chanting mournfully from a book of Hebrew prayers, swaying their bodies to and fro; some were prostrate (sic) on the ground, pressing forehead and lips to the earth; some were close to the Wall, burying their faces in the rents and crannies of the old stones; some were kissing them, some had their arms spread out as if they would clasp them to their bosoms, some were bathing them with tears, and all the while sobbing as if their hearts would burst. It was a sad and touching spectacle. Eighteen centuries of exile and woe have not dulled their hearts' affections, or deadened their feelings of national devotion.[182]

1889 — Mordechai ben Hillel haKohen

In 1889, Mordechai ben Hillel haKohen,[183] a Jewish tourist from Russia, described his reaction — so typical of Diaspora Jews who visited the Kotel for the first time.

"I started to organize my stay in the city (Jerusalem), but I soon realized that I did not have the strength to withstand the desire — nay! the urgent need — to hurry to the Western Wall. I remember nothing of the way I went; my legs bore me, and I went blindly like an animal following its herder. My eyes were lifted aloft all the time straining to catch the

---

181 Ted Bolen, The Master's College; Bible Places.com; Excerpted from *Jerusalem, Bethany and Bethlehem* (on openlibrary.org)

182 Reprinted with permission from Porter, Josias Leslie (1887). *Jerusalem, Bethany, and Bethlehem.* pp. 39–40.

183 Mordechai Ben Hillel haKohen, a Hebrew writer, Zionist and one of the founders of Tel Aviv.

first glimpse of the Wall. 'This is the Western Wall,' murmured my guide in a holy whisper; but I would have known anyway… I do not remember how my shoes left my feet, how I fell length on the ground, how I started kissing the flagstones under me or how I began weeping such copious tears they became torrents. My heart was in turmoil. I did not attempt to control myself or stop the flow of tears which I wept like a small infant without sense or words. The attendant did not approve and interrupted me, handing me a Psalter and showing me the verses which were to be recited at the Wall. Idiot! Did he not realize that at that the moment I had no need of any verses, of any prayer book or of any liturgy!?

"It was not want my eyes saw or the desolation at the Wall that so struck me but rather my inner soul-feeling. For in its appearance there is nothing in this Wall to so disturb the strings of a man's heart and to incite such a storm inside a Jew. There is not even destruction there. The stones have been burned with fire, the Wall is not destroyed, the rows of its stones do not cast the shadow of death and, generally, surely the terrible destruction deserves a more fitting memorial than that given by this Wall?!" After having said all this, I still must say that what this Wall does is truly awesome; for so great is the holy trepidation that falls on the Jew in this place that for the sake of the Wall and for its sake alone every Jew should make a pilgrimage to Jerusalem."[184]

"The place to which every Jew who visits Jerusalem turns first," is how A. S. Hirschberg, the author of *Eretz Chemda*, defined the Western Wall, which he first visited in 1901. These words and this small anthology, which has indicated the interest — both Jewish and non-Jewish — the Western Wall has aroused for many centuries, from the early days after the destruction of the Temple. This is what Hirschberg wrote: "On the day after I arrived, I went with one of my young friends to the Western Wall… We came to the vegetable market and from there we passed through narrow, crooked streets, some climbing and some descending, and through alleys, some of which were open and, most of which had stone Walls on both sides (for the Arabs build their houses inside the courtyards) until we came to a small, narrow alley. One side of this was the Western Wall and the other side was a solid wall of one of the hovels of the Magreb Quarter.

---

184 Reprinted with permission from: *The Western Wall*, Ministry of Defense Publishing House; Meir Ben-Dov, Mordechai Naor and Zeev Aner (1987) pg. 71-73

"When I arrived, there were only two men standing in front of the Wall praying and a few Sephardic beggars asking for alms. Some of the beggars were standing and some were sitting on the ground or on boxes that they had brought with them. The Sephardi beadle came over to me and made a tear in the side of my coat and gave me a little prayer book from which to recite the special prayer for one's first visit to the Wall. I began to mumble the prayer and suddenly I started to weep as I never had until that day, and I was not able to control myself. I was in shock. The walk through the squalid streets and filthy alleys, the appearance of the Arabs with their dirty children dressed in rags and barefoot, had depressed me so much that nothing I saw could impress me. When I came to the Wall, I did feel that I was standing in the holy place, but my senses were dulled and my heart laid waste. Then came this prayer touching on all ills man is heir to, replaying all the aches in the inner heart and the dam broke! All my private troubles mingled with our nation's misfortune to form a torrent. Here I was, standing before the Wall, this silent witness to Israel's glory of ancient times and against it I saw all those places and all those times of suffering and torture throughout the whole world and all history! The inquisitions and the pogroms that have been visited on our pitiful nation passed before my eyes — and these stones do not move... Tears blind me and the letters in the prayerbook dance before my eyes. My nerves jangle and my innermost emotions are totally shaken and sweep over me so that I am almost faint... I turned to escape like a fugitive from the Wall without finishing the prayer I had started, but the Beadle held me and gave me a wick to kindle in the small inferior oil lamp that stood at the end of the Wall. For me it was as though he had given me a memorial candle to kindle for the soul of our people dying there in exile.

"For the six months of my stay in Jerusalem, it was the Wall that attracted me most. It is the one and only memorial to our ancient greatness that is authenticated by our tradition and by scholarly research. The Jews of Jerusalem flock there regularly for prayers, particularly for the afternoon and evening services on the Eve of the Sabbath and festivals and for the additional services on those days themselves... They stand before the Wall in groups, and the recitation of the holy prayers never ceases. All kinds of Jews are there. Thin, scrawny, sharp-nosed

Yemenites dressed in poor, worn Arab robes recite the prayers in their unique pronunciation. A quorum of rich, fact, elegantly clad Sephardim, in their black coats with *tarbooshes* on their well-groomed heads, say the prayers solemnly and with great dignity. At their side is a group of Perushim, dressed in the weird mixture of East and West with medieval Polish fur hats on their heads; honored old men and earnest, pale young men screw up their faces to achieve that concentration fitting for prayer to G-d. And there are groups of Hasidim, in their kaftans of red, gold, or sky-blue silk and velvet, who shake themselves violently until their side locks flail, as they respond, 'Holy, Holy, Holy is the Lor-d of Hosts' in great ecstasy. And the women! The Ashkenazi women stand away off and jump little jumps as they respond to every *keddushah* prayer they hear. The Sephardic ladies love the Wall with a special love and most of them come to it enveloped in white sheets. Those who cannot read the texts of the prayers make modest prayerful signs to the Wall. All, when they leave, kiss each stone individually and back away as though they were leaving the royal presence, stretching out their fingers towards it with eyes raised on high.

"The square stones of the Wall, arranged one on top of the other, join together with no sign of cement; these stones which, scratched and cracked though they be, are not consumed in the teeth of time, are a symbol to the people that stands before them in prayer... How can they fail to excite and exalt the heart of every Jew who comes for the first time to the Wall?!"

Stories from 1930 to 1966

Rabbi Moshe Tsvi Segal - 1930 — The Shofar and the Wall[185]

Note: What follows is an excerpt (translated from the Hebrew) from the memoir of Rabbi Moshe Segal (1904–1985), a Lubavitcher Chassid who was active in the struggle to free the Holy Land from British rule.

In those years, the area in front of the Kotel did not look as it does today. Only a narrow alley separated the Kotel and the Arab houses on its

---

185 Reprinted with permission from Chabad.org http://www.chabad.org/library/article_cdo/aid/2246/jewish/The-*Shofar*-and-the-Wall.htm

other side. The British Government forbade us to place an Ark, tables or benches in the alley; even a small stool could not be brought to the Kotel. The British also instituted the following ordinances, designed to humble the Jews at the holiest place of their faith: it is forbidden to pray out loud, lest one upset the Arab residents; it is forbidden to read from the Torah (those praying at the Kotel had to go to one of the synagogues in the Jewish Quarter to conduct the Torah reading); it is forbidden to sound the shofar on Rosh Hashanah and Yom Kippur. The British Government placed policemen at the Kotel to enforce these rules.

MAN BLOWING SHOFAR DURING ELUL

The reverberating shofar reminds us of the time when the Jews in the desert blew the shofar every evening while Moses was on Har Sinai, concluding with Moses' descent on Yom Kippur. During the month of Elul, we too sound the shofar every morning to sense for ourselves the imagery of Moses climbing the mountain on the morning of the first day to receive the second pair of Tablets, marking G-d's forgiveness. Knowing that G-d forgave the Children of Israel after they sinned with the Golden Calf creates a climate in which tefillah, teshuva, and tzedakah may very well bring about G-d's forgiveness for our sins.

On Yom Kippur of that year [1930] I was praying at the Kotel. During the brief intermission between the Musaf and Minchah prayers, I overheard people whispering to each other: "Where will we go to hear the shofar? It'll be impossible to blow here. There are as many policemen as people praying..." The Police Commander himself was there; to make sure that the Jews will not, G-d forbid, sound the single blast that closes the fast.

I listened to these whisperings, and thought to myself: Can we possibly forgo the sounding of the shofar that accompanies our proclamation of the sovereignty of G-d? Can we possibly forgo the sounding of the shofar, which symbolizes the redemption of Israel? True, the sounding of the shofar at the close of Yom Kippur is only a custom, but "A Jewish custom is Torah!"

I approached Rabbi Yitzchak Horenstein, who served as the Rabbi of our "congregation," and said to him: "Give me a shofar."

"What for?"

"I'll blow."

"What are you talking about? Don't you see the police?"

"I'll blow."

The Rabbi abruptly turned away from me, but not before he cast a glance at the prayer stand at the left end of the alley. I understood: the shofar is in the stand. When the hour of the blowing approached, I walked over to the stand and leaned against it.

I opened the drawer and slipped the shofar into my shirt. I had the shofar, but what if they saw me before I had a chance to blow it? I was still unmarried at the time, and following the Ashkenazi custom, did not wear a *tallit*. I turned to the person praying at my side, and asked him for his *tallit*. My request must have seemed strange to him, but the Jews are a kind people, especially at the holiest moments of the holiest day, and he handed me his *tallit* without a word.

I wrapped myself in the *tallit*. At that moment, I felt that I had created my own private domain. All around me, a foreign government prevails, ruling over the people of Israel even on their holiest day and at their holiest place, and we are not free to serve our G-d; but under this *tallit* is another domain. Here I am under no dominion save that of my Father in Heaven; here I shall do as He commands me, and no force on earth will stop me.

When the closing verses of the Ne'illah prayer "Hear O Israel," "Blessed be the name" and "The L-rd is G-d" proclaimed, I took the shofar and blew a long, resounding blast. Everything happened very quickly. Many hands grabbed me. I removed the *tallit* from over my head, and before me stood the Police Commander, who ordered my arrest.

I was taken to the *kishle*, the prison in the Old City, and an Arab policeman was appointed to watch over me. Many hours passed; I was given no food or water to break my fast. At midnight, the policeman received an order to release me, and he let me out without a word.

I then learned that when the chief rabbi of the Holy Land, Rabbi Avraham Yitzchak Kook, heard of my arrest, he immediately contacted the secretary of High Commissioner of Palestine, and asked that I be released. When his request was refused, he stated that he would not break his fast until I was freed. The High Commissioner resisted for many hours, but finally, out of respect for the Rabbi, he had no choice but to set me free.

For the next eighteen years, until the Arab conquest of the Old City in 1948, the shofar was sounded at the Kotel every Yom Kippur. The British well understood the significance of this blast; they knew that it will ultimately demolish their reign over our land as the Walls of Jericho crumbled before the shofar of Joshua, and they did everything in their power to prevent it. But every Yom Kippur, the shofar was sounded by men who know they would be arrested for their part in staking our claim on the holiest of our possessions.

1944 — Shofar at the Kotel

"I was very early for a meeting in Jerusalem this morning, so I wandered around and stumbled upon a plaque containing the following tidbit:

"In the summer of 1944, after a nearly fourteen-year ban on Jews blowing the shofar at the Kotel, the Irgun (or Etzel) sent word to the officials of the British Mandate that they planned on blowing the shofar at the end of the upcoming Yom Kippur... at the Kotel. The Irgun warned that members of the British forces should keep clear of the Kotel at that time, and that the Irgun would 'punish' those who chose to ignore this warning. To everyone's surprise, the British took the warning seriously.

No British official showed up, the shofar was blown, followed by a spontaneous outburst of the singing of *Hatikva*.

Wow, our founding fathers sure had guts."[186]

SWEARING-IN CEREMONY
All IDF recruits receive their corps beret upon completion of their basic training at a swearing-in ceremony. Infantry units and some others, such as military police, swear in at the Western Wall. It is an emotional moment for family and friends as they celebrate their loved ones and their wholehearted allegiance to the State of Israel.

---

186 http://israelinthemaking.blogspot.com/2009/06/i-was-very-early-for-meeting-in.html, posted June 17, 2009

CHAPTER XXIV

1967 — Stories of Israeli Soldiers Who Took Part In The Liberation.

I want to share with you the following stories:

Dr. Moshe Amirav, a paratrooper, describes his first minutes at the Wall

We ran there, a group of panting soldiers, lost on the Plaza of the Temple Mount, searching for a giant stone Wall. We did not stop to look at the Mosque of Omar even though this was the first time we had seen it close up.

Forward! Forward! Hurriedly, we pushed our way through the Magreb Gate and suddenly we stopped, thunderstruck. There it was before our eyes! Gray and massive, silent and restrained — the Western Wall!

Slowly, slowly I began to approach the Wall in fear and trembling like a pious cantor going to the lectern to lead the prayers. I approached it as the messenger of my father and my grandfather, of my great-grandfather and of all the generations in all the exiles who had never merited seeing it — and so they had sent me to represent them. Somebody recited the festive *Sh'Hechiyanu* blessing: "Blessed are You, O L-rd our G-d, King of the Universe who has kept us alive, and maintained us and brought us to this time." But I could not answer "Amen." I put my hand on the stones and the tears that started to flow were not my tears. They were the tears of all Israel, tears of hope and prayer, tears of Chasidic tunes, tears of Jewish dances, tears which scorched and burned the heavy gray stone.[187]

I wrote the above story on June 8th, 1967 as I lay wounded in Hadassah Hospital in Jerusalem, waiting for surgery to remove a small piece of copper shrapnel in my head from the battle for the liberation of Jerusalem. Far more than my wound preoccupied me, I was overwhelmed by my encounter the day before with the Kotel. The paratroopers' meeting with the Kotel, which has been documented and filmed so extensively, symbolized, more than any other event, the magnificent victory of the Six-Day War for the country and the nation. I felt that we, all the paratroopers that participated in the battle for Jerusalem, became representatives, messengers of generations of Jews who sent us to liberate the city they yearned for, prayed and dreamed about for 2,000 years.

I knew Menachem Mendel, a frequent visitor to our home in Netanya, since my childhood. He was a strange and grumpy man. I never saw even so much as a shadow of a smile on his lips. My father once told me that he spent his life mourning "not for his family, but for Zion." My father also told me that he was a member of a group called Mourners of Zion which gathered in his home. "And what do they do?" I asked, and my father answered: "They miss the Western Wall." My curiosity, the curiosity of a twelve-year-old, was aroused. Thus, in 1957, I arrived at a Mourners of Zion meeting in Netanya. My mouth open in wonder, I spent the evening listening to Menacham Mendel's stories about the history of the Mourners of Zion throughout the generations and diasporas. "Even in the Treblinka concentration camp," Menachem Mendel told me, "we had a group of Mourners of Zion. One day a week, we would torment our souls by

---

187 Permission granted by Dr. Moshe Amirav (http://www.aish.com/jw/j/48964231.html)

fasting." I couldn't believe my ears! Even in the death camp people fasted as a sign of mourning for the destruction of the Temple!

When I parted from him, he told me something I remembered for many years: "It says in Tractate *Baba Batra*: 'Whoever mourns for Jerusalem will be privileged to see it in its joy.'" And thus, in those years, the years of my youth, while my friends spent their leisure time having fun, I was busy mourning a captive Jerusalem on the other side of the border.

On Monday, the 5th of June 1967, I arrived in Western Jerusalem as a soldier in a paratrooper brigade. All through that night, we advanced from house to house under heavy fire. The battalion advanced to the east; I knew that it was in the direction of the Old City and the goal was clear: the Western Wall. At the end of that night, which was the longest in my life, we arrived in the area near the Rockefeller Museum. I climbed up onto the roof of the adjacent building and in dawn's first light I was able to see — Jerusalem.

A Jordanian shell exploded on the roof of the building. As a result of the blast, I flew up in the air. I felt a piece of shrapnel ripping my face and it felt as though it was blowing up my head. Immediately, my face bled and all I heard were screams of "Medic, Medic!" Ofer the medic stopped the bleeding by bandaging me quickly and professionally. He calmed me down by saying: "In a few minutes, a rescue jeep will get here and take you to the hospital." I understood that for me, the war was over. "But I have to get to the Kotel!" I cried. Ofer looked at me as though I'd lost my mind: "That's what interests you now, the Western Wall?!"

A few hours later, I was already at Hadassah Hospital in Ein Kerem. I could hear the echo of shooting from the Old City. The next morning, we listened to the broadcast of the Voice of Israel reporter, Raphael Amir: "At this moment, I am going down the stairs toward the Western Wall... I am touching the stones of the Western Wall..." Sounds of gunfire could be heard in the background mixed with the elated cries of the soldiers and the sounds of shofar blowing. I could not continue listening to the broadcast. I got out of bed and told Motti, who was lying in the bed next to mine: "I am going to the Kotel!" I smile now when I remember how I ran to the Kotel, holding Motti's hand since I could hardly see where to go. We did not take our time — we ran quickly, past the Moghrabi Gate, pushing forward in a hurry. Suddenly we stopped, thunderstruck. Standing opposite us was the Western Wall: gray, huge, silent, and restrained. I remembered feeling this awe-struck only once before, as a child, when my father brought me close to the Holy Ark.

Slowly, I began my approach to the Kotel, feeling like a *shaliach tzibbur*, a cantor praying for a congregation; representing my father Herschel Zvi of Jerusalem and Lithuania, representing Grandfather Moses and Grandfather Yisrael who were slaughtered in Punar, representing my teacher and rabbi Mourner of Zion Menachem Mendel and his entire family that was killed in Treblinka, representing the poet Uri Zvi Greenberg whose poems I knew by heart and had sent me here.

Someone near me made the *Sh'Hecheyanu* blessing, but I could not answer "Amen". I just put a hand on the stone and the tears that streamed from my eyes were part water and part prayers, tunes, and longing of generations of Mourners of Zion.

I came back to the hospital later that day to undergo surgery to remove the piece of shrapnel from my head. The next day, lying in bed, I wrote "A Paratrooper's Story." The story was published in a book about the paratrooper's brigade, "Lion's Gate," and from there it reached other books and publications until a renewed adaptation found its rightful place in the light and glass exhibit — The Generations Center near the Western Wall.

Abraham Duvdevani's First Encounter with the Wall:

"Narrow alleys, filthy passageways, garbage at the entrances of shuttered shops, the stench of dead legionnaires — but we paid no attention. Our eyes were fixed on the golden dome which could be seen from a distance. There, more or less, it had to be! We marched faster to keep up with the beating of our hearts. We met a soldier from one of the forward units and asked him the way and hurried on. We went through a gate and down some steps. I looked to the right and stopped dead. There was the Wall in all its grandeur and glory! I had never seen it before, but it was an old friend, impossible to mistake. Then I thought that I should not be there because the Wall belongs in the world of dreams and legends and I am real.

Reality and legend, dream and deed, all unite here. I went down and approached the Wall and stretched out my hand towards the huge, hewn stones. But my hand was afraid to touch and of itself returned to me. I closed my eyes, took a small, hesitant step forward, and brought my lips to the Wall. The touch of my lips opened the gates of my emotions and the tears burst forth. A Jewish soldier in the State of Israel is kissing history with his lips.

Past, present, and future — all in one kiss. There will be no more destruction and the Wall will never again be deserted. It was taken with young Jewish blood and the worth of that blood is eternity. The body is coupled to the rows of stones, the face is pushed into the spaces between them and the hands try to reach its heart. A soldier near me mumbles in disbelief, 'We are at the Wall, at the Wall...' "[188]

Avraham Schechter: Was I dreaming? Was it real?

My commander touched me and asked "Are you wounded?" I leaned on the side, I couldn't move. I woke up and saw the Kotel. I came close, and started praying, and the words of the prayer, the words I say each day, were different. I felt as if I added on to them the wish that we will never return this place, it's so dear to us and we've paid for it with so much blood after long years of yearning for it. I said the *Amida* prayer and asked that this place always be ours, for eternity ours. I felt Someone was listening to my prayer up there, and pleased, and that it was accepted. I felt my body weightless. I was floating. Then I heard the shofar blowing and I got the chills and felt my body burning. Friends told me I cried like a child. I wrote home on a piece of scrap paper that I envied no one — I was in the unit that broke into the Old City and got to the Kotel.[189]

1973 — The Soldiers Are Weeping[190]

By Yehuda HaEzrachi

The Wall, did not only draw to it the soldiers, the public figures and the rabbis. It drew everybody! Among those who squeezed and pushed

---

188 Reprinted with permission from aish.com

189 Ibid.

190 Reprinted with permission from: *The Western Wall*, Ministry of Defense Publishing House; Meir Ben-Dov, Mordechai Naor and Zeev Aner (1987) , pgs.155-156

themselves into the packed prayer area, were representatives of the press from Israel and abroad; writers and poets, many of whom set down their impressions of those early hours for posterity. Among them was Yehuda HaEzrachi:

"I ran after a group of soldiers to the southwest corner of the compound (the Temple Mount), towards a little green gate, the Maghreb gate. The gate was wide open and soldiers were coming and going through it to the noise of their heavy boots and their heavy tired breathing. From it leads a narrow alley with a sharp right turn to narrow, steep steps — to the Western Wall.

"In this suddenness I at first saw only the stones. It was a suddenness long-awaited for interminable hours mingled with fire and explosions but sudden nonetheless. I saw the sacred stones and, wondrously, it was as though I had already been there only the other day. They are so familiar. No, not the other day, but generations ago! They are so old; breathing in the touches and the caresses and the weeping and the dirges and the supplications and prayers of generation after generation. And maybe, even before then, outside of time, when motionless, my mother stood by them, her frozen posture like a prayer to G-d. I first saw them and I had already known them for generations. 'The Stones,' my mother said then. Here they are, now, in front of me, in their courses. Suddenly, I remember their smoothness, every crack, every bit of roughness, every sign of the stone mason's hand, every erosion of the rain and the wind, every indentation where the strange bushes lay down their roots, every flicker of light and shadow. But first, I saw only the stones.

"They towered above me, course on course, and I stand by them. Then my gaze started searching for this secret places (sic), looking for redemption. Slowly it went up, searching from below, from the course my hands were touching, to the course above it; from the deep dimness like a waterless river pressing its dry banks, to the courses above it, higher and higher. So close! The stones of themselves lead my eyes from the depths upwards, until they come to the living roof, to the patch of sky.

"Soldiers are standing there. Standing in their sweat stained, dusty camouflage outfits, dirty with the smoke of shooting and the blood of wounds — maybe their own, maybe their friends' who were hit or killed while fighting at their side. They are wearing steel helmets and they are laden with rifles, machine guns, ammunition, mines, and frozen faces. Look! One of them stretches out his black hand, hesitantly, to the old stones and touches them lightly. Another pushes the palms of his hands against the stones, then his body and his face into the courses. Another looks up, to on high. And I see, astonished, tears flash in their eyes. Perhaps it is the Divine Presence, in the form of a white dove which cries human tears, that hovers above them in the little patch of blue sky. Hardened, frozen-faced soldiers are standing here — and they are weeping.

"My mother is standing here. She is wearing a large straw hat with a wide brim, shadowing her forehead. 'Mother,' I called to her. Her hand touched and did not touch these stones, known so well, so ancient, that rise up above us."

Israel's Defense Minister Moshe Dayan proclaimed:

"This morning, the Israel Defense Forces liberated Jerusalem. We have united Jerusalem, the divided capital of Israel. We have returned to the holiest of our holy places, never to part from it again. To our Arab neighbors we extend, also at this hour — and with added emphasis at this hour — our hand in peace. And to our Christian and Muslim fellow citizens, we solemnly promise full religious freedom and rights. We did not come to Jerusalem for the sake of other peoples' holy places, and not to interfere with the adherents of other faiths, but in order to safeguard its entirety, and to live there together with others, in unity."

Prime Minister Levi Eshkol — Israel's Peaceful Intent:

"Peace has now returned with our forces in control of the entire city and its environs. You may rest assured that no harm whatsoever shall come to the places sacred to all religions. I have requested the Minister of Religious Affairs to get in touch with the religious leaders in the Old City in order to ensure regular contact between them and our forces, so as to make certain that the former may continue their spiritual activities unhindered."

Yitzhak Rabin — No Time for Weeping

When Israeli military forces captured the Old City of Jerusalem on the third day of the Six-Day War, Yitzhak Rabin was commander-in-chief of the IDF, the Israel Defense Forces. He wrote about his experiences when they reached the most sacred shrine in Judaism, the Western Wall:

"Driving toward the Lions Gate, on the eastern side of the Old City Wall, we were surrounded by signs of the previous day's fighting. The smoldering tanks filed by the gate itself. The narrow alleys of the Old City, with their shuttered windows and locked doors, were totally deserted. But every now and then the eerie silence was broken by sniper fire from Jordanian soldiers who had failed to flee in time and continued to resist.

"As we made our way through the streets I remembered from child-hood, pungent memories played on my emotions. The sheer excitement increased as we came closer to the Western Wall itself. It is still easy for me to conjure up the feelings that assaulted me then, but it's very difficult to put them into words. The Wall once was and is our national memento of the glories of Jewish and pendants in ancient times. Its stones have a power to speak to the hearts of Jews the world over, as if the historical memory of the Jewish people is in the cracks between those ancient ash-lars. For years I secretly harbored the dreams that I might play a part not only in gaining Israel's independence but in restoring the Western Wall to the Jewish People, making it the focal point of our hard won independ-ence. Now that dream has come true, and suddenly I wondered why I of all men, should be so privileged. I knew that never again in my life would I experience quite the same peak of elation.

"When we reached the Western Wall, I was breathless. It seemed as though all the tiers of centuries were striving to break out of the men crowded into that narrow valley, while all the hopes of generations pro-claimed: 'This is no time for weeping! It is a moment of redemption, of hope...' We stood among the tangle of rugged, battle weary men who were unable to believe their eyes or restrain their emotions. Their eyes were moist with tears, their speech incoherent. The overwhelming desire was to cling to the Wall, to hold on to that great moment as long as possible."[191]

---

191 Thanks to Jewish Lights Publishing. Story by Yitzhak Rabin, "No Time for Weeping"
     Jewish Stories From Heaven and Earth edited by Dov Peretz Elkins

Reflections — Stones With a Human Heart

by Yossi Gamzu's Reflections[192]

Yossi Gamzu is a lyricist, most famous for writing the words to the following song:

A girl stood facing the Kotel
She drew her lips and chin close to it.
She said to me, the shofar's blasts are strong
But the silence is even stronger.
She told me: Zion, the Temple Mount
She was silent, about the reward and the right.
And what shone on her forehead at evening
Was the purple of royalty.
The Kotel, moss and sadness.
The Kotel, lead and blood.
There are people with a heart of stone.
There are stones with a human heart.
The paratrooper stood at the Kotel.
Of his whole division — the only one.
He told me that death has no image
But it has a diameter —
Nine millimeters only.
He told me, I'm not shedding tears
And again lowered his glance.
But my grandfather, G-d knows,
Is buried here, on *Har haZeitim* (the Mount of Olives).
The Kotel...
She stood, dressed in black, at the Kotel.
The mother of one of the infantry soldiers.
She told me, it's the eyes of my son that are shining
And not the candles on the Wall.
She told me: I'm not writing
Any note to hide between the cracks.

---

192   Reprinted with permission: Western Wall Heritage Foundation

Because what I gave to the Kotel only last night
Is greater than any words or writing.[193]

Yossi Gamzu Conveys his Feelings:[194]

The Kotel — moss and sadness
The Kotel — lead and blood.
There are people with hearts of stone,
There are stones with human hearts.

MAN BESEECHING G-D
"Hear our voices" (Shema Koleinu) is the 16th blessing of the Shemoneh Esrei, beseeching G-d to accept our prayers. Here the man has lifted up his hands (nasa kapav el) toward G-d.

---

193 (Translated from the Hebrew)
Reprinted with permission from: Western Wall Heritage Foundation, and thanks to
http://www.hebrewsongs.com/song-hakotel.htm
194 Ibid.

"The liberation and reunification of Jerusalem united more than the physical city itself. It united hearts and minds across the entire spectrum of the Jewish nation. From religious rabbis to secular poets; from old people who remembered touching the stones to young children who only had the memory of other people's memories... The liberation of the Old City, and particularly the Western Wall, carried immense implications for all."

Yossi Gamzu wrote these words only hours after the liberation of the Old City, while standing with a group of military reporters in the narrow alleyway of the Kotel.

"In contrast to the mass number of albums that glorified the war and its heroes," relates Gamzu, "In this song, I sought out the human stories."

Rabbi Zvi Yehuda Kook[195]

It is fascinating to note that Gamzu was not the first to find the heart in the stones of the Kotel.

In *"Behind Our Wall,"* Rabbi Zvi Yehuda Kook described the Kotel in the following way:

"...Even if the shame of the destruction covers its appearance,
even if the signs of destruction stand out prominently from its back,
and the clouds of desolation overshadow its radiance...
even if it is hidden behind the thicket of shady and filthy alleys,
and even if it is pushed aside and squashed in the battle of its neighbors
who surround it from every angle and try to invade its borders,
to diminish and wipe it out —
Like a stone fortress, it stands guard,
without moving and without its internal glory weakening,
pure and exalted in the strength of its identity...
Because it is a remnant of something holy and precious.
There are hearts and there are hearts —
there are human hearts and hearts of stone.
There are stones and there are stones —
there are stones that look like stones,
and there are stones which are actually hearts..."[196]

---

195   Reprinted with permission:The Western Wall Heritage Foundation [www.TheKotel.org]
196   Ibid.

"The Heart of the Matter"[197]

by Joseph Hermoni

What did the listeners, wherever they were, feel? Joseph Hermoni of Kibbutz Ayelet haShachar describes how he heard the news:

"Wednesday, 28th of Iyar, the third of the Six Days. We were sitting wherever it was, glued to a tiny transistor radio. The generation of the transistor — this little instrument with its batteries breathing their last — succeeded in letting us hear the beat of the wings of history. Just so!

"Those were the ten seconds when we accompanied the voice-choked reporter of the Israel Broadcasting Service on his way to the Wall. I do not know that broadcaster's name, but he deserves the thanks of all of us

AD HOC PRAYER — MINYANS
At all times of the day from dawn through nighttime, men coalesce around to form a minyan (quorum of ten men). This spontaneous, spur-of-the-moment assemblage for the purpose of prayer is man's connection to G-d. Indeed, prayer is founded on the premise that finite human beings can communicate with the infinite Holy One, Blessed be He. This appears to be an innate human need.

because he succeeded in suddenly making clear how stupid is the devious controversy over 'Who is a Jew?'

"(He) succeeded because he stood before us naked, vulnerable, after he had lost all his armor of professionalism. He did not talk with the newspaper man's objectivity, he wasn't articulate, he couldn't even control the recording machine he was carrying. That's why we all felt how history was beating its wings..."

Others' hearts ached because at such a time they were far away from what was happening. That is how Major General, Ezer Weizman, Chief of Operations in the GHQ, felt. On June 7, he had joined the forces which were meant to take Sharm El Sheik and in his memoirs, *'Yours are the Heavens; Yours is the Earth,'* he writes: We started to get organized there. I radioed: Tell Moti (Hod) that he should tell Dayan that everything is under control and the straits are in our hands, open to Israeli shipping. They answered, we cannot tell Dayan, he is at the Wall. I nearly fell over. Somebody was with me and I said to him, my lousy luck! For years I've been dreaming of it! And look. At this historic moment when everybody's at the Wall, where am I? Stuck in the most faraway place of the war!

"...My friend Benjamin has gone mad, he is screaming with all his strength: 'The Old City of Jerusalem — Jerusalem of Gold!' It is hard to describe how we look — dirty four-day-old stubble, dirty from the dust, from the soot of the shells, from the torn up tarmac of the roads. But morale is very high. About seven in the evening we are gathered around our only transistor radio to listen to the news. The transistor's batteries are weak and reception is poor. Seven pairs of ears are glued to the transistor. A cold evening in the desert. We are receiving the broadcast about the conquest of the Old City. We listen hard. The Chief of Staff is speaking and also Rabbi Goren. The broadcaster is describing how he is going down behind the soldiers to the Western Wall. His voice is excited; choked with tears. We, hundreds of kilometers beyond the border, are no less excited. On the radio, we hear the shofar. Staff Sgt. Harel, a religious fellow who prays every morning at dawn, cannot hold back his tears. After they said the *Kaddish* prayer at the Wall, we heard the *Hatikva*. There, at sunset in a yellow waste surrounded by purple ridges, we stood to attention spontaneously and joined the singing coming from the radio. Seven men in seven hoarse, tired voices sang. Before we finished the last stanza, the mobile artillery crew realized what had happened and they joined in and before they finished the half tracks crew also joined in. The desert echoed with the strains of *Hatikva* from the truck to the half track and from the half track to the tank...

MEN PRAYING AT KOTEL
What is prayer from a Jewish perspective? Is it a conversation with G-d? Is it an outpouring of the human heart? Is it man's quest for the Divine? Is it praise of the Almighty? Is it a petition or supplication? Is it a confession, meditation or thanksgiving? Jewish tradition maintains that there is a real G-d who hears the individual prayers of all mankind, rich and poor, powerful and weak. Moreover G-d Himself answers those pleas (Psalms 91:15) — there is a personal relationship between man and G-d. As such, prayer is all of the above and more.

"So it was... The scene at the Wall, on Wednesday, June 7, 1967, the third day of the Six-Day War was 'the heart of the matter.' In every place near or far, for soldiers as for children, for new immigrants as for old-timers, the heart of the matter touched every heart."

The Paratroopers Are Crying by Chaim Chefer [198]

This Kotel has heard many prayers
This Kotel has seen many Walls fall
This Kotel has felt wailing womens' hands and notes pressed between
its stones
This Kotel has seen Rabbi Yehuda haLevi trampled in front of it
This Kotel has seen Caesars rising and falling

But this Kotel has never before seen paratroopers cry.
This Kotel has seen them tired and exhausted
This Kotel has seen them wounded and scratched-up
Running towards it with beating hearts, with cries and with silence
Pouncing out like predators from the alleyways of the Old City
And they're dust-covered and dry-lipped
And they're whispering: if I forget you, if I forget you, O Jerusalem
And they are lighter than eagles and more tenacious then lions
And their tanks are the fiery chariot of Elijah the Prophet
And they pass like lightning
And they pass in fury

And they remember the thousands of terrible years in which we didn't
even have a Kotel in front of which we could cry.
And here they are standing in front of it and breathing deeply
And here they are looking at it with the sweet pain
And the tears fall and they look awkwardly at each other
How is it that paratroopers cry?
How is it that they touch the Wall with feeling?
How is it that from crying they move to singing?
Maybe it's because these 19-year-olds were born with the birth of Israel
Carrying on their backs — 2000 years.

---

198 Reprinted with permission: The Western Wall Heritage Foundation [www.TheKotel.org];
Thanks to 'Jerusalem Diaries'.

CHAPTER XXV

MAN RECITING SUPPLICATIONS

Supplications for refuah (recuperating from sickness), shidduchim (marriage match), parnassa (livelihood), to conceive, for healthy pregnancy, for teshuva (repentance), prior to childbirth, greeting the Rosh Chodesh (New Moon), going to the cemetery, pleading for virtuous and learned children, and more.

Stories after 1967

A Sincere Dialogue with G-d[199]

A man was being escorted to the *Kotel* (Kossel), obviously a blind man, guided by others on either side. He was a *Sefardic* Jew, his sharp, graceful features accentuated by thin, curly earlocks. He approached the *Kotel* (Kossel), and leaned forward to give it an affectionate kiss. He ran his hands over its surface, his super-sensitive fingers feeling centuries of history, glory, and suffering in every crevice and ripple. Then he began his dialogue with G-d. Yes, a dialogue, for although only one voice was audible, he knew that he had a responsive listener. He spoke directly, respectfully and with great clarity, exactly as if the conversation were with a person. He gestured with his hands to provide the necessary emphasis and description that his words required. At one point, he abruptly stopped, hesitated a moment and said, "Oh, I'm sorry. I already told You that yesterday."

Dr. Rabbi Abraham Twerski continues: "This was [a] simple and sincere prayer at its best. There was no doubt in this man's mind that what he had told G-d yesterday was heard, and that there was therefore no reason to repeat it. I turned back to continue reciting the Psalms, realizing that I had never really prayed before."[200]

---

199 *Generation to Generation.* Abraham Twerski. Lakewood, NJ: C.I.S., 1992
200 Ibid.

MEN RECITING SHEMONEH ESREI

"All prayer speaks of G-d; the Shemoneh Esrei speaks to G-d... One prayer is central to every worship service—morning and night, weekday, Shabbat, and holiday: the Amida, the"Standing" prayer, which is also known as the Shemone Esrei, the "Eighteen" blessings, or the Silent Devotion. It is the peak experience of the prayer service (and) is recited silently, standing, and occasionally bowing."[Rabbi Maurice Lamm, "Day To Day Judaism: Prayer"]

A Return to Jerusalem[201]

by Rabbi Mendel Weinbach zt"l

Remembering Shavuos 1967

"I rejoiced when they said to me — let us go to the House of *HaShem*."

We sang these words of King David, the Sweet Singer of Israel, as we walked to the *Kotel* in the wee hours of the morning many years ago. It was Shavuot Night, and countless thousands of Jews had been up all night studying Torah to make up for the shortcoming of their ancestors

---

201   Reprinted with permission: Rabbi Moshe Newman, Ohr Somayach Institutions [www.ohr.edu]

over 3,000 years earlier in sleeping the night before they received the Torah at Sinai.

Now those Jews were pouring out of all the streets onto the main thoroughfare leading to the Old City, forming a human sea brimming with song and ecstasy. For most of them this would be their first encounter with the

MEN PRAYING AT NIGHT
The Kotel is open twnety-four hours a day, seven days a week, all year long. There is a daily progression of fixed prayers: Shacharit in the morning, Minchah in the afternoon, and Ma'ariv in the evening. This cycle parallels the natural transformation of the day: the emerging sunrise, the looming sunset, and nighttime. True, nighttime is when most people normally sleep. But there are those who work nights and sleep during the day. For others, the nighttime solitude is like a magnet drawing them to the Kotel when they can be alone with G-d, separated from other people, whether considered as a welcome freedom from disturbance or as an unhappy loneliness.

Kotel. Many of them had not even been born when that last remnant of the site where once stood the House of HaShem fell into Jordanian captivity in the War of Independence in 1948. Others, like myself, had arrived in Israel only a few years before it was liberated by Israeli soldiers.

The *Kotel* had been in Israeli control for a week already, but the military authorities wanted to ascertain that there were not mines or snipers lurking on the way to the Old City before giving the public access to the *Kotel.* Some intrepid individuals had somehow infiltrated and brought back dramatic accounts of their inspirational experience. But the general public waited for the green light of the army, and it finally came on Shavuot.

Shavuot and the Kotel

What a combination!

It was an updated version of the historic link between Torah and Jerusalem expressed in the passage said and sung by Jews for generations when the Torah is taken out of its ark: For from Zion shall come forth Torah and the Word of HaShem from Jerusalem. Zion was the site of the *Beit haMikdash* with its celestial corps of *Kohanim* steeped in Torah and the sacred service of the sanctuary; Jerusalem was the seat of the Sanhedrin, the supreme authority on interpreting the Word of HaShem. Small wonder, then, that when Yehoshua ben Gamla initiated the first system of public education for Jewish children who had no parents to teach them Torah, he chose Jerusalem as his national center. Where else would a youngster have such shining models as *Kohanim* and judges of the highest court?

This extraordinary atmosphere of Jerusalem, suggests Rabbi Aharon Halevi, author of the classical *Sefer Hachinuch*, serves as part of the explanation for all of the commandments requiring a Jew's physical presence in Jerusalem. In four years of the seven-year cycle of tithes, a Jew was required to bring almost ten percent of his crops — or their monetary value — and consume them as a "second tithe" in Jerusalem. The same was true of all the fruit which grew on his trees in the fourth year of its life. Add to this the ten percent of the cattle born each year which he had to bring for slaughtering in the *Beit haMikdash* before he could eat their flesh, and you get a picture of the vast amount of food that a Jew could enjoy only in Jerusalem.

Too much, points out the author, for any family to consume during their stay in Jerusalem three times a year on *aliya l'regel* or on an occasional visit to Jerusalem to offer a sacrifice. It was therefore advisable, from a purely economic point of view, to have one member of the family permanently stationed in Jerusalem where he would have the opportunity to study Torah with most of his needs covered by the aforementioned foods whose consumption was limited to that city.

With such an opportunity to grow in the Torah atmosphere of Jerusalem this member of the family would eventually return home to serve as a sort of "family resident-scholar," capable of providing hands-on spiritual guidance for his relatives in a manner in which no communal rabbi was capable.

Kotel, Kotel, Kotel —

A Poem by Deborah (Shapiro) Hemstreet[202]

Stone upon stone upon stone
Polished by touch of hand.
Shining from multitudes' tears
Standing tall in an eternal land.
Touch upon touch upon touch
In tremors of joy and of pain
Centuries' old dream come true
Hearts linked to a Wall in a chain.

Tear upon tear upon tear
Shed in a stream that won't dry,
Praying for peace to come
That no more of her sons may die.
Land upon land upon land
Casting waves upon the shore
Determined from their hearts
To live free forevermore.

Kotel, Kotel, Kotel,
You've engraved your stones on my heart
So now I lay my prayer in yours

---

202   Reprinted with permission: Deborah (Shapiro) Hemstreet.

Trusting Him before whom you stand.
All that you are no man can see
But perhaps with this song it's a start.[203]

Winds of Remembrance —
Yom haZikaron Commemoration at Kotel, April 22, 2007[204]

By Judy Lash Balint

It is eerie how often the elements reflect events occurring here in Israel. At last week's *Yom HaShoah* commemoration at Yad Vashem, participants huddled together in the chill of the Jerusalem evening as the ceremony marking the systematic murder of six million European Jews unfolded. The youthful members of the choir were shivering in the frigid air. Six survivors delegated to light the memorial torches stood stoically at attention as a cold wind blew across the hilltop.

But just one week later, as the State of Israel pauses to remember her fallen soldiers, the ritual takes place as a soft, warm, almost comforting breeze envelops hundreds of bereaved families gathered in the plaza facing the Kotel. The flag at half-mast barely flutters in the gentle wind flurries, and the memorial flame remains virtually immobile in front of the subdued crowd. Those commemorated on *Yom Hazikaron* are not the mass victims of yesteryear's death camps, they are our youth who died and continue to die, defending the state and its citizens. We need the warmth and gentleness to reassure us, to enable us to look to the future.

It's slightly disconcerting to see the Kotel bereft of worshippers, replaced by rows and rows of men and women with sadness in their eyes. A significant number of the men choose not to wear any head covering — I cannot help wondering if it is an indictment of G-d or an expression of secularism that has nothing to do with their loss. Apart from the ultra-Orthodox who generally do not serve in the army, the full spectrum of Israeli society is represented at the service — national religious and secular;

---

203 http://www.hope-challenged.com/?page_id=205
204 Reprinted with permission: Judy Lash Balint

Ashkenazi and Sephardi; rich and poor; old and young. Bereavement itself is a social stratum here; according to the Defense Ministry, 23,305, soldiers have died in the fifty-nine years of statehood leaving thousands of families to join the ranks of the bereaved.[205]

Yom Kippur at the Kotel[206]

By Jenna Hopp on September 24, 2007

"My friends and I lit *yizkor* candles and then we headed for the Kotel. Doing the *Kol Nidrei* service while resting my hand on the Kotel Wall was one of the most emotional and moving experiences of my life. I have never felt so connected with my past and present and so close to HaShem. HaShem's presence was everywhere all around, knowing and listening. Regardless of setting, *Kol Nidrei* is the most emotional service for me because my mother and I used to do this service together. We would take a journey into each other's minds and search for meaning and depth in each other and we would also try to get and understand forgiveness from HaShem. Being at the Kotel for *Kol Nidrei* I felt as if I had finally made it into the woman I was meant to be. I have never felt as proud of myself as I did that night."

The Singing Stones of the Kotel[207] — Birds and Plants of the Western Wall

By Ilan Braun

The Kotel plaza sees a steady stream of visitors. Tourists and locals, young and old, Jews and non-Jews alike. They come to pour out their hearts, write a note to G-d, press their lips against the ancient stones. They pray, dance, sing, laugh and cry. But amidst all this vibrant humanity, one element of the Kotel is usually overlooked: the Wall itself is pulsating with life. If you listen closely, you may hear

---

205 From Jerusalem Diaries: http://www.jerusalemdiaries.com/doc/253

206 Reprinted with permission: Jenna Hopp

207 Reprinted with permission from the author: Ilan Braun http://www.chabad.org/library/article_cdo/aid/2174138/jewish/The-Singing-Stones-of-the-Kotel.htm

birdsong mingling with the prayers. The swift builds its nest in the crevices near the top of the Wall. Swifts are migratory birds, arriving in Israel during the month of February in huge flocks. The prophet Jeremiah notes, "The turtledove, the swift and the crane observe the time of their coming." Indeed, these birds never fail to arrive at the Kotel right on time!

Then there are the sparrows. Psalms (84:4) declares, "Even the sparrow finds its home and the free bird her nest where she laid her young." The sparrow is called the "free bird" because, although it can live very close to man, it is impossible to domesticate. The Talmud specifies that the sparrow's blood was used to purify lepers.[208]

We can hear the familiar turtledove's cooing. Could this bird be the incarnation of G-d's Presence (called the *Shechinah*) on earth, as some believe? The dove is the most persecuted bird, and so it is frequently found in the Bible and Talmud as a metaphor for the nation of Israel.

And let us not forget the plant kingdom — no less than seven different plants call the Kotel their home. The ephedra provides red berries for bird gourmets, and produces ephedrine, an alkaloid used in pharmacology to treat diseases of the bronchi. The golden henbane is described by the Jewish historian Josephus, who compares its blossom to the tiara of the high priest.

The Temple area is an idyllic rendezvous for certain bird species. Their link to the Western Wall is by an ancient connection. The swifts' (Apus Apus) annual return to the Kotel is marked with delight by both bird watchers and the Kotel worshippers. The common swift stops over at the Kotel to nest between the cracks in the ancient wall as it returns from wintering in South Africa. The crevices between the wall's massive limestone blocks are a perfect nesting site for the swift.

---

208 Talmud: *Yoma* 75b

Their neighbor, the horsetail knotgrass, exposes its tiny pinkish white flowers. According to the Mishnah, it was used as an antidote against snakebites. The thorny caper, with its large white flowers and cucumber-like fruits, is also found here. The Talmud notes that the caper bears fruit every day, and that all other trees will do the same during the era of Moshiach.[209]

Finally, one last wild creature peeks out surreptitiously between the ancient stones, emitting a curious sound ("tzit-tzit") before vanishing. The agile and hyperactive gecko is mentioned in the book of Proverbs (30:28), and the Talmud (*Shabbat* 77b) gives it as a natural remedy for scorpion bites: grind two geckos, one light-colored and one dark, then place the powder on the wound. Fortunately, no scorpion has ever been found near the Kotel! Human, animal, vegetable and mineral. Here at this most holy place, all four levels of existence blend together in perfect harmony.

Reprinted with permission from the Judaism site http://Chabad.org

[Ilan Braun is a retired wildlife conservationist and journalist who has lectured in Europe and Israel. He studied and lived in Israel, US, Australia and Europe. He is presently preparing a book on the clandestine 1946 aliyah of a group of Holocaust survivors from Italy.]

My Awesome Visit to the Western Wall Tunnels[210]

[The Times of Israel — Oct 8, 2013] by Heddi Keil

It is said that the Divine Presence still rests where the ancient Temple of the Hebrews once stood, beneath today's Dome of the Rock on The Temple Mount in Jerusalem.

King Herod built a retaining wall around the Second Temple circa 35 BCE. The Temple itself was destroyed by the Romans in 70 CE, and only a small portion of this Wall remains today visible above ground. It is at this Wall, "the Western Wall," that one can see Jews praying, rocking back and forth. They know they are close to where the Temple once stood and the "Holy of Holies."

"I have often looked at these people, wishing that I could feel even a fraction of their fervor, but I am not religious. I don't feel anything except

---

209 Talmud: *Shabbat* 30a

210 Reprinted with permission from: Heddi Keil & from *The Times of Israel* [8/10/13]

the suspicion that I am missing out on something, and appreciation that at least some people are showing respect to what might be there.

"This past week my cousin Carol came to visit us from the United States. It is her first visit to Israel, and amongst other sites like Masada and the Dead Sea, my husband Mark and I decided to take her on the Western Wall Tunnels tour.

CHILDREN PRAYING
Here a young boy and girl pray in the rear of the women's section as their mother prays closer to the Kotel. "The old men and old women will yet sit in the streets of Yerushalayim and the ruins of Yerushalayim will fill up with little boys and little girls playing in her streets." (Zechariah 8:4-5)

"We learned that the Western Wall actually extends much further to the north, but underground. Painstaking excavations have been done since 1967 so that today we can walk through a tunnel that stretches alongside the entire length of this ancient Wall. We saw the gargantuan stones that King Herod used, whilst our English-speaking guide enhanced our understanding of the site's history.

"Halfway along we came to a spot where women were praying. I immediately felt an aura of goodness, of warmth. Then we entered an alcove, perhaps three meters by three meters, where men were praying. This room has become an underground synagogue, and is reputed to be the closest spot to the Holy of Holies.

"We stopped here for a few minutes whilst our guide spoke. But I was not listening to him. I could feel pouring through the Walls a positive energy. It was Powerful. It was Good. And the more I allowed myself to focus on it, I understood that this energy was unaffected by time. It was as strong now as it had been 3,000 years ago when the Temple was first built. It might have originated hundreds of millions of years ago, but at the same time I felt that for It, Time was irrelevant. It always was, is, and will be. I felt through my very bones that there is something UnEarthly (sic) beyond that Wall.

"I had never felt anything like this before. I have never taken drugs, and am not imaginative enough to have conjured it. I kept asking Mark and Carol, "Do you feel it? Do you feel it? Do you feel the energy coming through the Wall?" They had their own thoughts — for Mark, intense happiness that we had brought our family to live in Israel; and for Carol, sadness at all the killing that has taken place here in Jerusalem because of religious intolerance.

"I wondered if the men praying were feeling the energy too, or just doing what they always do — showing respect and honor to our G-d; but I couldn't interrupt and ask them. Tears were coming to my eyes. My fingers were tingling. 'How much longer can I stand here with this inexplicable energy pouring through the Walls?' I wondered. Thankfully, our tour continued on its way. We emerged from the tunnel into the hyper-intense normalcy of Jerusalem. I was shaken and totally puzzled by what I had experienced.

"I am a logical person and am tempted to ask if any scientific instruments have been brought to that underground alcove to measure radiation, or a change in the magnetic field, or something, to bring some sort of scientific explanation to what I have felt there. And even, can they do this, if they haven't already? Perhaps this is too sacrilegious to ask. But I want an explanation!

"It is thought that fumes from an underground volcano in Greece induced visions in people who prophesied at its Oracle of Delphi; so maybe there is an explanation here too.

"This energy that I felt at the underground synagogue does not conform to my personal vision of the G-d of the universe, the one whom I appeal to when I want my family to be safe, or when I want my computer to start working again; but perhaps it is an emissary, and one of many sent throughout the universe.

"Up until now I had thought that the story of Moses receiving the Ten Commandments at Mount Sinai was probably true, but now I believe it is. If what I sensed in the underground synagogue has any semblance to reality, then the Israelites did witness something out-of-this-world at the foot of Mount Sinai. It was enough to have their descendants maintain their faith in G-d and abide by His commandments not only when living in the Promised Land, but also through the subsequent thousands of years of exile and persecution, and up to our glorious return to Zion.

"Will I return to the Western Tunnel? Probably; though I am a little afraid to — because either I will feel nothing in the synagogue the next time I go, or given a longer time in the alcove, I could be overwhelmed. I can't say that what I have experienced has turned me into a hat-wearing, kosher-keeping, religious woman; but it will propel me to try to be nicer, kinder. The 'Source' was sent here for a reason and I will try to respect and honor it in the best way I know."

Ani Zocher

by Jared Zaifman, ECRUSY (Spain / IP 2003)

"Israel is AWESOME! One of the most significant experiences I had in Israel occurred when we were touring the Old City. Our group was with a tour guide and he told us to close our eyes. We all then locked hands and started to walk not knowing where we were going; only being able to hear the story of the liberation of Jerusalem. Once we got to a point where we could see the Kotel, we opened our eyes and it almost felt like you could really experience the feelings felt by those who were in the battle of the liberation of Jerusalem."

Reprinted with permission from: Jared Zaifman (BA, MPA)

Photos

The photographs included in this book properly belong in the gallery of the human heart, our inner Synagogue. I would love to share with you the thousands more that are out there, but cannot due to space limitations.

The author gratefully acknowledges permission granted by the following organizations for the right to reprint photos from their collections:

GP=Israel National Photo Library

ACP=Library of Congress (American Colony Photographic Collection)

TB=Pictorial Library of Bible Lands. Credit to: Todd Bolen/BiblePlaces.com

IM=ImageBank Israel

Chapter XXVI

SOURCES ON THE KOTEL — SELECTIONS

"Never will the *Shechinah* budge from the Western Wall of the *Beit ha-Mikdash*, as it says: Behold, there he stands behind our Wall."[211]

"Behold, there he stands behind our Wall."

Behind the Western Wall of the *Beit haMikdash*. Why? Because HaShem vowed that it would never be destroyed.[212]

"Many peoples will go and say, 'Come, let us go up to the Mountain of HaShem, to the Temple of the G-d of Jacob, and He will teach us of His ways and we will walk in His paths.' For from Zion will go forth Torah, and the word of HaShem from Jerusalem... They shall beat their swords into plowshares and their spears into pruning hooks; nation will not lift up sword against nation, and they will no longer study warfare."[213]

"Our feet shall stand within the gates, O Jerusalem."[214]

"Walk about Zion and Go Round About Her."[215]

"For Zion's sake I will not be silent, and for Jerusalem's sake I will not be still, until her righteousness emanates like bright light, and her salvation blazes like a torch. Nations will perceive your righteousness and all the sovereigns your honor... Then you will be a crown of beauty in

---

211 Shir HaShirim 2:9; *Midrash Tehillim* 3:11 *Shemot Rabbah* 2:2
212 *Numbers Rabba* 11:2; Song of Songs, 2:9 (Shir HaShirim)
213 Isaiah 2: 2-4
214 Psalms 122:2
215 Psalms 48:13

the hand of HaShem and a royal diadem in the palm of your G-d."[216] [In the above prophecy, the Prophet Isaiah is conveying the following message: We will become a "crown of beauty" when the righteousness of our spiritual center will emanate like bright light to all the nations.]

"The old men and old women will yet sit in the streets of Yerushalayim and the ruins of Yerushalayim will fill up with little boys and little girls playing in her streets."[217]

"If I forget thee, O Jerusalem, may my right hand forget its cunning.

May my tongue cleave to the roof of my mouth, if I do not set Jerusalem above my highest joy."[218]

MAN KISSING THE KOTEL
A time-honored sign of love and respect is to kiss sacramental objects, such as the Torah as it is carried past. This extends to kissing mezuzah, tefillin, tzizit, sacred books (a chumash or siddur) and the Kotel. When approaching the Kotel, lean forward to give it an affectionate kiss. Run your hands over its surface, feeling the spirituality of 2,000 years with your fingers.

---

216   Isaiah 62:1-3
217   Zechariah 8:4-5
218   Psalms 137:5-6

CHAPTER XXVII

CONCLUSION

I owe you, my reader, a debt of gratitude for your patience in listening to my story about the Western Wall. We have both been enriched by the encounter. Together we traveled through many time periods to experience, albeit vicariously, the vicissitudes of Jewish life as it revolved around the Kotel and its worshippers. I would have been much happier had the *Beit haMikdash* still stood with all its glory. "It became the core of Israel's spiritual life and inspired lofty ideas that shaped the life of the nation for generations."[219]

Alas, the First Temple was destroyed due to three sins of which the Jews were guilty: idolatry, sexual indiscretions, and murder. The Second Temple was destroyed because the Jews were guilty of baseless hatred towards each other. One would think that after 2,000 years, our hope for a Third Temple would have faded away. This may be true for those whose belief has languished. But for the rest of us, whose faith is unwavering, the hope is very much alive. We pray three times a day for the return and rebuilding of the Temple in Jerusalem that had once stood as the First and Second Temples that were destroyed by the ancient Babylonians and the Romans.

I would be remiss if I did not share with you my thoughts. I link our collective future with Ezekiel's prophecy: that the *Beit haMikdash haShlishi* (Third Temple) will come before long and will be a House of Prayer for

---

219 *"The Western Wall"*, Ministry of Defense Publishing House; Meir Ben-Dov et al, 1987 , pg 19

All People with a sacrificial service (in some form or another). It will be a perpetual structure and an everlasting dwelling place for the G-d of Israel on the Temple Mount in Jerusalem.

May it be the will of the Creator that I and my fellow stones will join *Am Yisrael* (the nationhood of Israel) in witnessing its construction prior to, or in tandem with, the Messianic age.

About the Author

Israel Rubin, whose educational background includes a Degree in Engineering from The Cooper Union and a Master's Degree from M.I.T in Finance and Industrial Management, has worked with returnees to Judaism (*Ba'alei Teshuva*) for more than twenty years. His Torah background includes Mesivtah Chaim Berlin. An observant Jew, he now lives in Beit Shemesh with his wife. His children, grandchildren, and great-grandchildren all live in Israel.

He has authored three other books:

- *The How and Why of Jewish Prayer* — http://www.arbakanfotpress. com/ Arba Kanfot Press, 731 pgs., 2011
- *Who Were the Krymchaki?* — A vanishing remnant of Rabbinic Jews dating back 2,000 years. (Being readied for publication)
- *From Palestine to America & Back to Israel* —The author's autobiography, from his childhood in Haifa under the British Mandate; his arrival in America; his life experiences until 2005, when he returned to Israel with his wife, children and grandchildren. (Being readied for publication).
- *My Writings - The Power of the Pen* — a collection of hundreds of essays on Jewish religious issues, letters, stories, op-ed articles, and speeches, delivered on Jewish issues relating to Soviet Jewry and Pro-Israel activism. (Being readied for publication)

He is the process of writing:

- Concepts in Judaism - An Introduction — A selected compilation of Biblical, Halachic, *Talmudic* ideals, principles, thoughts and practices, drawn from *Tanach* (Torah, Prophets and Writings), *Mishnah, Talmud*, Codes of Jewish Law, *Midrash*, and Apochrypha.
- Jewish Ethics and Customs.

To Contact author: israel@ibrubin.com

About This Book

This book is an outpouring of the flood of images that have filled my mind over the past twenty centuries. No camera has ever been invented that can capture all that I have seen and experienced. I have encountered the full spectrum of happenings —from the sad, heartbreaking, and distressing, to the happy, joyful and lively — that have marked the years. I have chronicled every episode and can verify to its authenticity. No, I did not take down notes, nor was I able to make a recording or video. There was never a need to. I have been blessed with an extraordinary memory, as you shall soon see.

If you are one of the countless visitors who come to this, the most visited site in the Holy Land, you may have touched and kissed me as you stood to pray or recite psalms. If you have not yet been here, possibly your parents, grandparents or those that came before them were here to touch and caress me. The Divine Presence has never left us stones of the Western Wall. Here at the Wall, you will come into contact with something both palpable and ethereal. You will be able to experience a feeling both profound and inexplicable. Perhaps for the first time, you will sense the real essence of life.

To this day, the strong spiritual magnet that is the Kotel draws thousands of tourists visiting Israel from all over the world. The enticement is more than a visit to another archaeological site. Can you feel it? That special power that draws you to the Kotel stems from the special holiness that defines the Kotel. Only at the Kotel can they experience this inexplicable sensation and response. The encounter is mysterious as it is baffling. Young and old, pleading and questioning as they come face to face with the closest physical symbol of G-d's Presence on Earth.

MOSAICA PRESS

About Mosaica Press

Mosaica Press is an independent publisher of Jewish books. Our authors include some of the most profound, interesting, and entertaining thinkers and writers in the Jewish community today. There is a great demand for high-quality Jewish works dealing with issues of the day — and Mosaica Press is helping fill that need. Our books are available around the world. Please visit us at www.mosaicapress.com or contact us at info@mosaicapress.com. We will be glad to hear from you.